110 GREAT
SCOTTISH RUGBY
MOMENTS

STEWART WEIR

Black&White

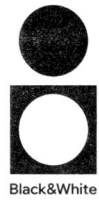

Black&White

First published in the UK in 2019 by Black & White Publishing
as *100 Great Scottish Rugby Moments*

This edition first published in the UK in 2025 by Black & White Publishing
An imprint of Bonnier Books UK
5th Floor, HYLO, 105 Bunhill Row,
London, EC1Y 8LZ

Copyright © Stewart Weir 2019, 2025

All rights reserved.
No part of this publication may be reproduced,
stored or transmitted in any form by any means, electronic,
mechanical, photocopying or otherwise, without the
prior written permission of the publisher.

The right of Stewart Weir to be identified as Author of this
work has been asserted by him in accordance with the
Copyright, Designs and Patents Act, 1988.

The publisher has made every reasonable effort to contact copyright holders
of images in the picture section. Any errors are inadvertent and anyone who
for any reason has not been contacted is invited to write to the publisher so
that a full acknowledgement can be made in subsequent editions of this work.

A CIP catalogue record for this book is available from the British Library.

ISBN: 978 1 78530 926 7

1 3 5 7 9 10 8 6 4 2

Typeset by Iolaire Typesetting, Newtonmore & IDSUK (Data Connection) Ltd
Printed and bound by CPI (UK) Ltd, Croydon CR0 4YY

The authorised representative in the EEA is
Bonnier Books UK (Ireland) Limited.
Registered office address: Floor 3, Block 3, Miesian Plaza,
Dublin 2, D02 Y754, Ireland
compliance@bonnierbooks.ie
www.bonnierbooks.co.uk

CONTENTS

Foreword by Gary Armstrong OBE   ix
Introduction   xi

PART I – 1970s

1. Telfer Try Wins the Day in France, 1969   1
2. The Calcutta Cup Makes up for Earlier Upset, 1970   3
3. Chris Rea's Try Against Wales, 1971   7
4. Peter Brown's Winning Kick Against England, 1971   9
5. Scotland Beat England for the Second Time – in a Week, 1971   11
6. Scots Star as Lions Show Their Claws, 1971   14
7. Scotland Retain the Calcutta Cup, Again, 1972   17
8. Andy Irvine's Kick to Beat England, 1974   19
9. Scots Lions Maul the Springboks, 1974   23
10. "Flower of Scotland" Comes to Bloom, 1974   25
11. A World-Record Crowd, 1975   27
12. A Lawson Double Wins the Day, 1976   30
13. Gordon Brown – Fighting with Opponents and Fitness, 1976   34

14. Scotland Hail a New Try-Scoring Sensation, 1977	38
15. Andy Irvine's Try Against Wales, 1977	40
16. Hawick Win Play-Off to Take Title, 1977	42
17. Hawick's Unstoppable Green Machine, 1978	45
18. *Superstars*, 1978	47

PART II – 1980s

19. The Very Worst and Very Best of Andy Irvine, 1980	53
20. All White on the Night as Scotland Beat Australia and the Elements, 1981	57
21. Scotland Have a Wales of a Time, 1982	59
22. Iain Paxton's Try of the Season, 1982	64
23. Scots Raiders Stew-Mel Take the Middlesex Sevens, 1982	66
24. Achievements for Irvine and Scots Down Under, 1982	68
25. When History of the Wrong Kind Was Made, 1983	70
26. Barbarians Exhibition Showcases Lafond and Rutherford, 1983	73
27. Free-Flowing French Win Historic Melrose Title, 1983	75
28. Not Even Lucky Jim Could End the All Blacks Hoodoo, 1983	77
29. A Season that Just Got Better, and Better, and Better Still, 1984	82
30. After a 46-Year Wait, a Triple Crown, 1984	86
31. And to Scottish Rugby, a Grand Slam, 1984	91
32. Scots Trial Verdict Has Appeal, 1986	96
33. Paul Thorburn and *That* Kick, 1986	99
34. Record-Breaking Scots Thrash England, 1986	101
35. Oh Calcutta Cup Debacle, 1988	106
36. Baa-Baas and the Three Bears, 1989	108

37.	Scots Lead the Pride of Lions, 1989	110

PART III – 1990s

38.	Chalmers' Key Role in Grand Slam Success, 1990	117
39.	David Sole on the March, 1990	122
40.	Tony Stanger's Match Winner, 1990	127
41.	Scott Hastings and *That* Tackle, 1990	132
42.	The Melrose Era Begins, 1990	136
43.	Big Gavin on the Charge, 1991	139
44.	Scotland Enter the Fashion Stakes, 1992	140
45.	Co-optimists "Select" Select Takes the Melrose Sevens, 1993	141
46.	England Loss Too Much for Hastings, 1994	143
47.	Scotland Win in Paris for the First Time in 26 Years, 1995	145
48.	Toony, Paris and *That* Pass, 1995	148
49.	Peters' Try Sets Tone for On-Song Scots, 1995	153
50.	The Year of the "Nearly Men", 1995	157
51.	Captain Fantastic Hammers Ivory Coast, 1995	161
52.	Doddie's Double Not Enough to Halt All Blacks, 1995	165
53.	Dods' Haul Sees Scotland to Win over French, 1996	168
54.	England Leave Scots so Near, yet so Far Again, 1996	172
55.	McGeechan and Telfer Mastermind Lions Win over World Champions, 1997	177
56.	Hail Cesar II, 1998	182
57.	The Future's Bright, the Future's Orange, 1998	187
58.	Now for Wales to Do Us a Favour, 1999	188
59.	Gregor Townsend – Individual Grand Slammer, 1999	192
60.	Wales Do Scots a Turn, 1999	195

61.	When Scots Won a Championship but Let a Bigger Prize Slip Away, 1999	198
62.	When Gala Partied Like It's 1999, 1999!	203

PART IV – 2000s

63.	England Denied the Grand Slam, 2000	211
64.	A High-Water Mark for the Game in Scotland – Literally, 2000	216
65.	Scots Wreck Irish Title Ambitions, 2001	218
66.	Bill McLaren Retires – and Scotland "Retire" from Winning in Cardiff, 2002	222
67.	Scotland Cast Aside 33 Years of Hurt and History, 2002	226
68.	Scotland Join the Century Club – Paterson Hits 40, 2004	230
69.	The Kicking Tee Delivery Business Just Got Real, 2006	233
70.	Hadden Inspires Debut Calcutta Cup Win, 2006	234
71.	Kicking Masterclass from Paterson Sees off Wales, 2007	237
72.	*That* Jersey and *That* Game, 2007	240
73.	Strictly Kenny, 2007	241
74.	Scots Well Beaten by New Zealand – or Maybe Not, 2007	243
75.	Out of the Blue, 2008	245
76.	Edinburgh Go for Artistry of a Different Kind, 2009	249

PART V – 2010s

77.	Scots Clean up in Dublin Thanks to Parks Department, 2010	253
78.	No Cries in Argentina as Scotland Take Historic Series Win, 2010	257
79.	Scotland Defeat the World Champions, 2010	261
80.	Edinburgh Live the European Dream, 2012	265
81.	Ansbro and Strokosch Spill Blood for the Cause, 2012	269

82.	Tonga Shocker at Pittodrie Ends Robinson's Tenure, 2012	271
83.	Hoggy and *That* Pic, 2013	272
84.	Ibrox Makes the Perfect Stage for Sevens, 2014	274
85.	Warriors Are Grand in Pro12 Final, 2015	277
86.	Scots Denied World Cup Semi-Final Through Referee Error, 2015	281
87.	Jade Becomes a Trailblazer, 2016	283
88.	Sevens Success for Scots Duo in Rio, 2016	284
89.	The Transformation Is Complete, 2017	288
90.	Hogg Double Has Irish in a Stu, 2017	290
91.	Watson Wallops Wallabies, 2017	292
92.	Driven Ford Becomes Scotland's Most Capped Player, 2017	296
93.	Doddie Weir's Big Entry, 2017	297
94.	Scots Waltz Past Ill-Disciplined Aussies, 2017	301
95.	Make Space for the Calcutta Cup, 2018	303
96.	Maitland Hits England with "Try of the Year" Contender, 2018	306
97.	George Is Head-Turner with Canada Hat-Trick, 2018	308
98.	Tommy Seymour Hat-Trick versus Fiji, 2018	309
99.	Calcutta Cup – a Match Like No Other, 2019	311
100.	Glasgow Hosts Biggest PRO14 Final Ever, 2019	318

PART VI – 2020s

101.	Memorable Scots Win – Then Something We'll Never Forget, 2020	323
102.	A Win at HQ – Nearly Forty Years in the Making, 2021	327
103.	Italian Job Completed in Record-Breaking Style, 2021	330

104.	Scots Tower Over French in Paris, 2021	333
105.	Third Successive Scotland Win Over Wallabies (Do We Get to Keep Them?), 2021	336
106.	Make Mine A Double Is Order of the Day, 2022	339
107.	You Wait 38 Years for One, then . . ., 2023	342
108.	Halfway To Paradise, So Near and Yet So Far, 2023	345
109.	One Is Always Enough, 2024	348
110.	Duhan's Treble Yell Pushes Scotland to the Four, 2024	352

FOREWORD

Anyone passionate about rugby will have memories of the games they've watched on television, the players they've seen, and the matches they've attended, be it at club level, internationals at Murrayfield, or perhaps on tour.

For me, my rugby memories feature some of my rugby heroes more than they do me and the games or teams I was involved with; such as watching Andy Irvine, Jim Renwick and of course Roy Laidlaw, a fellow Jed-Forest man, in action for Scotland.

Playing rugby, especially international rugby, was great, but greater still are the memories you have – and share – from those special occasions, like winning a Grand Slam, or the Five Nations, or a game or try you might have been part of.

All the key moments from the last 55 years of Scottish rugby are captured in this book; there are more than a few that will mean a lot both to Scotland's die-hard supporters and to the players who created those great memories for us all.

It's nice to see that my name features a couple of times, but then so do many legends and icons of the Scottish game over the past five decades; winners and great leaders, world-class players, and legendary names from the world of TV and radio.

And so I'm sure that *110 Great Scottish Rugby Moments* will definitely bring back some truly great memories for you.

Gary Armstrong OBE

INTRODUCTION

Arriving at the greatest moments in Scottish rugby over the last 55 years was something of an elimination process, and in parts, easier said than done.

Firstly, this book is about memories, and from my perspective, that always means living memory. To that end it was quickly established that there were not too many around who could reference first-hand Scotland successes pre-war, but in making it over the last half-century, we at least had a chance to speak to some of the greats about equally great days in the Scottish game and what made it special for them.

Secondly, there was the small matter of coming up with 110 magical, and some not so magical, moments. If you can imagine asking 100 people to name their favourite moment, and 93 answering "Tony Stanger", with 81 giving David Sole as their second choice, you will appreciate that the complexities of amassing over a century of significant achievements had to be a tad more scientific.

To all those who I annoyed on various occasions, a big thank

110 GREAT SCOTTISH RUGBY MOMENTS

you, and to those who said they remembered nothing about certain instances or important interludes, because it happened 20, 30 or 40 years ago, then spent an hour or more talking about it, an even bigger thank you.

If you have a special recollection that didn't make the top 110, then imagine it charted at 111 – which is also the room number where some of the instantly forgettable occasions are housed.

I hope you enjoy the 110 that are included.

PART I

1970s

1

TELFER TRY WINS THE DAY IN FRANCE

11 January 1969 • Five Nations, Colombes
France 3–Scotland 6

A Scottish win on French soil has been something of a rarity for a few generations now, although few could have considered that even possible back in 1969 when Scotland repeated their win from two years prior at the old Stade Colombes.

The scoreline, Scotland winning by 6–3, tells you virtually all you need to know about a disappointing game, which, as the famous voice of Bob Danvers-Walker summed up on the British Pathé newsreel of the match (yes, it was that long ago), "unfortunately didn't turn out to be quite the match that had been expected".

Scotland led 3–0 thanks to a penalty, kicked by Heriot's fullback Colin Blaikie, which gave the visitors a lead they somehow protected into the second half, thanks in the main to the usual quotas of French profligacy and some last-ditch defending, including Sandy Carmichael's try-saving tackle on Jean-Marie Bonal, just as the French winger appeared in mid-air, during his dive for the line.

Blaikie's counterpart, Pierre Villepreux, who had previously kicked abysmally, tied the scores with a penalty. However, it always looked as if one score could tip the balance of this game, and it came near the end. From a French scrum, replacement scrum-half Iain McCrae was alert to make the pinch, feeding on to no. 8 Jim Telfer, Scotland's widest man, on the right wing, and from close range he brushed past scrum-half Jean-Louis Bérot and charged through Villepreux for the match-clinching try.

Little did anyone realise that Telfer's score would end up something of a museum piece through time.

Jim Telfer recalls: "It was a try you'd expect a no. 8 or a back-row forward to score if they were alert to the possibilities. Not too far out, from my recollections, but the kind you would back yourself to score. Nothing special.

"What made it special, I suppose, was that it then took so long for Scotland to win again in Paris – until 1995 to be precise. All that time, my try was shown on TV, which for a time didn't look out of place, but through time, you were aware that Scotland hadn't won away to the French since television footage was in black and white.

"If you could have earned royalties from repeats and reruns, I'd have made a few quid over those 26 years..."

2

THE CALCUTTA CUP MAKES UP FOR EARLIER UPSET

*21 March 1970 • Five Nations, Murrayfield
Scotland 14–England 5*

By the time the final weekend of the 1970 Five Nations arrived for the Scots, there was arguably more interest in the head-to-head about to take place in Amsterdam – Mary Hopkin (UK) v Dana (Ireland) to decide the Eurovision Song Contest – than there was in the meeting of rugby's two oldest rivals at Murrayfield.

England had beaten the Irish and were slight favourites in Edinburgh because of it. There was also the small matter of Scotland's recent history of just two wins in their last 16 Championship encounters. Scotland's series had been calamitous over the opening three matches, starting with a narrow loss at home to the French and followed by losses in Cardiff and Dublin. The 16–11 reversal at Lansdowne Road saw Jim Telfer dropped as captain, replaced by his Melrose colleague, hooker Frank Laidlaw.

The first 40 minutes were Scotland's – Peter Brown kicked a penalty, then Ian Robertson's outside break was made doubly effective with John Frame confusing the England back division with a dummy scissors, enabling Jock Turner to set Alastair Biggar free to sprint home. Brown advanced the lead by another three points with the boot to 9–0, before a John Spencer try 13 minutes from time was converted by Bob Hiller, the England full-back having been kept at long range when Scotland had conceded penalties.

It was too close for comfort now, but Robertson, who gave his opposing outside-half Roger Shackleton a torrid afternoon, again produced some neat work to set up Turner for his try, Brown adding the extras. At the end, Laidlaw was chaired off the field by Rodger Arneil and Tommy Elliot in celebration, another occasion when Scotland's only win brought them a piece of cherished silverware.

No coincidence then that in a season when the Scots served up "All Kinds of Everything", Dana won... Former BBC radio commentator Ian Robertson states:

"If there was one match I really, really, really wanted to win, it was this one. I won my first cap two years before against England and lost that one, then won my second cap in 1969 at Twickenham and lost again. There was a heightened urgency to win this game because it wasn't often you lost three times on the spin against England and were invited back.

"The win in 1970 was followed by an away win against England – a rarity because we have never been outstanding at Twickenham, with the odd banana skin there – and we had another win at Murrayfield in 1972, so we had quite a grip on the Calcutta Cup around that time and haven't really since.

"There were some real names in the English back division that day at Murrayfield: Bob Hiller at full-back, [John] Novak on one wing, [Mike] Bulpitt on the other, and the centres were John Spencer and David Duckham, with Roger Shackleton and Nigel Starmer-Smith – another who made it into the BBC – at scrum-half.

PART I - 1970s

"It was quite a profitable match for the licence fee payers, getting two future correspondents out of the one match. They weren't that fussy who they got. They just ended up picking the names out of a barrel.

"Actually, the England captain that day, Bob Hiller, did *Rugby Special* on TV from time to time. He said his demise began when they had the headlines for the show, and they'd show a few tries and great moments, and then Nigel Starmer-Smith would say, 'Welcome to *Rugby Special*. Tonight we are doing this and this.'

"Bob said he bowed out because in the opening sequence he dropped a high ball, when the Irish had kicked it up to him; he didn't attempt a tackle on a Welsh try scorer. Then they showed him knocking on a few metres from the line, and finally, he was shown being tackled, throwing the ball over his head, from which France scored a try. He said he was never watching the programme again, at least not until five minutes into the broadcast because the opening was a character assassination.

"One thing that upset me about that Calcutta Cup win was that it was the last match shown in black and white; colour TV came in for the game the following year. I was furious. Imagine, my greatest moment forever recalled in black and white.

"I was fortunate to have some good players around me in that Scotland team, and somewhat blessed having a back row of Tom Elliot, Rodger Arneil and Peter Brown, who did all my tackling for me. I said I've got one pair of shorts which need to last me a season, so if you don't mind getting dirty ... and they didn't.

"A few times I was quite thankful I was on their side.

"I had got my blue at Cambridge in 1967, played for London Scottish at the start of 1968, then that summer, I started as a teacher at Fettes, and then played for Watsonians.

"But 1970 was the end of my Five Nations career. I went to

Australia, my final Test, then in the December played for Blues against Whites in the first Scotland trial at Murrayfield, was double-tackled and did my knee, and that was it. I lost three of the four cartilages and had suffered medial ligament damage in one knee and cruciate damage in the other, and I never recovered from that. I was 25.

"Nowadays, there'd be something they could stick in, or some form of corrective or reconstructive surgery that could perhaps salvage your career. But back then it was all very primitive.

"But as huge compensation, Cliff Morgan flew up from London and said now that I was retired, would I like to come and join the BBC? It was as simple as that. I had met him twice, briefly, and in other people's company, and he was a wonderful entertainer, the life and soul of the party, and we had a couple of great evenings. But he came up to Edinburgh and said, look, Bill McLaren does the rugby but he's a school teacher as well and can't get time off to do everything, so the BBC decided Cliff was to switch to television and would I like the radio job? I thought that would go down rather well, and that was that.

"Out of the misery and the suffering of not being able to play after one Scotland trial match, I landed a dream job – the job of a lifetime – which I clung to for 47 years..."

3

CHRIS REA'S TRY AGAINST WALES

6 February 1971 • *Five Nations, Murrayfield*
Scotland 18–Wales 19

The 1971 Five Nations match against Wales at Murrayfield will forever be remembered for John Taylor kicking a conversion in the closing seconds to win a dramatic match for the men in red. Even that most unbiased of gentlemen, the late Bill McLaren, conceded at that moment, had he access to a shotgun, the Welsh flanker may have been his target. It was a disappointing conclusion to a marvellous match, which may explain why a try from centre Chris Rea is overlooked. The reason it hasn't been here is that it did, of course, feature in the BBC's *100 Greatest Tries* video.

For younger readers, that was a thingy, full of tape, that you could record programmes on. Think of it as a hard drive, which occasionally would unravel but had the mystical power to keep cats amused for hours (less so mothers who didn't see the funny side of your household moggy ripping six hours of *Crossroads* to shreds).

Talking of shreds, Scotland have always excelled at living off them, and Rea's try typified that.

Winning a line-out on the Scotland 10-yard line, McHarg fed Dunky Paterson, who launched a bomb on Welsh lands. Winger John Bevan dithered, then had his kick charged down by opposite number Billy Steele. Welsh hands retrieved, in the form of JPR Williams but he was consumed by Rodger Arneil, sending the ball loose and stoating into the hands of Rea, who burst through the tackle of John Dawes, then fended off wing-forward Dai Morris to score.

The conversion was missed by PC [Peter] Brown. Ach, sure, it was only two points and anyway the Scots led by four – but that was soon wiped out by a Gerald Davies try and that Taylor kick. Scotland lost 19–18...

4

PETER BROWN'S WINNING KICK AGAINST ENGLAND

20 March 1971 • Five Nations, Twickenham
England 15–Scotland 16

Prior to 1971, Scotland had last won at Twickenham in 1938. The odds were against Scotland rectifying that lengthy trend, having lost to France, Wales and Ireland in their three previous Five Nations matches that season.

New caps Arthur Brown (full-back) and hooker Quintin Dunlop had been drafted in to freshen up the Scottish ranks, but when England ran the ball back at the Scots, wing Jeremy Janion igniting the attack – which eventually saw England run and pass their way through a statuesque Scottish defence – the white-shirted Bob Hiller finished out wide.

Scotland came back with a fine try of their own. Dunky Paterson cleared up a messy heel just outside the English 25, feeding to Chris Rea, who engaged with wing Alastair Biggar, cutting in off the left flank. He was eventually apprehended, but not before connecting with Nairn MacEwan, the flanker passing to Gala teammate Peter Brown, who touched down, then added the extra points. Hillier, with his end-on kicking style, banged over a couple of penalties to give the home side a

9–5 half-time lead, although their advantage was cut to just one when Paterson, who was making a habit of living off minimal rations, landed a timely drop goal to keep Scotland in touch.

When Paterson fumbled off his own put-in, his opposite number, Jacko Page, pounced in a flash. He threw a pass wide to the evasive Janion, who sent Tony Neary in for the score. While Hiller was off target with the conversion, his next penalty pushed England 15–8 ahead. Just eight minutes remained.

Scotland, with nothing to lose as they attempted to avoid yet another Twickenham loss and a Five Nations whitewash (the wooden spoon was ours already), upped their game and the tempo.

When Rea made decent yards, Paterson sent a deft kick over enemy lines. The ball should have been fielded by debutant Dick Cowman, but the English no. 10 spilled the ball and the ever-hungry Paterson scored. Nevertheless, England had both the scoreboard and the clock on their side.

In the final minutes, Scotland once again attacked, producing what proved to be the match-winning move.

From a shortened line-out on the right, Rodger Arneil tipped the ball into the clutches of Paterson, who released the hard-charging Ian McLauchlan. A call for a high tackle on the prop could have scuppered the Scots, but French referee Charles Durand allowed play to progress, Scotland winning the ruck. Paterson gathered, his snipe read perfectly by clubmate Peter Brown, who, with an unorthodox one-handed, lobbed pass, released Rea, who, despite the attentions of England skipper John Spencer, dived in to score.

The only thing that remained was for Peter Brown, displaying the newfangled round-the-corner kicking technique, to add the extra points, which he did with aplomb. Never in doubt.

5

SCOTLAND BEAT ENGLAND FOR THE SECOND TIME – IN A WEEK

27 March 1971 • Centenary International, Murrayfield
Scotland 26–England 6

You wait all year for a Scotland–England game, then two come along at once. It was something of an anomaly in 1971 that we would have two such fixtures on successive weekends. The first game, won by Scotland – or rather Peter Brown's trusted right boot – had been your standard (if there was ever such a thing) Five Nations, Calcutta Cup encounter.

Game two, however, was something a tad special – a match to commemorate the centenary of the first Scotland–England tussle at Raeburn Place. If the level of dignitaries in attendance was better than usual – both the Prince of Wales and Prime Minister, Edward Heath, were at Murrayfield – then so too was Scotland's performance, resulting in a 26–6 win over their oldest rivals.

Having won by just a point at Twickenham, the Scots, with the same starting XV as the previous week, were rampant from the off in front of their home crowd.

Dick Cowman, winning only his second match (having been a debutante in the first leg of this double-header), threw a daring pass along his own goal line as England tried to run back the kick-off, only for John Spencer to drop it. John Frame touched down and his Gala colleague Arthur Brown, who would end the day with four conversions, obliged with the extra points. Not a minute had passed.

Peter Brown and Cowman exchanged a penalty and a drop goal to make it 8–3, only for the former to add a try just after the half-hour. Scotland took one against the head, then Dunky Paterson kicked ahead and retrieved his own kick after Alastair Biggar's work on the chase, feeding Brown to twist his way in for the try and an 11–3 half-time lead.

There was no living with the Scots second half. Centre Chris Rea cross-kicked to enable Frame to grab a second try, and although Hiller cut the leeway by three from straight in front of the uprights to make it 16–6, Billy Steele, having turned in a defensive masterclass with tackles on Jeremy Janion on the left, followed almost immediately with another saving tackle on Tony Bucknall, scored off a flowing Scots move.

Scotland's fifth and final score came when English centre Chris Wardlow was engulfed by a blue wave including Rodger Arneil, Alastair McHarg and Peter Brown, their rucking churning the ball out for Rea – overlooked for the forthcoming Lions tour in favour of the hapless Wardlow – to run in the score.

It was a win befitting of the occasion...

Scotland and Lions loose forward Rodger Arneil describes a week the victors have never been slow to recall: "Cowman, the England stand-off, had made his debut in the Twickenham game. We had a pretty simple ploy of ruffling him up in that one. It worked so well, we just repeated the dose. The poor chap took his eye off the ball a bit, so their backs fell into disarray.

"People said we played offside. That was just an illusion. We were just very close to it, very...

PART I – 1970s

"We had a good back row, with PC [Peter] Brown, Nairn MacEwan – who used to travel silly miles every week from Inverness to Gala and back, just to train – and myself.

"But we were able to enjoy a bit of autonomy up front because our tight five – Ian McLauchlan, Quintin Dunlop, Sandy Carmichael, Al McHarg and Gordon [Brown] – were just so damn good at tying up our English counterparts.

"I always thought Scotland around that time were just about good. What I mean by that was we had a lot of great players, men who would play for the Lions and the likes, but with Scotland we never quite got the results consistently enough. That season, we had the beating of Wales, I felt, but John Taylor kicked his conversion and we lost by a point. Frustrating.

"Winning at Twickenham, then Murrayfield – I mean, that was a real pleasure. I played in four successive wins against England, but I only mention it if asked – or occasionally if I'm in the company of someone who might need reminding.

"I remember I was playing golf at Muirfield and my guest was Budge Rogers, a former England captain no less. Peter Brown, for some reason, was sitting having breakfast as well. I hadn't seen him for a while, but the first thing he said was: 'Hey, Rodger, how are you? Do you remember when we beat England?'

"Budge choked on his bacon and eggs – and he hadn't even been playing. Peter was never the most tactful of people."

6

SCOTS STAR AS LIONS SHOW THEIR CLAWS

1971

Compared to the playing schedule current British & Irish Lions touring parties face, the 1971 trip to New Zealand, led by Welshman John Dawes, lasted more than three months and entailed 26 matches, including four Test games. By comparison, the 2017 tour comprised just ten games, three of those Tests.

In addition to Doug Smith as the Lions tour manager, Scotland provided seven players for the squad: Rodger Arneil, Alastair Biggar, Ian McLauchlan, Sandy Carmichael, Gordon Brown and Frank Laidlaw. Chris Rea also made the trip, eventually replacing the injured English centre Chris Wardlow.

While Carmichael's tour would end prematurely through facial injuries received against Canterbury, his fellow Glasgow and Scotland prop McLauchlan made the team for the first Test in Dunedin and scored a crucial try, charging down Alan Sutherland's clearing kick to score in a 9–3 win.

McLauchlan would eventually play in all four Tests; the second was lost 22–12 in Christchurch, while Gordon Brown replaced Delme Thomas of Wales for the third Test, the Lions winning 13–3.

It all hinged on the final game, the fourth Test in Auckland,

PART I - 1970s

where the Lions earned a 14–14 draw to take the series.

Brown had cemented his place in the Lions boiler room alongside Willie John McBride, and they would pair up again in three years' time in South Africa. McLauchlan, meanwhile, had earned a reputation for his destructively ferocious scrummaging and the nickname "Mighty Mouse" (at 5'9" and 14st 6lb), his status becoming legendary on the tour after dismantling the "Taranaki Tank" – 19-stone All Black prop Jazz Muller, who also sported a 20-inch neck and a four-inch height advantage over the Jordanhill man.

As Muller would have found out, it's no' the dog in the fight but the fight in the dog.

Ian McLauchlan on "emigrating" to New Zealand:

"I left in April and didn't come back until August. We had two weeks in Eastbourne to get together, went out via Hong Kong, had a couple of matches in Australia and then on to New Zealand, which was nothing like Eastbourne.

"I didn't get paid for being off work so it didn't really bother me – though it did my wife Eileen because she had nae money. But that was just the way it was. You knew you'd be there for a while, although you maybe don't realise quite how long it was.

"I think we were there longer than some people who had emigrated there managed to last. It was hard. The pitches weren't great – some were cricket fields, some were cow fields – and the weather isn't kind to you. You don't really have issues like that in South Africa, but New Zealand was hard graft.

"All of the provincial sides reckoned they could beat you and would do whatever it took to achieve that. They came at us, sometimes not that intent on playing rugby either, and you just had to deal with it.

"I've met up with guys like Tane Norton, Fergie McCormick when he was still with us, and Alex Wyllie – 'Grizz'. I have punished them very badly for some of their misdemeanours, unseen by many, felt by some. Wyllie said to me once, 'You are the only b*****d I know who can't count.' I asked why?

"He said, 'Well, you swipe me, I swipe you back, and you hit me again and say that makes us even. How the f**k does that make us even?'

"I just said it was an attitude of mind and he should get used to it.

"There was a lot made of the Muller thing by the New Zealand media. I read an article where he said he'd met Mighty Mouse, who'd made him look like Mickey Mouse, and I thought that was sad. I contacted a friend of mine and asked if the next time I was out, he could arrange for me to meet Jazz Muller again. I didn't want him to feel that way.

"Those tours were good for me and good for any of the Scots boys on them. It's where you learn – the intensity sees to that. In South Africa, the Scots boys made up a quarter of the Test team. That kind of experience you can't create elsewhere."

7

SCOTLAND RETAIN THE CALCUTTA CUP, AGAIN

18 March 1972 • Five Nations, Murrayfield
Scotland 23–England 9

They say winning becomes a habit. Against England in the early 1970s, it was a habit the Scots were showing no sign of kicking either.

The 1972 Five Nations was rendered null and void when both Scotland and Wales decided not to visit Dublin in light of the heightening political tensions. There was, however, one prize still to play for – namely the Calcutta Cup, which Scotland had become very attached to.

Because of the match rota, England would complete their entire itinerary in Edinburgh – not that they had anything but some face-saving to play for after losing to Wales and Ireland at Twickenham and being resoundingly beaten in Paris. It did not get any better for Peter Dixon's side further north in a match where the hosts were never headed.

Nairn MacEwan gave Scotland the lead through a try after just four minutes. Lionel Weston, the England scrum-half, who ironically played his club rugby for West of Scotland, threw an aimless reverse pass infield, which new cap Geoff

Evans failed to hold. Colin Telfer applied his boot to the loose ball, and although full-back Bob Hiller tried to clear up the mess, Telfer collected him, leaving the attentive MacEwan to score.

Alan Old and Peter Brown swapped penalties, before the latter scored a try off Billy Steele's long throw-in at a line-out. Arthur Brown failed with a second conversion, although Scotland were well placed by the turnaround, Telfer kicking a left-foot drop goal, as if to prove the treatment he had been receiving for a knock to that leg had worked.

Old kicked two penalty goals to make it 14–9, but calmly, the Scots started to amass a bigger haul of their own – Arthur Brown finally hitting the target with a penalty, then Peter Brown with two to help Scotland take an unglamorous but nevertheless needed win.

England gathered the wooden spoon, Peter Brown the Calcutta Cup, which would later be inscribed with his name as a captain who had recorded back-to-back wins in the fixture, becoming the first Scot since Dan Drysdale in 1927. A rare honour, indeed.

8

ANDY IRVINE'S KICK TO BEAT ENGLAND

2 February 1974 • Five Nations, Murrayfield
Scotland 16–England 14

As someone once said: "There is no such thing as a lucky, dodgy, narrow, tight or jammy win over England; they are all glorious." So said a certain George Wilson "Doddie" Weir, more than once – a man who never experienced what it was like to win against the red rose.

Back in the early 1970s, you would have been upset to have been a Scotland player who didn't sample such a delight, and those selected to do battle at Murrayfield dined out on their success for many a year.

For the first time since the 1880 fixture, the game against the Auld Enemy wasn't the final game of the spring series. Instead, Scotland aimed to pick up the pieces after a 6–0 loss in Cardiff, and those beaten by the Welsh were given a chance to redeem themselves.

Andy Irvine, still just 22 and winning only his eighth cap, pinged over a penalty from just shy of the England ten to give Scotland a lead, increased to 9–0 with Irvine's conversion after Wilson Lauder's try, the Neath wing-forward at hand to take a Duncan Madsen pass after the hooker had pounced on Jan Webster's spill.

A Fran Cotton try and an Alan Old penalty brought England back into the fight, 9–7 down. England, in terms of their pack, were a muckle unit, none more so than no. 8 Andy Ripley. A 400-metre runner, his charging break from the halfway line after an orchestrated tap penalty from scum-half Jan Webster cut like a bulldozer through jelly.

Irvine partially halted the athletic Ripley (who would later be one of the leading lights in the BBC's *Superstars* compendium of sporting tests), but he got his pass off to Tony Neary in support and England were up 11–9, only for Scotland to score an unconverted try of their own as Colin Telfer switched play to the right, with Nairn MacEwan the conduit, to find Irvine in full flow, and his dodging run saw him elude three defenders to score in the corner.

England then led 13–14 (not quite following the script of the game at Bannockburn more than six centuries earlier), after Coventry full-back Peter Rossborough had sent a howitzer of a drop kick between the Scotland posts, picking up on Telfer's hacked clearance.

It looked as if the spoils and the Calcutta Cup, in a contest where the lead had already changed hands three times, were headed south of the border. Instead, with the match well into injury time, Andy Irvine – by now established as the picture boy of the Scottish game and already with a try, a conversion and a penalty to his name – yanked the trophy and win from English clutches.

When Alan Old missed his touch kick to end the game, Irvine countered, passing to Drew Gill, who booted ahead. In a moment of panic, as the English desperately tried to snaffle the ball, David Duckham was blown for being offside as he picked up.

Irvine steadied himself, then from 40 yards, on the angle and

PART I – 1970s

wide out on the flank, parted the posts, his successful effort signalled by the referee's whistle, which also brought an end to the game.

It was so typical of the brilliant Irvine, who looked almost embarrassed as Alan Lawson, Gordon Brown and Alastair McHarg attempted to hoist him aloft. He didn't want that – and neither did he want for a headline writer. He wrote his own, as he describes here:

"I remember scoring a try in that game to put us in the lead, and then England scored one of their own and eventually took the lead. I also remember Peter Rossborough hitting a massive drop goal from quite a distance, which was one of those scores in a game that came when you least expected it.

"It didn't deflate us as such, but we had put a lot into the game up until that point and you wondered, firstly, if you had a bit more left to give you a chance, and secondly – and more importantly – if you would have enough time remaining to get another chance.

"In the last seconds, David Duckham encroached offside. We knew that it was time up and so it had to go over. If it missed, we weren't going to get the ball back, so there was a lot riding on it.

"Back in those days, with the open terraces at Murrayfield, for some reason I was as happy kicking from that right side as I was from the other, because it wasn't considered the natural side for a right-footed kicker. It was a bit outside in, so to speak, turning the ball across the posts, rather than hooking it in. You would have thought I'd be more at home on the left, in the shadow of the Main Stand, given my style, but I just felt more comfortable on the right and it may have been because of the way I kicked the ball – who knows?

"Anyway, I didn't really have a choice that day. It was still a difficult kick, because of the swirl, but I pulled it in nicely. And the rest is history. I have to admit, if anyone is thinking it, that I missed a few like that as well. But on that day, it went over.

"That game had to be one of the highlights of my whole career, because at the end of that season, I went to South Africa with the Lions, which was an unbelievable experience for me as a relatively young player.

"But in terms of my career, ironically, the game I enjoyed the most came at the very opposite end of my career – my last Five Nations match and my last in the UK, in Cardiff in 1982 against Wales, when we gave them a real hammering.

"We hadn't won there for 20 years, and while I didn't score any tries and only kicked a few goals, being captain of that team that day was just a wonderful experience. They always had great teams, and not many teams won in Wales. To go there and pull that kind of result was just massive.

"While I would play in Australia, I didn't know then it would be my last game for Scotland. Not a bad way to bow out.

"When we came back from the Australian tour, I took about three or four weeks off and then started to train again. I went out for a run and my calf muscles tightened up. So I left it a week and tried again, and the same thing happened. Instead of clearing up like it had previously done, it just got progressively worse, and what I'd done was my Achilles, and that's why I retired.

"My whole game was built on stamina and outright speed, and if you can't train, though ultimately, very, very painful, there isn't much left for you other than to call it quits. I was only 30 when I played my last Test."

9

SCOTS LIONS MAUL THE SPRINGBOKS

1974

Whatever the perceived rights and wrongs of the British Lions going to South Africa in 1974 were, no one could deny that on the rugby field, the Lions, having won in New Zealand three years earlier, confirmed their status as the best around – and did so emphatically while touring the Cape.

Six Scots made the touring party – Andy Irvine, Billy Steele, Ian McGeechan, Ian McLauchlan, Sandy Carmichael and Gordon Brown – as Willie John McBride's Lions created history, going through the entire tour unbeaten – 22 matches in all. Had it not been for a highly contentious decision in the fourth and final Test – when referee Max Baise refused to award a try when it appeared that Fergus Slattery had grounded the ball for a score – then their record would have been played 22, won 22.

The last Test was drawn, but by then, the Lions had wrapped up the series, winning 3–0.

They won the first Test 12–3 in Cape Town, with Steele, McGeechan, McLauchlan and Brown in the side, and that same quartet also faced the Springboks in Pretoria, Brown grabbing a try in an emphatic 28–9 win.

The third Test saw the Lions secure the series win in Port Elizabeth, Irvine replacing Steele on the wing, while Brown was again amongst the try scorers. However, the West of Scotland giant had to sit out the final Test in Johannesburg with a broken hand (acquired in one of the many altercations with the Boks pack), while Irvine contributed a try and a penalty in the 13–13 draw, meaning McLauchlan and McGeechan played in all four tests, with only Carmichael failing to secure a Test berth.

What they had secured, however, was a place in Lions history.

10

"FLOWER OF SCOTLAND" COMES TO BLOOM

1974

There was a time when McDougalls was the flour of Scotland. However, that all changed in the early 1970s when, in front of millions of TV viewers, "Flower of Scotland" was delivered as a rugby anthem, sung passionately by Scots – and Welsh and Irish and even English.

The song itself would have been known only to those who were devotees of the Scottish folk duo The Corries. However, during the summer of 1974, it was presented to a slightly different audience – namely the British Lions touring party to South Africa.

Langholm, RAF and Scotland winger Billy Steele was the instigator. Needing material for the regular and popular camp singalongs, Steele gave a rendition of the tune, which has, over the years, become famous the world over.

One subtle amendment was made: "proud Edward's army" became "the Springbok army" as the song was sung pre- and post-match during trips and in-camp evenings.

So when the triumphant Lions, undefeated during a 22-match tour and Test series winners against the Boks were given centre stage during the BBC's Sports Personality of the Year awards ceremony from Television Centre in London that November, the show broadcast to millions across the British Isles, the Lions launched into a rendition of what had become a favoured battle anthem. And, as they say, the rest is history.

It was a few years before the Scottish rugby team adopted it as their national anthem, but their lead was followed by other sporting teams and, ultimately, by the nation itself.

Billy Steele reflects, "It's funny now seeing as everyone knows the words and how the rugby crowds have adopted it as their national anthem. But the first time I sang it on tour, I don't think any of the other Scots knew the words. They soon learned, as did the rest of the Lions. It was just a great tune to lift you, to motivate you. It worked for us on that trip, when at times you felt you weren't just playing the Springboks but taking on all of South Africa."

11

A WORLD-RECORD CROWD

1 March 1975 • Five Nations, Murrayfield
Scotland 12–Wales 10

Attendance records set in Scotland was always part of sporting history. Ibrox – when staging the New Year Old Firm game in 1939 – clocked 118,567, the biggest league audience ever seen in the UK. Meanwhile Hampden Park, a colossus of a bowl in its day, had held the biggest crowds for both an international and a Cup Final in the UK at just shy of 150,000, those numbers reached in the space of just a week in 1937.

For rugby, however, Murrayfield wasn't in the same league, more because no one really knew how many it could hold and it had never been near full to find out. That all changed on St David's Day, 1975, and by chance, it was the Welsh who were in town.

There were contributing factors: despite a loss in Paris, Scotland had beaten Ireland, in their opening game, with some aplomb, enough for Lions and Irish captain Willie John McBride to declare that the Scots were "the team to beat". A first Triple Crown since 1938 was doable, almost anticipated.

There was also a concerted attempt to build interest in the game, although little encouragement was needed for the expected 30,000 Welshmen, who thought Rose Street would be the ideal venue to toast the good health of their patron saint. The new commercial radio stations – Radio Clyde in the West and the recently launched Radio Forth around the capital – also talked up the occasion, while snippets appeared in the printed press that suggested this might be a game of significance.

The Herald carried word that 16,000 ground tickets and 7,000 enclosure tickets had been sold for the game. Others, however, focused on those numbers and suggested there would be ample space for all in the 80,000-capacity venue. The aforementioned broadsheet had also handily hooked in would-be supporters by mentioning the ticket sales at the end of a front-page story telling of the abandonment of the Friday friendly between Harris Academy FPs of Dundee and visitors Pontypool United, where the referee called a halt to proceedings, under appeal from the home skipper, after three of his players had suffered facial injuries during the first half, resulting in two eye wounds and four lost teeth.

Thankfully the game on the Saturday was less damaging, unless you were a Welshman with Grand Slam ambitions or had been buffeted and squeezed trying to get into Murrayfield. That the terraces and standing areas had overspilled to within a few feet of the playing surface suggested this was a crowd like no other.

Having run in points aplenty against France and England, the Welsh pack was bullied and largely stymied at Murrayfield. It meant play was fragmented and sporadic, and turned into a kicking duel between Douglas Morgan and Steve Fenwick in the first half, each Morgan penalty cancelled out by the Bridgend centre, until the Scotland scrum-half edged his team ahead 9–6 before the turnaround.

It remained that way until seven minutes from time, when from a Scots heel, Morgan executed the perfect dive-pass to find partner Ian McGeechan, his left-footed drop kick from the Welsh 25 tumbling high over the bar.

PART I - 1970s

Wales, down 12–6, were not done, and from a line-out on halfway, and already four minutes into time added on for injuries (although they were minor compared to Friday's battle in Dundee), Wales launched a final salvo – spinning the ball along the line, Gerald Davies was brought into play on the right but cut back across field, seeking red jerseys and ground populated by fewer Scots. Wales took play all the way out to the left, mainly through replacement Phil Bennett and Gareth Edwards, who, at full pace, threw a reverse pass back inside to keep the move alive. This was in the days before "phases".

Scotland killed a ruck, enabling Edwards to take a quick tap and, once more, head right. Ray Gravell and Terry Cobner maintained the momentum, with JPR Williams bringing Gerald Davies back into play. He danced his way into the Scots 25, before the loop run of Trefor Evans completely wrong-footed the Scottish defence, and the Welsh wing-forward crashed through Alastair McHarg and over in the corner.

McHarg was still prone on the touchline, receiving treatment, as Welsh lock Allan Martin – an old-fashioned end-on kicker – sent his kick into the grey Edinburgh sky and, thankfully for every Scot, wide of the right-hand upright.

Scotland were thus in pole position for the Triple Crown at Twickenham a fortnight later, but unfortunately the wheels came off in West London.

Nevertheless, 104,000 remains a record attendance, unlikely ever to be bettered on these shores and only beaten 24 years later when the Sydney Olympic stadium hosted the Bledisloe Cup match between Australia and New Zealand, when 107,042 attended – though this was surpassed a year later in the corresponding fixture by a crowd of 109,874.

If only they hadn't locked several thousand outside at Murrayfield back in 1975.

12

A LAWSON DOUBLE WINS THE DAY

*21 March 1976 • Five Nations, Murrayfield
Scotland 22–England 12*

The Five Nations that term hadn't begun particularly well for the Scots. A frustrating defeat against France at Murrayfield was followed by a crushing loss in Cardiff. As things would have it, the Welsh would eventually play France in an epic Grand Slam decider at the Arms Park.

For Scotland, following those initial losses, modifications for the Calcutta Cup contest at Murrayfield were significant, the main amendments from the Welsh defeat coming at half-back where Dougie Morgan was dropped, giving way to Alan Lawson and his London Scottish partner Ron Wilson, the new cap preferred at outside-half, with Ian McGeechan switched inside to centre. Lawson possessed a long, flat pass; Wilson, just turned 22, a rather mighty boot. Both would serve the Scots well.

Alan Tomes of Hawick, a banker in Gateshead by day, also made a first appearance, with Alastair McHarg dropping back to no. 8, thus utilising his often less-regimented approach.

Visitors England had personnel changes of their own, both through injury. Martin Cooper and Tony Morley were initially

PART I – 1970s

selected but were eventually replaced by Alan Old (brother of England cricketer Chris Old) at stand-off, while winger Ken Plummer was drafted in for fellow Bristolian Morley. This would only be Plummer's second cap, his first coming seven years before. The fact Welsh winger Maurice Richards ran in four tries against him that day may have played a part in Plummer's lengthy absence.

But for the width of the touchline, Plummer would have had a try, while David Shedden's covering tackle on David Duckham meant the hosts stayed in the contest as England piled on the pressure. In an instant, however, the Scots gained relief and a score. Derek Wyatt, a replacement for Duckham who never recovered from the almighty clattering Shedden had inflicted, hooked his attempted cross-field kick backwards. The West of Scotland winger – again on the wrong side – collected the bouncing bladder inside his own 25 (we hadn't gone metric then) and set off, passing out of the tackle to the supporting Mike Biggar. For a second, Plummer's waterworks were tested, as he was confronted by seven charging blue jerseys, among them Sandy Carmichael, by now with ball in hand, and the veteran Lions prop weaved through England's last line. Tomes provided the link to Lawson, who ran in from the 25 to score.

Sitting 12–9 down at the turnaround, Andy Irvine kicked Scotland level, and from there they never looked back.

The ever-aware David Leslie charged down Old's attempted clearing kick to score, then, when the Scots back division cut across field from left to right, Wilson recycled the ball in the tackle. Billy Steele's dive-pass was burst upon by Irvine, who went through Leslie to Jim Renwick, an injury replacement for Shedden, who was concussed having halted the rampaging Andy Ripley earlier. For once, the Hawick man threw a misplaced pass inside to Irvine, but Lawson, having a day to remember, was on hand to run in his second try of the afternoon.

"What a day he's had," Bill McLaren proclaimed, keeping a lid on his inner emotions. Can't be every day your son-in-law scores twice against the Auld Enemy.

Man of the Match, Alan Lawson says, "What I remember of the actual match is all rather fragmented. I just think there was so much happening on the day that you just get caught in the game, and 80 minutes becomes rather blurred.

"For the first try, we'd all retreated when David Shedden gathered a kick in the corner and just started running, and it all flowed from there. The whole of England charged towards our line, going in one direction, then suddenly having been retreating, we were running in numbers at them. Someone likened it to the football scene in *Bedknobs and Broomsticks*.

"Because play had switched direction so quickly, all of our forwards, who normally wouldn't be in the clear, were our most advanced players and were passing the ball between one another like backs. I always remember Ian McLauchlan telling me, 'You could have passed to me – I was only a few yards behind,' and me replying he wasn't – but he bloody well was! I knew I was going to score, take the tackle and just go over, but it was a very nice feeling to finish it off. A great moment.

"The second try involved some lovely running and handling as well, and again, I was in a great place to pick up and score the clinching try.

"We did have a good team around the time with some really fine players. Ron Wilson, who was at London Scottish as well, was stand-off that day, winning his first cap. I was one of the first at scrum-half – and certainly was at international level for Scotland – to develop the spin pass. Sometimes it worked, sometimes it didn't. When wet, the balls back then were just like a bar of soap. If you didn't get your pass right, it could

PART I – 1970s

come out at all angles, and Ronnie, who was also a great buddy, made me look good by taking passes off his toes, or above his head, or behind him. And having him in the team helped me.

"Jim Renwick, David Leslie, Gordon Brown, all great players. Dave Shedden was 10st 8lb. We used to jokingly call him 'Strolling Bones'. And Sandy Carmichael, the first Scotland player to reach 50 caps, which in any generation is an achievement, but it would be like 100-plus today.

"I owe Sandy everything because it was him who ran over Ian 'Spivey' McCrae and broke four of his ribs to get me my first cap. It was planned. No, actually, what was planned was that me and Sandy had worked out a ploy the French would run at a line-out. Sandy stood beside Colin Telfer, ready for a throw over the top to scrum-half Jean-Michel Aguirre, and Sandy, being our best tackler, would be waiting – except no one told Spivey, so when he tackled Aguirre around the ankles, Sandy smashed Jean-Michel and tramped on Ian. What is it they say about other people's misfortune?

"The Queen was at Murrayfield that day in 1976 when we beat England and was presented to the teams in advance of the game, and that was quite a big honour. I always remember, the Royals, historically, ask questions, like have you played the opposition before, who do you play for and where were you born? I recall eyes being raised once when that was asked of Nairn MacEwan and he replied, 'Dar es Salaam.'

"I was lucky enough to play England five times, winning in 1972, 1974 and 1976, drawing in 1979 and being hammered 26–6 in 1977, when England had a big lad at centre – a doctor, Charles Kent, who played for Rosslyn Park – who was an immensely powerful runner.

"Funny, I remember more from that game, probably as I had a good chance to see England close up all day!"

13

GORDON BROWN – FIGHTING WITH OPPONENTS AND FITNESS

*11 December 1976 • Inter-District Championship, Murrayfield
Glasgow 15–North and Midlands 18*

The six degrees of separation theory works on a great many things, often across seemingly the most diverse and disassociated individuals, groups or teams. Occasionally, however, even the most obscure names, from different genres, can be a lot closer than you first believe. Take for instance Noel Edmonds, he of radio, TV and Mr Blobby fame, and the SRU, custodians of the game in these parts. What could possibly connect them – or, more accurately, who?

That connection is down to one person, former Scotland and Lions giant the late Gordon Brown, who, in 1976, when Edmonds was in his pomp at the Beeb, found himself on the wrong side of the administrators north of the border, much of it because of TV evidence.

Edmonds was then the first host of BBC's flagship Saturday morning entertainment *Swap Shop*, the tame, smiley, sanitised offering which was up against, for several years, the utter chaos and mayhem offered by *Tiswas* on commercial telly.

To show just what a national brand *Swap Shop* was, they

PART I - 1970s

would send Keith Chegwin out around the shires and cities, the game being to guess where he was, then spontaneously turn up to be part of the show and, if you were lucky, explain to a national audience why you were seeking an ABBA LP, or a Scalextric track, or a skateboard, swapping it for something you had but didn't want, like a sister.

The guessing game was easy though, as seven or eight times out of ten, you only had to find out which match *Rugby Special* was highlighting to work out what town or public space they'd be in.

In December 1976, Murrayfield became Cheggers' port of call, so maintaining the kids–rugby partnership.

The reason Murrayfield was in action was simple – a week earlier, winter weather caused both Inter-District matches to be cancelled. With an international trial beckoning, Scotland's top players needed game time, so the next series of games became a double-header at the national stadium, guaranteed to take place, of course, because of Murrayfield's famous "electric blanket", or undersoil heating as it is more commonly known today. But back then, it was revolutionary.

The meeting of Glasgow versus North and Midlands would be one of the games shoehorned into Nigel Starmer-Smith's weekly round-up, at best enabling us to see a few tries and perhaps a few potential international candidates.

On this particular day, however, we – and the Beeb – got more than we bargained for, for not only did young Donald from Oxgangs swap his hockey stick for a Johnny Seven OMA (and was no doubt instructed to swap it back again), but the BBC got their match action, plus a news item.

Unfortunately, the aforementioned news article involved some rather unsavoury out-of-shot foul play from North and Midlands hooker Allan Hardie but highlighted the far more public revenge attack by Brown – who, with blood streaming from a gaping head wound, chased his adversary across the pitch, intent on doing damage to him.

A nasty incident at any time. But the fact it had been on the late evening news round-up almost turned this into the first trial by television. Indeed, at the time, it was suggested the punitive sanctions meted out by Scottish Rugby Union to both players appeared to have been influenced by the fact the incident had been viewed across the country.

As a result, Brown was suspended for 12 weeks. Hardie, accused of kneeing then stamping on Brown's forehead, was banned for 16 months.

Brown missed the entire Five Nations of 1977; the first three games because of suspension, the last because the SRU selectors overlooked him. His lack of fitness was cited. He never played for Scotland again. Yet, less than a week after the defeat to Wales, the giant "Broon frae Troon" – a stalwart of the Lions tours to New Zealand in 1971, and Willie John McBride's "Invincibles" of 1974 in South Africa – was selected for the British Lions tour to New Zealand that summer. Fitness?

Brown would overcome that obstacle. However, forgiving and forgetting Hardie proved more difficult. As he admitted years later, being denied the opportunity of dealing out some revenge of his own always gnawed at him. That was until he took up meditation. Big Broon being into meditation? I know, but it's true.

Brown played 30 times for Scotland and in eight Tests for the Lions.

Sadly, after a battle as brave as any he fought on the rugby field, Gordon succumbed to non-Hodgkin's lymphoma in March 2001, aged just 53.

Former Rangers and Scotland defender Tom Forsyth explains how his boss Jock Wallace went about getting Broon's 6'5", 17st 9lb giant frame into shape: "There were always players from

PART I - 1970s

other clubs, juniors and the likes, coming in for treatment at Ibrox so seeing a new face wasn't that strange. We'd even seen one or two boxers there, but the first time I saw Brown I wasn't sure if he was a boxer, or an out-of-shape goalkeeper or a really out-of-shape centre-half!

"Our manager, big Jock Wallace, took a real shine to Gordon. It was him who I think invited him in to train. Jock was always grabbing us and roughing us up, putting us in a headlock. He was daft that way. I think it went back to his days as a soldier in the jungle, but that was how he was and it was all good fun. I think he grabbed Gordon once – then realised that the big man's 'playing' was a lot rougher than even Jock expected.

"It was the old Ibrox back then, with the stepped terracing. Jock sent Gordon running up to the top, then back down. Up and down. After a few climbs, Gordon stopped, exhausted, coughing as if he was going to throw up.

"'Are you okay?' asked Jock.

"'I think so,' Gordon replied.

"'Well, I never telt yi tae stoap. Go!' barked Jock.

"Gordon was a big fella, imposing, and very strong, but a lovely, lovely guy. I was coming back from a hamstring injury and did some sprints against him.

"I felt like I was flying, quicker than I'd ever been before. I was putting it down to having had a bit of a rest, then really getting myself into shape, stretching properly, making sure I was really warmed up and supple. I felt great. Who'd have thought after a lay-off for that kind of injury I'd come back in the best shape possible?

"Eventually, I got back to training again with the rest of the Rangers squad. I couldn't wait. I mean, I was like a greyhound now.

"And that's when I realised how slow big Broon actually was; I'd been racing against a coo!"

14

SCOTLAND HAIL A NEW TRY-SCORING SENSATION

19 February 1977 • Five Nations, Murrayfield
Scotland 21–Ireland 18

If ever there was an example of justifying the selectors' faith then it came in the shape of Bill Gammell's dramatic debut for Scotland against Ireland in 1977.

Gammell, the gangly Edinburgh Wanderers wing, was one of two new caps to face the Irish (the other being Hawick prop Norman Pender). However, given the 26–6 leathering the Scots had taken in their opening tie against England a month previously, that new pair were two of eight personnel changes made to Scotland's starting XV.

After penalties were exchanged between Andy Irvine and Mike Gibson, Gammell scored his first try, left with the simplest of finishes from just a yard out after Ian McGeechan's pass had been deflected from an Irish hand.

By the turnaround, Ireland were 9–7 up thanks to a Mick Quinn drop goal and another Gibson penalty, however, the home support was soon hailing a new hero as Gammell picked up a loose ball and galloped home from 30 yards.

Irvine landed a penalty, Duncan Madsen scored a try and

PART I – 1970s

Dougie Morgan dropped a goal, Ireland's only response being a Quinn penalty to leave Scotland comfortable at 21–12.

However, two minutes into stoppage time, the scoreline was made to look slightly better for the Irish when Tom Grace's kick and chase wrong-footed Jim Renwick, enabling Gibson to score then convert. Scotland 21, Ireland 18.

Gammell's glorious debut wouldn't be repeated. Although a reserve that summer for the Lions tour to New Zealand, he made just four more appearances for Scotland, while failing to trouble the scorer, his last cap coming during a dire 15–0 loss to England at Murrayfield.

The kind of result that had assisted his promotion to full cap status in the first place subsequently proved to be his downfall.

15

ANDY IRVINE'S TRY AGAINST WALES

19 March 1977 • Five Nations, Murrayfield
Scotland 9–Wales 18

There was a period in time when Scotland could make tries out of nothing. It was more than coincidental that period was during the years Andy Irvine regularly donned the dark blue jersey. Whether at full-back or winger (a position where his blistering pace was utilised to great effect, especially during Lions tours), Irvine was a potent force and a magnificent finisher.

While one would always like Scotland's best moments to come as part of glorious victories, occasionally even gallant losses throw up their own magic moments, and the 1977 game against Wales happened to be such an occasion.

Having been royally stuffed in Paris a fortnight earlier, the full house at Murrayfield (although not quite as full as two years prior) must have thought that, against all odds, Scotland were going to turn over a Welsh side which had Triple Crown ambitions as they built a 9–3 lead thanks to Irvine's try and conversion.

After Phil Bennett had cancelled out an Ian McGeechan drop goal during the first half, the second period saw Scotland

PART I - 1970s

awarded a scrum on the Welsh ten. A quick heel down the no. 1 channel saw Douglas Morgan pick up and scuttle across field. McGeechan's run from stand-off was a decoy, Morgan instead targeting Jim Renwick on the crash ball. The Hawick man brushed off Terry Cobner, shirking Bennett's tackle and drawing JPR Williams, before passing to Irvine outside.

The Heriot's star collected at pace, his natural arc taking him inside and out of harm's way and behind the posts, though the outcome might have been different had Clive Burgess tackled Irvine, not the supporting Renwick.

Ahead by six, Scotland couldn't land a knockout blow and were felled themselves by tries from JJ Williams and a classic counter-attack and try from Phil Bennett, which ironically came about after Wales returned Irvine's probing, attacking chip kick.

16

HAWICK WIN PLAY-OFF TO TAKE TITLE

*12 April 1977 • Scottish Div 1 Championship Play-Off,
The Greenyards, Hawick 15–Gala 3*

These days in sport, play-offs are all the rage. In football, they are well established now as a means of adding extra interest, intrigue and injections of additional cash to league competitions that previously had been predictable and run out of steam. So too in rugby, where gone is the straight, round-robin league format in many countries in favour of that only being the process to decide which teams will have the honour of going for the big prize, in either a Premier or Grand Final.

Imagine then the interest there was to be had back in 1977, when, through chance rather than design, the Scottish Division One title was decided in a winner-takes-all finale.

Thus, it came to pass in March that year when Hawick, Gala and West of Scotland found themselves tied at the top of the table entering the final round of games, though West required a try-fest against Edinburgh Wanderers due to their inferior scoring record.

At start of play on the last day of term, Gala had a superior differential of five points over Hawick, and in beating Highland

PART I - 1970s

at Netherdale by 31–3 appeared to have done enough, given Hawick trailed away to Selkirk 19–7 at half-time. Amazingly, however, Hawick recovered to score nine tries in the second half, eventually winning 52–19.

When the arithmetic was done, West were out of the running, having only secured a 16–6 win against Wanderers. However, Gala had 270 points for, 84 against, while Hawick had a balance of 301–115, leaving both with an identical difference of plus 186 points. Having identical records of played 11, won nine and lost two games, this became 18 points.

Although provision had been made for such eventualities, no one had considered a tie on all counts.

As if to prove nothing has ever been simple in the club game in Scotland, the Scottish Rugby Union championship committee, who had instructed the clubs to agree their own arrangements for the title showdown, became the court of arbitration, as neither club could agree on the format for the fixture.

Hawick, who had won all three previous championships since the competition's inception, were happy to participate in the play-off on a Saturday already scheduled for a Border League game between the two at Netherdale, Gala's home, provided the play-off would be on neutral ground.

Gala, on the other hand, wanted the two games played separately, but would agree to such a postponement of their home match against Hawick if they received financial compensation for the cancellation of the Border League match, which would have been required to switch to a midweek date.

In the end, the championship game became a midweek fixture – the date of 12 April was finally decided upon – at the neutral Greenyards, home of Melrose, selected ahead of Selkirk's Philiphaugh and Murrayfield itself, which although favoured by some (because it would have saved the SRU rent money elsewhere) was dismissed as an option because even a substantial five-figure crowd would be lost in a stadium which only a few years before had accommodated 104,000.

If a form guide was required ahead of the play-off, then it suggested Hawick would start favourites, having two weeks earlier scored an 11–4 win over Gala at Netherdale in that Border League tie, in addition to defeating the men in maroon 14–6 way back in the November.

In the end, Hawick won the play-off, a match which, for all the hype and expectation, came up short on excitement for the 10,000-plus crowd who squeezed into the Greenyards. While the history books will show the telling score in a 15–3 win came from Donnie McLeod, the Hawick no. 8, who had only returned to the Green Machine pack after an ankle injury, the most telling tally was the number of injuries sustained by Gala, who were forced to play short-handed after injuries to Andrew Whitehead and Vic Chlebowski (recall, this was in the days before injury replacements had been sanctioned). That imbalance handed the defending champions a fourth consecutive championship.

17

HAWICK'S UNSTOPPABLE GREEN MACHINE

1978

The Scottish Rugby Union introduced the six-division league championship format in 1973, thus replacing the old merit system, the first of its kind within the home unions.

From the off, Hawick stamped their authority on the Scottish domestic game, reeling off five successive titles between 1974 and 1978, with West of Scotland as runners-up in that inaugural season, followed by Gala for the next three seasons – and only after a play-off in 1977 – with Boroughmuir the second-placed team in 77/78.

Yet, it was Heriot's FP who brought an end to Hawick's monopoly when taking the spoils in 1979.

Through that period, the Mansfield Park club was a valuable source of talent for the Scotland team at international level, with Jim Renwick, Colin Telfer, Ian Barnes, Alastair Cranston, Alan Tomes, Norman Pender, Colin Deans and Brian Hegarty all appearing in national team colours during that window.

After the three-year hiatus, Hawick were indeed back as Scottish champions, winning it in 1982 to end Gala's ambitions of claiming a hat-trick of titles, with Hawick themselves dominating once more, taking the national crown in 1984, 1985, 1986 and 1987.

Ten championships in 14 seasons, as Hawick achieved, has never been equalled, let alone surpassed.

18

SUPERSTARS

1978

Long before social media, PR managers, agents and personal sponsors, the only way international rugby players would be recognised would be for their exploits on the pitch. When the BBC bought into the American concept of the sporting elite going head-to-head across various disciplines and sports that weren't their stock in trade, they had a ready-made winner in *Superstars*, in effect a light-entertainment show involving sport, which was scheduled accordingly.

Instead then of rugby players only being given a Saturday afternoon to showcase their talents, suddenly they were projected on to TV screens to a peak viewing audience, so becoming household names.

Several Scottish rugby players made guest appearances but none quite as successfully as Andy Irvine, the pin-up boy of Scottish rugby, who showed millions of new fans just what a superb all-round athlete he was.

"Superstar" Andy Irvine recounts his exploits: "In those days, we were all amateurs and you just didn't have the time to do everything. The players then were working during the week, doing a day job, or studying for exams as I did. There were some who did athletics, or cricket during the summer, but much of the time we were on tour, so any thought of an athletics career never really came to much.

"It's also worth saying that I found athletics quite a lonely sport, quite boring, because you needed to do so much of it on your own, so I had started playing rugby because I enjoyed the team environment. Everything you did was with teammates, and there was a bit of camaraderie and a bit of craic when you were doing that. Athletics is a very individual, singular thing, a bit like swimming. Don't get me wrong, I liked the competition element to it, but I just wouldn't have fancied that kind of training so it wasn't anything I was very interested in pursuing.

"Foremost, we all played sport to enjoy ourselves and I did playing rugby. It might be different now, with the professional generation, where it's more of a business. The guys playing now, it's their livelihood and they don't tend to deviate from that.

"I don't know if I'd have liked that. We played for pleasure – and loved every minute of it. I'm not so sure the guys today can say that. I'm sure today the professional players must look forward to just having a day off, but it's about what you're used to, I suppose.

"However, in my day, there was a bit of scope to try other things.

"*Superstars* was a great experience, meeting a lot of different sportsmen from different sports and disciplines. It was a big deal back in the day, primetime TV when you only had three channels. It certainly brought you to the attention of many non-sporting folk.

"But while the US version had athletes competing in Hawaii and Florida, I think we got Bath and Cwmbran.

PART I - 1970s

"One of the heats I was involved in included Phil Bennett of Llanelli and Wales, who I had toured with a few times with the Lions. A bit of a busman's holiday.

"We both did the 100 metres and I knew he'd be quite quick over the first 50 metres, but I did fancy myself over the full distance, and so it proved.

"I won a steeplechase race as well and qualified for the Grand Final, where I finished third. It was something that was different, but hugely enjoyable and very competitive. There was a lot of pride to be defended, and one or two egos that were threatened. But good fun.

"For the same reasons as I mentioned earlier, you just wouldn't get the top sportsmen from rugby, football, judo, athletics, boxing and whatever racing each other on bikes or going head-to-head in the gym. Very different days..."

PART II

1980s

19

THE VERY WORST AND VERY BEST OF ANDY IRVINE

16 February 1980 • Five Nations, Murrayfield
Scotland 22–France 14

If one match epitomised the greatness of Andy Irvine then perhaps this was it. It was also a game which showed how fickle life could be as an international player, especially for a place-kicker. Scotland's game record entering this match was utterly shambolic, having failed to win in their previous 13 matches, their last victory being against Ireland in 1977 (albeit with a few draws thrown in along the way).

Against the French, the Scots could have been out of sight but instead trailed 14–4 (Scotland's points coming from a John Rutherford try). This deficit owed everything to the inaccuracy of Irvine, who was so wide of the mark with several kicks that the golden boy was being jeered.

With a terrific late rally, however, the Heriot's full-back almost single-handedly won the game. First, with just 15 minutes remaining, the instrumental Irvine rounded off a high-speed break, the ball having passed through the hands of Rutherford, Jim Renwick and twice through David Johnston and Bruce Hay, to score in the left-wing corner, picking up and diving over after

French full-back Serge Gabernet had attempted to bat the ball away. Irvine converted arguably his most difficult kick of the day to make it 14–10. Scotland, throwing caution to the wind, again attacked from well within their own territory. Renwick pinched possession, Roy Laidlaw and Alan Tomes kept the ball alive and the subsequent interplay between Renwick, Johnston and Rutherford enabled Irvine to finish the move by the posts, this time with Renwick converting.

Irvine landed two penalty goals, one awarded for offside on the French ten, the other from obstruction midway into the French half, to complete the win. The Scotland full-back had scored 16 individual points in just 14 minutes, a remarkable feat in any circumstances, but exceptional given the torrid afternoon he had endured earlier. Having been booed previously, his final contribution was heralded by a chorus of "Irvine, Irvine." How wonderfully Scottish.

Broadcaster John Inverdale, a fan and admirer of Andy Irvine, recounts why the Scotland full-back made rugby box office: "I do remember this match vividly. It was what we had come to expect from Andy Irvine, a player who, for me, was like no other.

"I think the great thing is that for me you can't think about Andy Irvine without thinking about JPR Williams. If you are of a certain age and you played in the back three – although that phrase didn't exist when those two were at their peak; you were a full-back or a wing – then you were either in the JPR camp or the Andy Irvine camp. I belonged in the latter.

"On one hand, you had this rugged, no-nonsense last line in what was a great Welsh side, who of course was a doctor, who appeared intent on making some opponents his customers. Remember that famous shoulder-charge tackle on Jean-François Gourdon in the 1976 Grand Slam decider against France? Andy would never have done that. He'd have asked, 'Would you mind terribly if I tackled you into touch?'

PART II - 1980s

"Andy played and looked like nothing I'd seen on the rugby field before. Had The Beatles been Scottish, he could have qualified as the fifth member. He was of the time, with his long hair, and a master of the 'new' side-foot kicking style. Great as JPR was, there was loads about Andy that set him apart and appealed to a teenage schoolboy who fancied himself as a number 15. Going to school in Bristol, there were several Welsh kids in our school, and we would argue endlessly about their individual merits and who was best. For me, they were both great players but chalk and cheese when it came to style – and Irvine had an abundance of that.

"If I ever missed a tackle, I would tell myself Andy would make up for it by doing something else, like going on a dazzling run. Occasionally, a fundamental lack of talent would prevent me from making amends. Make that the majority of the time. However, I was just one boy who began to really get into rugby because of the excitement Andy Irvine generated.

"We had been used to seeing the full-back catch the ball then kick it out of play. That was basically what you did, and you'd occasionally come up in the line, but that was often more by accident than intent. Then suddenly this bloke came along who, whenever the opportunity arose, would just take off at high speed. I don't know, maybe his kicking and punting, to start with, wasn't one of the strengths of his game and he just felt more confident running.

"But Andy had the ability to run from almost anywhere on the pitch and turn any kind of possession into a potential attacking option. It was almost as if he was ready-made to play for the likes of the Barbarians, with their style and approach.

"If you say 'Andy Irvine' to anyone, they never say, 'Oh, wasn't that an amazing tackle he made.' No, they speak of his blistering pace, that break, his eye for an opening and the way he could just weave his way around players, all because of his amazing speed.

"He had a hint of Gerald Davies about him, perhaps not with the dancing, twinkling feet, but he had that natural, raw pace.

"What I think is forgotten, or seldom gets mentioned, is that invariably, Irvine always found himself in the right place, so he read the game brilliantly. He was a very clever player, an amazing rugby intellect. Put all of those parts together and you can see why he was promoted so quickly to being a Test player with the Lions in 1974.

"He ran great support lines as well, so if there was an opening or opportunity made by a Rutherford or Renwick, Andy was often on their shoulder, having read what they were going to try.

"The fact that Andy ran like an absolute demon – that wasn't the norm. We're used these days to Stuart Hogg playing like Stuart Hogg does. But in the early to mid-1970s, Andy Irvine played like nothing we'd seen before.

"When you look at the modern world, and when Hogg is playing or isn't playing, it was the same if Irvine played or didn't play. It is, and was, generally accepted that if either of them was missing, the game was not generally going to be quite as exciting as when they played. I think that is one of the greatest things you can ever say about any sportsperson, whatever the sport.

"How Hogg approaches the game is the accepted way, but when Irvine broke into the Scotland team, it was really something quite revolutionary. I never tired of watching him."

20

ALL WHITE ON THE NIGHT AS SCOTLAND BEAT AUSTRALIA AND THE ELEMENTS

19 December 1981 • Autumn Test, Murrayfield
Scotland 24–Australia 15

In general, recollecting matches of 30-odd years ago can be troublesome. However, the mere mention of snow has many folk zeroing in on one game in particular.

Australia's tour to the British Isles in 1981 actually lasted into the following year, their final Test on the trip coming in early January, by which time Britain was in the midst of its coldest and most prolonged winter in nearly 20 years. And to think, they could have had a Christmas barbie on the beach back home.

Instead, they had to endure the kind of weather featured on TV adverts and festive cards from that time of year as they prepared to meet Scotland a week shy of Christmas itself.

Preparation for the game in the Scots capital – following a win in Dublin and an 18–13 loss in Cardiff – were far from ideal. Indeed, they had to go seeking out a playable pitch on which to train on the Thursday, the nearest available being 20 miles away at North Berwick. While Scotland used straw bales for tackling practice on the back pitches at the national rugby stadium, the

Aussies were given access to the snow-free international surface on the Friday by the generous SRU.

Just like Easter Road and Ibrox – the only two grounds in Scotland to stage Premier League football matches that weekend – the benefits of the Murrayfield undersoil heating proved invaluable.

With piles of snow around the edges of the pitch, the Australians appeared to have no trouble with the cold. Indeed, with ball in hand, they were absolutely red hot in the first half, leading 15–12 at half-time with three tries from Simon Poidevin, Brendan Moon and Andrew Slack. Scotland kept in touch, just, through Andy Irvine.

However, had his counterpart in the kicking stakes, Australian centre Paul McLean, taken all of his opportunities, his team would have been 27–12 to the good. Instead, he landed just one of six. Such inaccuracy proved costly.

Irvine's fifth penalty tied the scores, and after a quarter of virtual inactivity, John Rutherford dropped a goal to give the hosts the lead at 18–15, before Jim Renwick popped in for a try which was again converted by Irvine, equalling his previous international best of 17 points in a match.

If snow had been an issue, it was nothing compared to what befell Britain by mid-January, when the nation was in the grip of a record-breaking freeze, the temperature dropping to –27.2 in Braemar – by which time the Australians had gone home.

21

SCOTLAND HAVE A WALES OF A TIME

20 March 1982 • Five Nations, Cardiff
Wales 18–Scotland 34

There was a time (some may say there still is) when Scotland set off for Cardiff assured in the knowledge that well-rehearsed excuses would be required come the end of 80 minutes against Wales. Prior to this encounter, Scotland hadn't won in the principality since 1962, and only three times during the century.

Those ghosts, however, were well and truly laid to rest on that spring afternoon when the Scots turned in an exhibition of running rugby. Yes, it was unexpected, but what no one had seen coming was the ease and manner of the Scottish triumph, by five tries to one, thus securing the country's first away win in the Five Nations since toppling Ireland in 1976.

Having wrapped up the wooden spoon convincingly the previous year, a draw at Twickenham was greatly received; losing to Ireland in Dublin – or more accurately the boot of Ollie Campbell – as the men in green secured the Triple Crown less so. However, a comfortable win against the French in Edinburgh at least had brought some respectability to this campaign. There was, therefore, a more relaxed atmosphere within the Scotland camp as they concluded their domestic international season, ahead of a summer tour to Australia.

Scotland included just one new cap, Gosforth winger Jim Pollock. The prefix of "lucky" hadn't yet been applied.

Scotland fell behind to a Gwyn Evans penalty. Indeed, it was the Maesteg full-back who maintained any level of respectability for the hosts during the afternoon. Iain Paxton's try soon turned the momentum though and gave Scotland an insight into what kind of day it would be.

Having cashed in on the Welsh kicking possession away, Scotland profited once more when Rob Ackerman spilled the ball midway inside the Scotland half when he was unable to hold Ray Gravell's pass. John Rutherford was first to the ball, popping it up for Calder, who passed to the numberless Jim Renwick (his shirt had been ripped in an earlier skirmish), who, from just inside his own half, won the foot race against some notable flyers, Ackerman and Clive Rees in particular, to touch down under the posts – a try to go with his earlier opportunistic drop goal from distance.

At half-time Scotland led 13–9. Eight minutes into the second half, Pollock made it a debut to remember. After David Johnston had hacked upfield, with Colin Deans providing his usual nuisance factor, the Scots – with Iain Milne proving an immovable backstop – won a ruck in front of the Welsh posts, from which Roy Laidlaw scampered right to put the ball through Rutherford, Renwick and skipper Andy Irvine to tee up Pollock for a score in the corner. Derek White, operating at no. 8 after Paxton's demise, picked up and crashed over for yet another Scotland try off a five-metre scrum.

Scotland were set back on their heels momentarily when Eddie Butler rounded off a great running move to score for Wales. But this was only a momentary misfire. Scotland roared

PART II – 1980s

back, and with 12 minutes remaining – and with Welsh captain Gareth Davies preoccupied by Rutherford's positioning for what looked like another drop goal attempt (he had scored one earlier in the half) – the future Lions stand-off was able to release centre Johnston on his outside, the Watsonians centre running the perfect arc to grab the clinching try. Irvine kicked his fourth conversion to complete an incredible 34–18 rout.

It was a day never to be forgotten – possibly because there had been nothing to remember in Cardiff for the two decades previous.

Jim Renwick on Scotland not needing Andy Irvine to beat Wales: "The night before the game Wales had lost Terry Holmes at scrum-half and no. 8 Jeff Squire, but Keith Robertson had the flu so we had to bring in a fella Jim Pollock from Gosforth, winger, or 'Lucky Jim' as he became known, for good reason.

"Them having the call-offs – especially big players like that – gave us a wee edge – well, it gave me a wee edge, and even though we had a terrible record down there, I think we were all feeling quite relaxed.

"I've watched the game a few times – I think I deserved it seeing some of the results I found myself on the end of – and every wee chance we got, we counter-attacked. Wales were hard on their boys after that game, but it was improvisation – off-the-cuff stuff from us. It wasn't planned, so reading it and defending it, that was very difficult.

"It was all about using the ball; you've got the tool, as they say – use it. I suppose that's the way we're playing now when we get the ball, using it at every turn.

"Even back then, we were using video to watch the opponents. I had noticed Gravell at outside centre drifted wide. I said to Andy, as captain, that if we could suck him in, and get the ball to Andy coming through, we could be in business.

"Andy watched the tape and agreed, and said, 'Right, Jim, this is what we'll do. On the first play, we'll miss one out and give it to me; the second time, we'll do the double dummy and throw the ball out to me; the next play, we'll go with the double scissors and out to me, and then the dummy scissors and miss, out to me.'

"I said, 'If you don't mind, I'm getting missed out all the time.' He says, 'Jim, the game isn't all about you.'

"That's Mr Irvine for you – honest.

"Unfortunately, that turned out to be Andy's last Five Nations game for Scotland. Unusually, he was quite quiet, probably because other folk were doing all the scoring – maybe we should have tried that a bit earlier!

"Sometimes games come your way, but that was a game Andy – who, let's be honest, had won so many games for Scotland in the past – didn't need to go looking for. We were never really chasing it.

"We had scored two tries; the one big [Iain] Paxton was involved in and Jim [Calder] scored, and then there was another one nobody mentions. That would be mine. Wales got back into it at half-time, as we were only four points up.

"But to have a second half like that was just magic. I suppose maybe we shouldn't have been too surprised. We had some cracking backs, but every play, either planned or spontaneous, we looked like scoring.

"Rud [John Rutherford] scored a drop goal, after I'd kicked one in the first half. Literally, anything we went for or tried worked.

"For a good few years – for as long as I could remember – we had lost a lot of games narrowly, just the odd point, or odd kick or mistake costing us. We weren't consistent enough, but we did have some good players – world-class players with the likes of Andy, who so many times had been a match winner.

PART II - 1980s

"I don't think we were shy of self-belief, or belief in our ability. We had a good tour to New Zealand in 1981 – we came close in the first Test, not so close in the second – but we had a lot of good players, and the pack that summer won the Grand Slam three years later. The talent was there – putting it all together was where we struggled a wee bit.

"Cardiff was special. That folk are still talking about it nearly 40 years later shows how special it was. It might have been because no one did that to Wales in Cardiff back then. If the supporters enjoyed it, so did the players. I'd had a few cracks with Ray Gravell over the years, especially when Steve Fenwick played alongside him, and we didn't come out on top too often.

"But after that game, Gravell and the other centre, Alun Donovan, never played again for Wales. Neither did the fella [Gerald] Williams that replaced Holmes.

"I don't think the Welsh took it well."

22

IAIN PAXTON'S TRY OF THE SEASON

1982

Throughout their history, even in barren spells in terms of results, the Scots have always had the ability to score fantastic tries, often when least expected, regularly turning the proverbial scraps into a thing of beauty.

Their opening score in Cardiff back in 1982 was exactly that, making and taking something from nothing to manufacture one of the best remembered tries in history.

With the hosts 3–0 up, Wales looked to press home that early advantage, skipper Gareth Davies chipping behind Scots lines, his kick fielded by Roger Baird. However, instead of the Kelso winger seeking the sanctuary of touch, he counter-attacked, setting off from just ten yards off his own line and with the narrowest of channels to negotiate on his left wing, so catching the Welsh completely by surprise.

Baird sped up the touchline, his pace and direction only matched by no. 8 Iain Paxton, who, with giant strides, bounded from inside his own half to the 22, where he was tackled (and accidentally injured) by Clive Rees. The Selkirk man, however, still managed to offload to his South colleague Alan Tomes, who,

PART II - 1980s

with a basketball pass, connected with Jim Calder to dive over.

It was a try that left Wales bewildered, Scotland ebullient. "That surely must be the try of this season's internationals," suggested Bill McLaren, having called home the score with his usual precision. Few argued at the time or since.

23

SCOTS RAIDERS STEW-MEL TAKE THE MIDDLESEX SEVENS

8 May 1982 • Middlesex Sevens, Twickenham

Long before the proliferation of Sevens rugby, there were one of two "jewels in the crown" that would be particularly treasured. One was, of course, the Melrose title, where this particular branch of rugby first took root; the second would be the Middlesex Sevens, which in addition to being populated by the big London clubs (and there were big London clubs back then) would also have their own list of invitees.

In 1982, Stewart's-Melville FP headed south, unfancied by many but confident within their own ranks, despite having made up the numbers and little more in competitions nearer to home.

The visitors – aiming to become the first guest side since Heriot's FP in 1949 to take the coveted title – reached the sharp end of proceedings with a 20–10 win over Exeter University, a team that had clocked up 162 points in their preliminary rounds but were no match for the Scots visitors when Andy Blackwood cut loose to grab a hat-trick of scores.

Beating London Scottish 18–12 in the quarter-finals was merely an overture for better things to come – namely a 12–0

PART II – 1980s

semi-final victory against holders Rosslyn Park (Andy Ripley et al.), where scrum-half Dougie Morgan took all the points, leading to a final against Richmond, favourites and winners in five of the previous eight years.

A towel would have been thrown in had the final been a boxing bout, the men from the Scots capital scoring a thumping 34–12 victory in the decider: Blackwood with a brace – making him leading try scorer in the tournament with six – Jim Calder and winger John Mackenzie (with a treble) the try scorers, with the amazingly reliable boot of Morgan doing the rest. No wonder he celebrated with a handstand when the final whistle sounded.

Finlay Calder on a day to remember at sunny Twickenham: "That was a Seven and a half; Dougie Wyllie and Dougie Morgan were the half-backs and me, brother Jim and Alex Brewster made up the forwards.

"We would win plenty of ball, and the two Dougies knew what to do with it, but it was out wide where we had the real cutting edge. Most teams had a flying winger, but we had two wide players – John Mackenzie and Andy Blackwood, who had gears others couldn't imagine.

"It was an impressive unit, and I'm not just saying that because I was part of it; five full internationals by the time their careers were finished, and three were British Lions, out of the one club. Amazing.

"It was great – although you're not aware of maybe how great it was at the time. Easy to get sentimental, but I'd have backed that team against many 'exponents' today."

24

ACHIEVEMENTS FOR IRVINE AND SCOTS DOWN UNDER

4 July 1982 • Summer Tour, Brisbane
Australia 7–Scotland 12

In amongst international news headlines such as the ill-fated Falklands taskforce ship HMS *Sheffield* may have been carrying nuclear weapons, or that the newly born second in line to the throne would be known as William, and that his mother may celebrate his birth and her 21st birthday with a glass of champagne, Scotland's rugby players were about to write a few headlines of their own for the back pages.

Victory in Cardiff had raised confidence – and expectation levels – ahead of the summer tour to Australia. If Scotland could win in Wales for the first time in donkey's years, then a first-ever win in Oz would naturally follow.

Brisbane's Ballymore Stadium would host the first of two Tests that summer, with the Scots selecting a side which ranged from the most experienced player still playing – full-back and captain Andy Irvine, who was winning his 50th cap – and a pair of newcomers: Gerry McGuinness, the West of Scotland loose head, and London Scottish centre Rick Gordon.

Bettering Mark Ella's attempt, which struck a post, a John

PART II - 1980s

Rutherford drop goal gave Scotland the lead in one of their few meaningful forays into the land of gold and green, annulled by Mike Hawker, deputising for the absent Paul McLean, Australia's leading international points accumulator.

Sheer horsepower up front saw Scotland assert themselves in the second half, and when Colin Deans pinched one against the head 12 minutes after half-time, Roy Laidlaw cut to the right, brought Rutherford into play and his vision and accurate toss out to the unmarked Keith Robertson brought Scotland a somewhat unexpected lead.

Irvine's touchline conversion was sound, unlike Hawker's effort on the hour off his own try. Scotland led 9–7, although the story would have been much edited had the Australian wing not been wide with four penalty attempts. In contrast, with around ten minutes remaining, Irvine remained composed to sink a penalty – and Australian hopes – after Wallabies skipper Tony Shaw had punched Deans.

A first-ever win in Australia was thus secured. Now for the series, or not. Australia, with McLean reinstated, won 33–9 at the Sydney Cricket Ground, McLean kicking 21 of those points, including five penalties – the same number Hawker had been presented with a week earlier.

In what proved to be his last outing in a Scotland jersey, Andy Irvine surpassed the joint-caps record he shared with Sandy Carmichael, while Gordon doubled his count with what would be his second and final Scotland appearance, thus having played out his entire international career 10,000 miles from Murrayfield.

25

WHEN HISTORY OF THE WRONG KIND WAS MADE

5 March 1983 • Five Nations, Twickenham
England 12–Scotland 22

Had Scotland managed to hold out just a few minutes longer against England in their epic Calcutta Cup clash at Twickenham in March 2019, they would have rewritten history and erased an unwanted fact in the process – namely that not since 1983 had a Scotland team beaten England on their own patch.

The very name Twickenham has become a painful reminder of missed opportunities and of days of coming second to England, occasionally by a distance. All of which makes the tale of 1983 even more mythical.

Scotland, under the guidance of coach Jim Telfer, travelled south hoping to avoid a Five Nations whitewash after a two-point loss to Ireland, and four-point defeats in Paris and against Wales. Narrow margins and, in general, the Scots hadn't been playing badly. The arithmetic, in terms of points though, totalled nil. You don't get rewarded for coming close.

When it came to beating England at HQ, Scotland's last win had been in 1971, although they did wangle a draw in 1979, an Andy Irvine penalty securing a 7–7 draw. So, with history

PART II - 1980s

– both distant and short-term – against them, Scotland trooped south more in hope than anything else.

There was one small ray of sunshine on the horizon, however. The game would be refereed by Tom Doocey, a hotelier from Christchurch – not Dorset but New Zealand – and therefore more likely to be forgiving and "tolerant" of Scotland's rucking style.

England led almost immediately, John Horton landing a drop goal, equalised by Peter Dods with a penalty after Steve Smith had tackled Jim Renwick, minus the ball when a penalty try should have been forthcoming. Maybe the referee was from the south coast after all.

There was still nothing between the teams at half-time, England full-back Dusty Hare with a brace of penalties, each matched by Dods. After the switch of ends, however, Scotland turned pressure into points. Firstly, scrum-half Roy Laidlaw led England's back row a merry dance to score, drifting outside Nick Jeavons and past John Scott for a try which Dods converted. Hare, whose coming together with winger Tony Swift had given Scotland the scrum from which Laidlaw scored, made some amends with his third goal.

It took three attempts – the first two from John Rutherford and Renwick, winning a record-equalling 51st cap – before Keith Robertson slipped over a tidy drop goal to put Scotland a score in front, leaving Gala giant Tom Smith, making his debut, to apply the *coup de grâce*, showing some of his basketball-playing dexterity to work space at a goal-line line-out to plunge over.

Tom Smith was the first Scot to be a double international at basketball and rugby union since Pringle Fisher. He says:

"International rugby was all new to me, although we had an inspirational leader in Jim Aitken, as he would prove the following year.

"England had some big lads up front, but, not being the most mobile, compared to Leslie and Beattie and Paxton, the idea was to keep moving forward, and keep moving their pack around the field. And it worked.

"Did I think people would be talking about me 30-odd years later? No, not really."

The English perspective from Gloucester and Lions lock Steve Boyle: "My background first: my father was Scottish, and I still get a buzz when I go home to the Borders. He's passed now but I have two sisters and a stepmum who call Scotland home. Around 1976, I was given a choice: play for Anglo Scots versus someone on a wet Wednesday night or tour Canada for six weeks with the England U23 squad. I chose Canada but sometimes wonder what would have been had I chosen the Anglos.

"Scotland had replaced Cubby [Bill Cuthbertson] with [Iain] Paxton, and he made a difference around the park.

"I still feel we had chances to win the game, but Roy's try was a beaut and he took it well, having the perfect blindside gap to aim for, and he scuttled one beautifully. Tom Smith went over from a line-out and we failed to cross the whitewash at all, despite a few chances.

"All in all, we were off the pace and Scotland were fairly comfortable by the end. Laidlaw and Rutherford were superb on the day and probably made the difference."

26

BARBARIANS EXHIBITION SHOWCASES LAFOND AND RUTHERFORD

26 March 1983 • Commemorative Match, Murrayfield
Scotland 13–Barbarians 26

The opening of the new East Stand at Murrayfield required an event to mark the occasion. The invitation to the Barbarians to partake in a special commemorative game not only attracted Princess Anne (as she was still known then) to the capital but also the BBC's cameras (for viewers in Scotland only). Thankfully, they were able to record, for posterity, some exhibition rugby from the Baa-Baas, but also some world-class fly-half play from John Rutherford.

"Rud" had been one of the key players earlier in the month as Scotland recorded a victory at Twickenham against the English, and faced with several others from that nation – along with a good helping from France and Wales, and Springboks trio Errol Tobias, Danie Gerber and Hennie Bekker (whose rather substantial frame did serious damage to Keith Robertson's shoulder) – he turned in another headline-grabbing display with two tries.

His first came after Peter Dods had scythed through the Barbarians backs, racing half the length of the pitch and linking with Jim Calder inside before he lobbed a basketball pass wide to Rutherford to score unhindered.

The game as a contest was over (the Barbarians eventually won 26–12) when Rutherford finished off a move that emanated on the Scots 22. The Selkirk stand-off – who would be part of the Lions tour to New Zealand that summer – set Jim Renwick off and running, play taken on by Jim Calder again, who set up a ruck. From there, Roy Laidlaw broke clear, swapping passes with John Beattie before giving the ball to Rutherford, wide left, who checked back inside to score.

If Rutherford's tries were good, in terms of team involvement, then the *pièce de résistance* came from the as-yet uncapped French full-back, Jean-Baptiste Lafond.

His countryman, prop Robert Paparemborde, making an international farewell, delivered something of a hospital pass to the 21-year-old, having to field a bouncing ball on his own 22 while confronted by Rutherford. The Scot appeared to have felled Lafond, but he somehow managed to maintain traction and he was gone, dancing past Laidlaw. When shown the outside by covering wingman Jim Pollock, he accelerated around Scotland's last-line tackler.

A memorable score on a memorable day.

27

FREE-FLOWING FRENCH WIN HISTORIC MELROSE TITLE

9 April 1983 • Melrose Sevens, The Greenyards

There have been many big-name winners of the Melrose Sevens, but few managed to capture the imagination quite so stylishly as the winners of the Centenary tournament in the spring of 1983.

The French Barbarians squad was star-studded, and they delivered with the kind of flair and panache that would have delighted the inventor of the shortened version of the game one hundred years earlier, local butcher Ned Haig.

While the Anglo-derivative of the select side, with five international players in their ranks, succumbed to Royal High in their opening tie, the French Baa-Baas overcame a stubborn Watsonians amalgam which led twice through tries from Gordon Forbes and Euan Kennedy, but was eventually seen off with a Patrick Mesny try on the final whistle.

It was an easier passage through the next couple of rounds, defeating Glasgow High/Kelvinside and Heriot's FP in the last eight, but at a cost: hooker Philippe Dintrans took an accidental kick to the mouth during the second tie and played no further part. They then lost another squad member, the livewire Didier

Camberabero, who withdrew following a comprehensive semi-final victory against Richmond with a hand injury.

That left Stewart's-Melville FP between the French exhibitionists and the Ladies Cup. The Edinburgh club had beaten hosts Melrose, Gordonians and Bangor, before tackling Kelso in an absorbing semi-final, which saw the Borderers lead 14–0 through scores from Andrew Ker, Eric Paxton and Jim Hewit, only for Stew-Mel to strike back in the remaining four minutes with tries from Finlay Calder, the rapid Andy Blackwood (who would conclude the tournament as the leading try scorer) and Dougie Wyllie. Dougie Morgan converted all three on his way to 33 points on the day.

How Stewart's-Melville had anything left in the tank after that epic tie was beyond most folk, but while their seven – which also included the Brewster brothers and Simon Scott – pushed the French side all the way, they fell just shy. Long-range tries from Éric Fourniols – one from 70 yards, the other from his own line after he gave Blackwood the slip – earned Fourniols, Serge Blanco, Jean-Baptiste Lafond (who days earlier had sparkled with the Barbarians at Murrayfield), Jean-Pierre Elissalde, Jean-Luc Joinel, Mesny and Marc Andriou their place in history.

28

NOT EVEN LUCKY JIM COULD END THE ALL BLACKS HOODOO

12 November 1983 • Autumn Test, Murrayfield
Scotland 25–New Zealand 25

The phrase "impact player" is well and maybe overly used today. The term describes a player who may change the course of a game, perhaps a season. However, few of today's generation has ever made anything like the impact Jim Pollock made

An unknown to the wider public, Jim Pollock was plucked from relative obscurity to make his international debut when Scotland beat Wales in Cardiff for the first time in 20 years.

His second came when Scotland overturned England at Twickenham after a gap of a dozen years, while cap three was earned when Scotland gained their best-ever result against the mighty All Blacks in 1983, a 25–25 draw at Murrayfield, while appearances four, five and six – against England, Ireland and France respectively – produced a Calcutta Cup, a Triple Crown and a Grand Slam.

And to think someone once asked, "So, how did you come by the nickname 'Lucky Jim'?"

Where perhaps his good fortune ran out momentarily was when the Scots faced the All Blacks in 1983, a tour which only came about because New Zealand's planned trip to Argentina was cancelled. Something to do with the Kiwis backing Britain when they reclaimed the Falklands.

There had been enough Scots on the summer tour to New Zealand with the Lions, including coach Jim Telfer, to know what the All Blacks were capable of. Yet, in that autumn Test, Scotland came as close as they'd ever done to beating them, and had Peter Dods not missed the conversion off Pollock's last-gasp try, history could have been different.

What many forget was that Pollock was also involved in the game's final act – a tackle on the ball-less Bernie Fraser, which should have given New Zealand a penalty. But referee René Hourquet, after consulting Scots line judge Brian Anderson, decided not to bother.

Jim Pollock on getting a call, a try or two, and a punch on the nose: "The Anglo Scots were around in those days and I had been playing quite well for them and my club, Gosforth. Down in London, I had scored a couple of times against South in the old Inter-District games, and maybe that brought me some recognition. Duncan Madsen, the former Scotland hooker, he had an affinity with Gosforth and had by now become one of the Scottish selectors.

"Then there was a guy by the name of Graham Law, who was a young trainee journalist studying in Newcastle, who I'm sure was tasked with finding out how Scottish I actually was. And a certain Ally McCoist, who was at Sunderland – his name was mentioned as well. Don't ask me how. 'Scots Mafia', let's say.

"I had been teaching at Kenton Comprehensive – my first job, state school and loved it – when one Thursday morning the school secretary – in her heels – ran across the field to tell me a Mr MacGregor [Ian] had been on the phone. You know how it is – who's taking the piss?

PART II - 1980s

"But it was legit, and he told me Keith Robertson had tonsillitis and to get myself on the train from Newcastle down to Cardiff and on to the St Pierre Golf and Country Club where the Scots lads were going to be staying.

"The school were delighted. It was the first time they'd been recognised in this way and they couldn't have been happier. They weren't even a rugby school, but after that I created a couple of teams and they were a rugby-playing school.

"On my journey to Wales I vividly remember sitting next to a guy who was in the Army, who had about 35 cans of beer and managed to spill a good few over himself, over the table and over me. When I arrived at the hotel I was stinking of drink.

"My first introduction to the rest of the team was when we had a run around, doing a few backs moves, which almost did for me because I went for a miss-one move and I went into a bunker.

"Fortunately, there weren't any traps like that at Cardiff Arms Park. Jim Telfer decided that we weren't going to soak up the atmosphere so we only arrived an hour or so before kick-off. I think his thinking was he didn't want us to get overawed by the crowd or the place. You could say it worked.

"I picked up a jar of Vaseline, or at least I thought it was – turned out to be Fiery Jack, so I couldn't feel anything during the game, or indeed after I came out the shower.

"What a match to be involved in. Andy Irvine – what a player – passed for me to score in the corner, which was nice of him. A wonderful experience and a wonderful team.

"The games I played in where we won were never in doubt. We stuffed Wales – and England at Twickenham. It had been a long time since we had won there, nothing like what it's like now.

"The 1984 game, we never felt under pressure, and then we

thumped Ireland in the Triple Crown game; Peter Dods was immense, Keith scored a great try – he had come back into the team at centre after big Euan Kennedy was injured in the England game – and Roy [Laidlaw] scored a couple, though I'm sure he could have given one to me.

"And France was like the England game – always in control, always with something in reserve, although that's how I saw it.

"The only game we didn't win in the spell was against the All Blacks. It was a fantastic result, though a win would have been better, but there was so little footage of the game shown at the time because there was a strike amongst broadcast staff and technicians, I don't really remember. But I do recall it wasn't on TV, which was a crying shame. That happened in a few big matches around that time.

"I scored a try in the last minute to tie the scores, but it was right out on the corner and it left Dodsy [Peter Dods] with an impossible kick to win it.

"The two things I took from that game were: one, it was a great chance to get a first-ever win, and two, I ended up getting a bop on the nose from Bernie Fraser, the Kiwi wing.

"He had scored twice already and I was just determined he wouldn't get a third, so I tackled him. Unfortunately, he didn't have the ball, but he did have a good right hook, and just off the pitch he gave me a good smack.

"It was one of the first times I can recall the touch judge getting involved for foul play. Reality was I'd have done the same.

"What a spell in my life though – I suppose I didn't do rehearsals or warm-up games, did I?

"Another match I played in was against the Barbarians. There was some problem as well with the BBC for the game to open up the new stand at Murrayfield.

"Rud [John Rutherford] scored a couple of tries and Keith got injured when the biggest South African in the world, Hennie Bekker, went down like a tree on him. That was some Baa-Baas team with Danie Gerber and Errol Tobias in it as well.

"What I remember most of that game was the French winger, Lafond, carving up the pitch, picking it up on his own try line, running around the entire Scotland team, and giving a half sidestep just to throw me as I arrive, having covered 60 yards to get near him.

"A while later I was sitting watching *A Question of Sport* and that try came up as a question: 'Name the French player scoring the try and the Scotsman missing the tackle?' Missing the bloody tackle? There were about ten of them before me who missed him!

"There was nothing lucky about that."

29

A SEASON THAT JUST GOT BETTER, AND BETTER, AND BETTER STILL

1984

From the first game in January, in Cardiff, until the showdown in March against France, Scotland pieced together this campaign, bit by bit, match by match. And, other than when edging home 15–9 against Wales, there was a prize to be had in each game thereafter.

While some were just a few appearances into their international careers when the call came, good for them. Iain Milne, "The Bear from Goldenacre", was a five-year veteran in Scotland colours who had seen it all before.

Or, at least he thought he had, until that day in 1984: "It maybe wasn't as unexpected as many have believed. Over a number of years, there had been building blocks put in place. The tour to New Zealand in 1981 was the first time we had come under Jim Telfer's control and tutelage. We had a terrific win in Cardiff in 1982, then the following year we beat England at Twickenham, many of the boys went with the Lions to New Zealand, and although they destroyed us in the Test series, in a more parochial context, we saw those from England, Wales and Ireland up close and realised most of them were no better than us, maybe even deficient in one department.

PART II – 1980s

Drawing against the All Blacks at Murrayfield in the November before the Five Nations continued the progression. Taking those results as indicators, Scotland was certainly going down the right road.

"We didn't think that going into 1984, we were title contenders, but we knew on our day, we probably could match any team.

"We kicked off in Cardiff, which after the result in 1982, didn't carry any trepidation. We were well prepared, and again, the team contained some very good players. All of those characteristics applied to the England match as well.

"Because of the old Five Nations format, there was a week where you would sit out – not ideal but it was the same for everyone. However, England kicked off their season at Murrayfield and were a bit underdone in terms of prep, whereas we were up to speed and had rid ourselves of the rough edges in Cardiff.

"While the score never ran away from England, similarly, neither did I ever feel England posed any great threat to us. Again, this was only the second fixture in for us and the biggest thing that day was retaining the Calcutta Cup.

"If those two fixtures were relatively relaxed, in terms of the build-up and expectation, Ireland was the complete opposite because there was a major prize up for grabs. It isn't being unkind to say Irish rugby was in disarray in a year between two successful terms. They still posed a problem, at Lansdowne Road, but ultimately it was about what we did – play like we had been playing and we would win.

"We got off to a perfect start, and any nerves or anxieties there had been in the lead-up to the game quickly dissipated. In the end, it was immensely comfortable. The game was won by half-time; seldom can you say that in international sport, never mind rugby.

"We had a bit of a luxury where we could enjoy half of that

game and listen to the crowd singing with 20 minutes to go.

"It's something that's seldom talked about, but I reckoned that with the training we did under Jim Telfer, we were by far the fittest team in the tournament. I felt that when I went down to play for Harlequins, post-Grand Slam, there weren't many who were my equal in terms of fitness and stamina – again, not something that would be the first thing you would say about a Telfer team. It was just the product of him working us so hard when we were doing other things, especially for the forwards and front five.

"We had won the Triple Crown for the first time since 1938 when we beat Ireland. I think that was always seen as the big achievement. The Grand Slam was almost the icing on the cake. We had already beaten England to win the Calcutta Cup as well, so this was always going to be seen as a very successful season when weighed up against previous years – indeed, dating all the way back to pre-war times.

"My recollection of the France game was that we were absolutely stuffed in the first half. If it hadn't been for the Welsh referee Winston Jones, I do think France could have been out of sight. They were a tremendous team, hot favourites, and had Jean-Patrick Lescarboura at stand-off, who was a tremendous goalkicker and set all kinds of points records that season. But Mr Jones was extremely diligent and observant on a number of occasions when our scrum came under pressure. I think he cast an eye more to why France were gaining an advantage, rather than how we might actually just be struggling.

"You always knew that if you could hang in against the French to within a score, they always had the potential to implode, in terms of their discipline.

"Rives lost it, and they reacted badly when David Leslie collected Jérôme Gallion, although maybe not as badly as he

PART II – 1980s

took it, knocked cold. It was an accumulation of things. Once they began putting punches through from the second row when you were scrummaging, you knew then their frustration was growing, and – although this is down to my rather stupid psychology – that if they were hitting me, they couldn't be pushing at the same time.

"That was when their scrum began to slowly disintegrate. You wouldn't have witnessed it from the touchline or stand, but you could feel it. When that happened, it was job done.

"The enormity of what we did never really sank in for me. We had a very good night and that was it. We won it, and then it was on to the next season – and beyond. Then the 1990 team had their success, and I believe at that point, our achievement was slightly devalued, almost because winning Grand Slams and Triple Crowns was considered the norm for Scottish rugby.

"Nearly 30 years on from the last Grand Slam, and I think what we achieved is now being recognised and appreciated properly, daft as that might sound. Historically, Scotland has only ever won three Slams, and that's why those days in the 1980s into the 1990s are so utterly unique, given the players we had – many of them world class – and the results those players produced."

30

AFTER A 46-YEAR WAIT, A TRIPLE CROWN

3 March 1984 • Five Nations, Dublin
Ireland 9–Scotland 32

The wins against Wales and England, and the sequencing of the Five Nations matches, meant that after just three games, Scotland had arrived in Dublin with their biggest prize in nearly half a century at their fingertips.

If there had been nerves or apprehension at the task in hand prior to the match then they were quickly blown as easily and quickly as the Scots blew away the opposition, running in five tries against just one from the Irish to seal an emphatic and richly deserved 32–9 victory and, with it, the Triple Crown.

Both sides were almost as pristine as they'd been running out of the tunnel when Roy Laidlaw opened the scoring after four minutes, the Jed-Forest scrum-half celebrating becoming Scotland's most capped no. 9 when he retrieved from a ruck, cut right, then jinked back inside to wrong-foot Moss Finn and opposite number Tony Doyle to score.

Peter Dods converted, then added two penalty goals to give Scotland a 12–0 lead. This was all remarkably easy considering, and made all the more simple when Ireland conceded a penalty

PART II – 1980s

try when no. 8 Willie Duggan dived into a scrum to prevent a pushover score. Dods, in front of the posts, served up the afters, 18–0.

By half-time, the contest was as good as finished. From a scrum almost on the Irish try line, Laidlaw again picked up, but rather than checking back as he had done with his first try, he zeroed in on the corner, scoring despite the attentions of the Irish fringe defence.

Laidlaw went off at half-time, concussed. The Irish must have felt the same. Though their gloom was lifted slightly when John Murphy kicked a penalty, then converted a 56th-minute Michael Kiernan try. However, Scotland sealed a memorable afternoon with two scores of their own in the last six minutes.

Firstly, from a line-out delivered by Colin Deans on the left, his Hawick clubmate Alister Campbell, making an impressive debut, batted the ball down while Gordon Hunter, Laidlaw's deputy, ran across field. His Selkirk teammate John Rutherford broke the Irish defensive line before passing to Melrose centre Keith Robertson to score. A try manufactured in the Scottish Borders.

Despite being 28–9 ahead, Scotland were still desperate to finish in style. A Scots counter-attack won them a scrum midway inside the Irish half. Iain Paxton tossed the ball back out to Rutherford, who, with a change of direction, speeded up the move, passing through Robertson, who had looped around his stand-off, to David Johnston and Roger Baird who gave the scoring pass for Dods to dive in at the corner, giving him 16 points in the match.

The celebrations began immediately for the Scots, and painfully for Gordon Hunter, who had his cheekbone smashed after a fan ran into him. Scotland had a glittering prize, but they also had an injury crisis surrounding the scrum-half berth ahead of the Grand Slam decider with France.

Whoever said it would be simple?

Try scorer Keith Robertson on how the Scottish backs got to show their stuff:

"I don't ever think we were under pressure going into the Ireland game, even if there was a lot to play for. I don't think the Scotland support didn't have huge levels of expectancy. Remember, in 1983, we only won one Five Nations game and that was against England at the end of the season, not enough for anyone to get too carried away with winning a couple of games in 1984.

"The big thing for some of us was that we had a dozen Borderers in the squad, who talked a lot, socialised a lot and played together a lot. We knew each other and how we played, and one thing that was impressed upon the guys from those who came back from the Lions tour in New Zealand the previous year was that those from the other home nations weren't any better than ourselves.

"Suddenly, there was a realisation that we could take these teams on and beat them, as we'd done with Wales and England. That was all the thought was, just winning matches. Then we are into a Triple Crown game.

"There wasn't nervousness; for me it was just the excitement about getting a wonderful opportunity to play in a game that you'd always dreamed of playing in. Rather than a side that was expecting to win it, we still hoped we could, so we never got too carried away.

"The Irish pack could be physical, aggressive, hard. But we had a game that, on the right day, could do real damage to them.

"Being honest, that was an Irish team that had started to get old. We wanted to get out and set the tempo of the game, which would be a lot faster than the Irish felt comfortable with. If it

PART II – 1980s

was slow, they could use their strength and make it a long, prolonged game; if it was quick, they would struggle.

"That was always the way we'd intended to play it, but because of the start we'd made, they played into our hands because they needed to respond, and the only way that was going to happen was if they quickened up their own play. They got back into the game after half-time, but that had taken a helluva effort from them and they'd nothing much left. But once I'd scored, that was it.

"It was the players – the backs – who decided how we would play. 'Creamy' [Jim Telfer] directed the forwards, how to win ball and recycle ball, how to get the set pieces right. But the plays that we ran, they came from us [the backs].

"It was great to win a Triple Crown but really pleasing to have done it in a fashion that pleased us, calling moves, scoring tries, finding holes; fast, quick, open rugby which came easy given the players we had.

"Dodsy [Peter Dods], for instance, was a self-confident individual and a lot quicker than he got credit for. Some won't be aware that he ran as a professional sprinter in a really strong school of sprinters headed up by a guy called Wilson Young. Peter won the big handicap sprint at the Jedburgh Games (regarded as the Blue Riband meeting in the Borders circuit) in 1980.

"We knew that when you were putting Dodsy away, through a gap or wide, then not many – if any – were catching him. But it was just about getting the time and position to use it. We had a load of different moves on split scrums – when the scrum is roughly in centre field and you can go one side or the other – and for our last try, which was a move we hadn't run before.

"As soon as I'd run around behind Rud [John Rutherford], a very simple move, it meant we had an overlap out left with

Peter as last man. And when Roger [Baird] gave him the pass, he was gone. It would have been nice to have run that play earlier, rather than at the end, but we didn't need it, or get the chance, because Roy [Laidlaw] had decided to do it all himself. He was brilliant for half that game. But we always had moves like that up our sleeve.

"I was back playing at centre that day, but it never bothered me where I played, wing or centre. Jim Telfer always maintained I wasn't big enough, in his mind, to play centre. I never weighed much more than 11.5 stone, but I could tackle and I made the max of what I had.

"Jim might have a point today compared to some of the monsters that play centre now, but back then, not an issue. As I say, I won half my caps as wing, half at centre. I loved being involved in calling plays and moves, so I'd have maybe preferred in the middle. But I never really gave it a thought. It was just about playing.

"I got to mix in all the success that year, but if you look at Jim Renwick, who should take a lot of credit for how we developed our game – and was a great thinker and reader of the game, who helped me and Rud develop as players, whether with South or with Scotland – he wasn't there in 1984.

"But probably he wouldn't have cared then where he'd got a game; he'd just have wanted to be there. I was just fortunate."

31

AND TO SCOTTISH RUGBY, A GRAND SLAM

17 March 1984 • Five Nations, Murrayfield
Scotland 21–France 12

Like the three previous matches in that Five Nations season, everything hinged on what would happen over the next 80 minutes, although by now, Scotland knew beating France would bring them the biggest prize in Northern Hemisphere rugby.

Perhaps it was because this season had already been declared a success – with the Calcutta Cup and a Triple Crown already celebrated – that the Scots appeared remarkably at ease with the world going into the French game.

Peter Dods scored first with a penalty, then suffered a blow to his eye, which meant he spent the remainder of the match looking as if he'd come off second best over 15 rounds.

France led 6–3 at half-time courtesy of a try from Jérôme Gallion, whose support of Jean-Charles Orso off the back of a scrum was rewarded with a scoring pass.

The machine-like Jean-Patrick Lescarboura converted, then kicked a penalty for France to lead 9–3.

Fortunately for the Scots, Lescarboura kicked far too often

with ball in hand, rather than spinning the ball along the talented French backline. Frustrations were evident.

While the one-eyed Dods had missed a couple of kicks, he had still managed to find his range with another three, tying it at 12–12 after Lescarboura's 40m drop goal had edged France in front.

A score of any kind could be crucial; a try, manna from heaven. Thankfully, it was the Scots who would dine first.

Off a Scots line-out, Colin Deans aimed for David Leslie at the back, but the ball rebounded off a French hand and Jim Calder gratefully received the assist.

Dods converted, then in the closing minutes, Serge Blanco took out the Gala full-back as he set off in pursuit of his own kick. While Dods lay winded, the ball pitched on the French 22, from where Dods, his right eye now completely closed, stroked home his kick for 17 points in the game.

Scotland were Grand Slam champions.

Try scorer Jim Calder on living life on the edge:

"Over the years since, you get asked about what it was like, then you don't get asked as often, and then there's an anniversary or something, and it all becomes relevant again.

"Because of the match sequence, we scored a regulation win over England and straight away the Triple Crown was on the agenda.

"What I do recall was because we won the 'mythical' Triple Crown, beating the Irish so comprehensively, we sort of had overachieved already. I know that might have people ask where was your ambition, but you have to remember Scotland had won nothing for goodness knows how many years. To get our hands on a prize, mythical or not, was everything most of us had dreamed of.

"I didn't think about – or I can't recall at least – even contem-

PART II – 1980s

plating the Grand Slam until we came home and people were talking about it.

"There wasn't huge pressure and there just wasn't the media interest in us like there would be today. I don't think I would have coped with or enjoyed that.

"It was lowish key, no one getting too carried away. For me, and I suppose Jim Telfer, the main concern was around Roy Laidlaw, who had an incredible first half in Dublin, and then went off with concussion. But his deputy, Gordon Hunter from Selkirk, who'd come on as replacement, smashed his cheekbone by bumping into a supporter as he ran off the pitch at full time, a completely freak accident, but we were in the middle of a scrum-half crisis with our first two picks down. Thankfully Roy recovered in good time, but I might say that was the only thing that may have been a deviation from the norm.

"We came back from Ireland on the Sunday, and I was back at work on Monday. You will hear mention today of staying grounded and going about your business as normal, but back then our business as normal was doing whatever you did for a living, 9–5 during the week.

"At that time, I was a sales representative for a subsidiary of Johnson & Johnson, covering all of Scotland, so during the week I'd be meeting doctors and surgeons, and a lot of them were interested in sport, and rugby in particular. You were therefore never totally removed from the build-up to the big game, but it wasn't the full-on, under-the-microscope stuff that you would expect to get today.

"That was one of the good things about being one of the amateur generations, but I think most of us, had it been around back then, would have fancied a crack at professionalism, even if it appears to be full-on every day.

"The closest I came would have been 11 weeks away in New

Zealand with the Lions: train, practise, play games, virtually no distractions. I did enjoy that, and quite a few of us who had been on that trip were now on the brink of a Grand Slam against France, who were the tournament favourites, stacked with some all-time great players and desperate to land the Grand Slam for themselves.

"The game itself was what you'd expect from a French side: hard, direct, dubious both tactically and in their discipline. We just put in a good all-round performance, right across the team, but as he was me on the other side of the scrum, I thought David Leslie was just outstanding, winning ball in the loose, first-up tackling when he got at their half-backs, as a ball carrier – and, of course, his hit on Jérôme Gallion shook him and the French to the core. It wasn't malicious. It was a long throw over the top and David took ball and took out the man at the same time. They got all upset at that, like they needed an excuse to get all upset.

"Iain Milne, 'The Bear', was another key man and anchored our scrum. The French couldn't get a move on him, even though they tried all sorts of manoeuvres. It was another game, under real pressure, where Peter Dods kicked beautifully and was, in my mind, the match winner with all the points he scored. I'm not trying to play down my try, but there really was nothing to it – right place, right time.

"Actually, it maybe wasn't quite the right place, probably offside by about six inches. What France did was leave me against their captain, Jean-Pierre Rives, three from the tail on a line-out right on their line, with Jean-Luc Joinel occupied marking Leslie because he was such a threat off the back.

"I remember thinking that Rives, great player as he was, wouldn't be used to taking up that position, as normally he'd be right on the end of the line so he could get in amongst it in the

PART II – 1980s

midfield. So I just took a step forward then wandered through the gap, because he had no intention of doing any blocking, and when the ball was deflected off the throw from Colin Deans – Joinel was so desperate to disrupt the throw which was going to David [Leslie], he just flapped at it – I was already standing waiting for the ball to drop into my hands.

"It was slightly fortuitous, I suppose, but it was quite instinctive. I had worked out the scenario and it had worked out perfectly for me."

32

SCOTS TRIAL VERDICT HAS APPEAL

4 January 1986 • Scotland Trial Match, Murrayfield
Blues 10–Reds 41

It is doubtful in the annals of Scottish rugby a similar epiphany had ever taken place. Regardless of the circumstances that helped Scotland's international selection panel arrive at naming their team for the Five Nations opener against France, it proved both a revelation and a revolution.

International trials, more often than not, were dour contests, which offered up little enlightenment when it came to deciding who between the possibles and the probables would get the nod. Not so the Blues (for all intents and purposes a Scotland XV, the holders if you prefer) versus Reds (the "challengers") on the first weekend of the new year.

1985 had been a disaster for the Scots – they'd gone from lifting the Five Nations title to custodians of the wooden spoon upon entering the new season.

Changes were being demanded; an outing of the old guard and an infusion of new blood the proposal, but how would the selectors vote, and would the trial give them a steer? As it transpired, the Reds won by a landslide, 41–10.

PART II - 1980s

Robin Charters, the convenor of Scotland's international selectors, admitted afterwards: "It could be an exciting time ahead. A lot of young players are bursting to come through."

He wasn't joking.

Eight of those who had started for the Reds found themselves in the side to play France, with six new caps recruited to start in the first Five Nations Test against France – Gavin and Scott Hastings, Matt Duncan, Finlay Calder, Jeremy Campbell-Lamerton and David Sole. Or, to couch it slightly differently, there were two future Lions captains and a future Grand Slam skipper amongst that sextet.

"No one could ignore a result of 41–10," said Charters when making the announcement.

He wasn't joking about that either.

Fortunately for him, the selectors' confidence was well founded; Scotland beat France 18–17.

A loser and a winner from that trial game, John Rutherford reflects:

"Trial games had historically been quite dull, no one really giving too much away because you didn't want to blow your chances. But that year, they just hammered us. Brilliant!

"You can laugh now, but there wasn't much to laugh at after that game. There were a few of us worried. I had been in the Blue team. I remember Roy [Laidlaw] and I sitting in the dressing room after it and thinking that's us, goners; are we going to keep our places? Look at the players who came out of that game.

"I think – or I'd like to believe – that the selectors looked at all the young bucks they planned on playing and thought, *Well, we'll need a bit of experience at half-back*. They looked kindly on us and we edged into that team.

"I always thought the trial was a great thing to have. It was a way of putting your marker down against the player directly vying with you for selection – although maybe I didn't think it was such a great thing having been on the receiving end that day.

"We used to get some decent crowds at those games, but of course, the professional game ended that.

"The equivalent today would be the Edinburgh–Glasgow Inter-City games in the PRO14, especially the ones at Christmas and New Year, when you have 30 boys all up against each other trying to play their way into the Scotland team. That is where all of our talent is on show, although it's a bit more structured compared to some of the things that took place at the official trial – especially the madness of that 1986 game."

33

PAUL THORBURN
AND *THAT* KICK

1 February 1986 • Five Nations, Cardiff
Wales 22–Scotland 15

Not all memories are happy memories, no. 3.

You don't need to know the context, the date, or even the player's name. If you mention Cardiff and *that* kick, those Scotland fans with a bit of history behind them will instantly recall the monster kick Paul Thorburn landed to drive a stake through Scots hearts.

The new-look Scotland team were more than in the contest, albeit 16–15 down despite outscoring their hosts three tries to one. However, in attempting to keep Wales deep in their own 22, the Scots targeted Jonathan Davies, perhaps a little too robustly, Finlay Calder's charge on the Welsh fly-half as he cleared resulting in a penalty from where the ball landed.

Thorburn suggested to his captain David Pickering he might go for goal rather than touch. The only problem was, he was a yard the wrong side of the 10-metre line – the Wales 10-metre line.

"It's miles to those goalposts," said a somewhat shocked Bill McLaren.

But from a full 70 yards out, Thorburn's howitzer went over,

Gavin Hastings on the other side of the posts almost dropping the ball in disbelief.

Thorburn celebrated like someone who'd scored in the final of the football World Cup. However, that kick may have deflated the Scots but it didn't defeat them. No, Thorburn clinched the 22–15 victory with a short-range effort – from the halfway line.

And what of those magic boots?

In 2018, Thorburn donated them for auction on behalf of the My Name'5 Doddie Foundation.

34

RECORD-BREAKING SCOTS THRASH ENGLAND

15 February 1986 • Five Nations, Murrayfield
Scotland 33–England 6

There have been games against the Auld Enemy best forgotten, others that have been no more than dull, even boring arm-wrestling contests, where a Scots win has meant they have been gilded to make them appear even better, but very few matches that have been gems for the Scots crown. One jewel which will forever stand out, however, was Scotland's trouncing of the English in 1986.

Scotland's Five Nations campaign had begun with a win against France, 18–17, the mercurial French scoring two tries, through scrum-half Pierre Berbizier and Philippe Sella, the world-class centre – good efforts nullified by the howitzer-like boot of debutante Gavin Hastings, the Cambridge University student kicking all of Scotland's points with six successful attempts out of 11, such was the levels of French indiscipline and, some might say, the levels of inaccuracy from Hastings.

Against Wales, Scotland outscored their hosts 3–1 on tries but were dealt a hammer blow when Wales full-back Paul Thorburn kicked a penalty goal from inside his own half to set his side up for victory.

Nevertheless, such were the performance levels of the side Colin Deans captained that a win against England wasn't beyond reach, and at 12–6 up at half-time, thanks mainly to England fly-half Rob Andrew only making two of his six kicks count, things were looking good for the Scots. In the second half, however, it got a whole lot better.

Scotland produced three great tries. Matt Duncan, a try scorer in Cardiff, took a pass from Gavin Hastings as Scotland explored the narrow side to go in for the try. Then when Maurice Colclough threw a horrid pass at Andrew, Finlay Calder pounced on the ball, with John Beattie in support. He lobbed a pass to Roy Laidlaw, who moved possession on to John Rutherford.

While the corner and wingman Roger Baird were options going left, with a swing of the hips and a step inside, the Selkirk stand-off wrong-footed four would-be defenders, and not even the desperate attempts of Graham Robbins could deflect his dive for the line.

Then, to round it off, Scotland scored a wonderfully fluent counter-attacking try, started deep inside their half when the hapless Colclough again lost possession. Baird set off down the left, evading two tackles before tossing a pass inside as a third pursuer arrived. Naturally, Beattie, Calder and John Jeffrey were in unison to progress the break inside the English 22, the "White Shark" and Rutherford exchanging the ball to Scott Hastings, who, after a minor juggle, ran in the score, punching both arms above his head in delight.

If there was a way to finish with style, this was it.

Brother Gavin made his third conversion look as easy as the other two, and with five penalties, and 21 points in total, broke the record he'd set against France a month earlier.

A win against Ireland in Dublin rounded off a good Five Nations for the Scots, tying with France at the top on six points.

PART II - 1980s

Reward then for some excellent performances, but nothing compared to the rewards some of that team would bring in future years.

Architect of that record-breaking effort, John Rutherford explains where the game was ultimately decided: "It was such a great game for us. It just felt like a good day for playing rugby, and it was such a pleasure to play in that team.

"The one thing we had was exceptional mobility in the pack. The selectors and coaches, especially Derrick Grant, had been quite radical that season – it was hard not to be after the trial match – and in this shake-up had decided to play to our obvious strengths, which was, of course, having some very mobile forwards.

"Iain Paxton, who I obviously knew well from Selkirk and was usually an eight, had been brought in again to play lock, with JJ [John Jeffrey], Fin [Finlay Calder] and a Lions no. 8, John Beattie on the back row. Add to that Alex Brewster, who had started as a flanker, at prop, and Colin Deans as hooker, who was like an extra wing-forward, and you could see what our game was based around.

"It was a great set of forwards to have. Al [Alister] Campbell was a Grand Slam winner from two years before, but arguably – although there wouldn't be much argument about it – the most important player in the pack was The Bear [Iain Milne], who was a rock who tied down one side of the scrum, and maybe a bit more, and let everyone else run around daft.

"We could hold our own in the scrum so long as Bear was there and that allowed the rest to go marauding.

"The English forwards, in the main, were big and a bit cumbersome in comparison, although they had some great players, like Peter Winterbottom at flanker. But the longer the match went, the more they slowed down, having been dragged around the field chasing all the runners we had.

"The fitter and more expansive set of forwards came into its own and we were in full flow. Nowadays, because of replacements and substitutes, you rarely see that kind of tiredness, and that's probably a good thing in terms of player welfare. Player safety is crucial and I'm all for that, as it has become such a physical game. Today, you would freshen the team up by throwing on eight replacements, empty the bench.

"It's something I have thought about in the modern game – are we making use of too many replacements? Is the next move having an entire team on the sidelines? Are we headed the way of the NFL where everyone is covered on the bench – who knows? But in those days, 30-odd years ago, you played 80 minutes; there was no such respite for us amateurs.

"You knew then if you had superior fitness, with 20 minutes to go, that would be an advantage you could use. Gavin kicked a lot of points that day, and that was because the English forwards were so fatigued, even during the first half and the longer the game went, that they were lying all over rucks and at breakdowns.

"It took a while to break England down. They always were tough up front – that was where they'd try and beat you up, but it's hard to do that when those you're trying to beat up just take off and are playing 40 yards away.

"Eventually we broke them up front, and that's when we scored our tries. We just cut loose. We were blessed at that time with so many good players. We had an exciting, quick back division, who could be quite brilliant in an attacking sense.

"It was a great time for Scottish rugby, and for me, playing with some wonderful – now legendary – players. That was the thing I remember most – that and being able to score some incredible tries.

"That England game came in the middle of a fantastic period

PART II – 1980s

for me, career-wise; I'd gone with the Lions to New Zealand in 1983, won the Grand Slam the following year, been part of the new-look Scotland team in 1986, including that win over England, and would then go to the first World Cup in New Zealand the following year. Great times, and up there with the best of them, that game against England."

35

OH CALCUTTA CUP DEBACLE

1988

Don't go looking for any highlights of the 1988 Calcutta Cup game at Murrayfield; there are none. This game, and any portion of it, was never going to find its way on to a "best" of compilation, unless it was one designed to induce sleep.

But oh, how the SRU – and indeed their English counterparts (of a fashion) – had wished those involved in that game had been driven to their beds early that night. Instead, what unfolded was one of the most talked about incidents ever to emerge from a Calcutta Cup game, one which almost lost the famous trophy for good.

After what had been a rather chaotic post-match banquet, where the quantities of alcohol far outweighed the amount of food thrown, the famous old trophy – dating back to 1878 and sculpted from silver rupees – was borrowed, snaffled or kidnapped and taken into the Edinburgh night on tour.

It visited various establishments along the way, via Rose Street, and even a brief appearance at Buster Brown's nightclub, while being carried, passed, thrown and even kicked like an old rugger ball.

By early Sunday morning, the Court of Inquiry had begun, the first question being: "Where is it?"

PART II – 1980s

However, on establishing its whereabouts, what unveiled itself was not the pristine, priceless artefact that had earlier been presented to winning skipper Nigel Melville but something that would more likely have a scrap value.

That week, the SRU staged a press conference where they presented the battered and dented Calcutta Cup – or the "Calcutta Shield" as one old sage quipped – to the media where an audible gasp was heard around the room. People knew it had been damaged but not to that extent.

It was repaired by Hamilton & Inches jewellers, who, while not through the best of circumstances, probably made it a better pot than the original design had been, although still not sufficiently robust to take out on a pub crawl.

And what of the protagonists? Dean Richards of England, still a serving police officer at the time, was given a one-match ban and a severe reprimand from the chief constable of the Leicestershire constabulary.

John Jeffrey of Scotland was banned from all rugby for five months.

Dean Richards says: "What happened? I don't know, I was drunk. On the way home, I went by train. A supporter said I looked as if I had been enjoying myself last night when I was tossing around a fake cup."

John Jeffrey recalls: "If that was what my punishment was to be, then so be it. I had to take it and get on with it. The only thing that rankled with me was Deano getting one game. And he moaned about that and still does!"

36

BAA-BAAS AND THE THREE BEARS

8 March 1989 • Mobbs Memorial Match, Northampton
East Midland 22–Barbarians 34

Over the past half-century several siblings have appeared in Scotland colours. The Hastings brothers, Gavin and Scott, shared Grand Slam success in 1990, Gavin appearing 61 times for his country, but outdone by Scott with 65 caps. Meanwhile twins Jim and Finlay Calder were Grand Slam winners in different years – 1984 and 1990 respectively.

Peter and Gordon Brown, Gordon and Alan Bulloch, Peter and Michael Dods, Thom and Max Evans, Zander and Matt Fagerson, Richie and Jonny Gray, Peter and George Horne, Sean and Rory Lamont are among the other brotherly combinations in the past 50 years, as are John and Martin Leslie who were Five Nations champions in tandem in 1999.

There were also international appearances for Bryan and Jimmy Gossman, who in the early 1980s amassed four caps between them, while we shouldn't forget 1990 Grand Slam winner Craig Chalmers and sister Paula, who both represented their country with distinction.

However, the Milne brothers – Iain, Kenny and David – top

PART II - 1980s

all comers during this period of Scottish rugby history with all three winning caps, although not at the same time. However, they did provide the front row for the Barbarians against East Midlands in the 1989 Mobbs Memorial match.

While in Scotland colours, Iain won the Grand Slam in 1984, an achievement matched by Kenny six years later. David meanwhile won his cap as a replacement, playing the last 20 minutes of Scotland's opening tie in the 1991 World Cup against Japan as sub for skipper David Sole.

Still, they all count.

37

SCOTS LEAD THE PRIDE OF LIONS

1989

By the time the 1989 British Lions tour to Australia came around it had been six years since their last sojourn abroad, which ended in a 4–0 "blackwash" at the hands of New Zealand. In 1983 it had been Jim Telfer who had coached the tourists. This time around, another Scot, Ian McGeechan, would look after the playing side, with countryman Finlay Calder as captain.

It would be the first time the Lions had set foot in Oz since 1971, and their first entirely Australian venture in 90 years. With both history and expectation to be satisfied, McGeechan's side made a winning start, assisted greatly by the Scots contingent who had made the 10,000-mile trip; in addition to Calder, Gary Armstrong, Craig Chalmers, Peter Dods, Derek White, David Sole, John Jeffrey and the Hastings brothers, Gavin and Scott, were present.

The Lions were six out of six in their provincial games, including narrow wins against Queensland and New South Wales. The first Test, however, was a rude awakening for the Lions – they were beaten 30–12 in Sydney, their heaviest ever loss to the Wallabies. After seeing off ACT in their midweek

PART II - 1980s

fixture, there were wholesale changes made to the Lions starting XV for the crucial second Test; Jeremy Guscott and the fit-again Scott Hastings replaced the Irish/Welsh duet of Brendan Mullin (his omission meaning there were no Irishmen in the side for the first time in Lions Test history) and Mike Hall in the centre, Rob Andrew preferred to Craig Chalmers inside them, while up front, Robert Norster and White made way for Wade Dooley and an injury-free Mike Teague. It was win or bust. And win it was, helped greatly by a Gavin Hastings try which gave the Lions the lead with just five minutes remaining.

Calder bypassed the usual half-back union, slinging a long ball to Andrew, then to Scott Hastings, who threw a wild pass outside as he tried desperately to exploit the overlap. Thankfully for him, and the Lions, the loose ball was gathered by Hastings [Gavin] to score. Guscott scored a brilliant individual try to win this bruising and bloody encounter 19–12, nicknamed "the Battle of Ballymore", for the most obvious of reasons.

The Australians were up in arms over events during that tie to such an extent that their captain, Nick Farr-Jones declared: "To me, basically, it's open warfare. They've set the rules, they've set the standards. As far as I'm concerned, if the officials aren't going to control it, we're going to have to do something about it."

No Lions team had recovered from losing the opening Test to then win the series. That was until the third and deciding Test back in Sydney, when once more Gavin Hastings played a pivotal role, capitalising on Australian indiscipline to kick five penalties, though the match will always be recalled for a try from Ieuan Evans, contrived by some comical decision making from David Campese.

The Lions concluded the tour with two more wins, but the headline result came in the Test series: 2–1 to the Lions, making Finlay Calder a series-winning skipper.

Winning Lions captain Finlay Calder talks flights, fights and fringe benefits:

"After the Scotland–Wales game at Murrayfield, Clive Rowlands, who would be the Lions tour manager, came across, introduced himself and said something along the lines of, 'We'll be seeing more of each other over the summer.' At that point I thought, *Brilliant, I'm in the frame for selection for the squad*, not imagining for a moment that I'd even be considered as the Lions captain, even though at that time I'd been captaining Scotland.

"But then events unfolded; so often sport is about a combination of things, and don't ever think luck, misfortune, good fortune, call it what you will, doesn't play a part. Will Carling, who had done a great job for England, and who, for me, was the standout candidate and would have made a terrific Lions captain in my mind, just couldn't go: ruled out long before the tour, suffering terribly from shin splints, and told to do nothing during that summer. From my perspective, his injury came at the right time.

"Will's luck was out. Where my luck was in; it was in having the most fantastic squad of players there, all fit most of the time. Clive and Ian McGeechan, as coach, were very good together, and having Ian there, as a fellow Scot for me, was a real blessing. The other thing was Ian really got what the Lions meant, 100 per cent. We saw that then and since.

"We had a fantastic bunch of blokes with us, with a real determination and belief, and we played as one. However, losing that first Test, it wasn't a nice feeling. Fair play to them and their coach Bob Dwyer. They shredded us. That was the low point. There was a meeting of minds, management, coach, me as the captain, the players. Our attitude was: if you think this is bad, we have another month of this if we don't win next Saturday. There were no doubters after that.

PART II – 1980s

"It was a long week until the next Test, decisions had to be taken. But we knew we could do it. Sometimes you could look at the opposition and think, no, we're kidding ourselves, this is too good a side. I don't think anyone thought that against Australia. We knew we could do it – and we'd convinced ourselves we would.

"The second Test, we won it, fair and square. The Australians said certain things about how we approached the game, but all they saw was what we should have shown in the first match. We showed our teeth. They didn't like it and they made that known. But we'd rattled them, we knew it, and it just made us more determined to do the same again and they couldn't handle that, which is probably why they conceded so many penalties in the deciding Test. Plus, Gavin kicked superbly.

"I remember in that final Test, Robert Jones, who, let's be fair, wasn't known as a scrapper, picking a fight with Nick Farr-Jones and Wade Dooley calming him down. Things you'd never think you see. But we really had a belief, a steel, and that saw us through. But that's not to diminish the talent we had.

"Graham Mourie, the All Blacks captain, used to say 'ripeness was all' in rugby: if the team was ripe, you could achieve greatness; too early or too old, suddenly you are chasing it. The players I had in Australia were prime, and because of that we achieved great things. I was blessed to lead them.

"Anyone who has ever had the captaincy bestowed upon them will know the feeling, the emotion, of being given the very privileged position of leading the Lions on tour. For me, it's the most enormous honour you can have as a British or Irish rugby player.

"It was highlighted for me in 2016 when those Lions captains who were still with us were all flown over to Dublin for a dinner, and you were in the same room as some of the greatest names in the sport. I think 12 of the 13 living captains were present – only Sam Warburton was missing because of playing commitments – going all the way back to Ronnie Dawson of Ireland who led the tour in 1959.

"We'd all had different lives since; some in business, some in rugby, there were those who had been professional, but ultimately we all had one thing in common, leading the Lions – some more successfully than others, I could add. But that would be to ignore luck, chance, fate and the likes, which through no fault of any captain, can shape the outcome of a tour or a series. Everyone there was an equal because of that bond, that link of having led the Lions.

"It was humbling being in that gifted and very talented company, part of a club with a very exclusive membership.

"There was a spin-off too for Scotland from 1989, just as there was in 1983. That year eight went to New Zealand, including my brother Jim, the following year, they did the Grand Slam. In 1989, we had nine Scots in the Lions party, and the following year, another Grand Slam.

"Coincidence? Maybe. But Scotland benefitted from having guys who had played solid rugby for 18 months. Both Grand Slam teams had a core of Lions, that ripeness about them ..."

PART III

1990s

38

CHALMERS' KEY ROLE IN GRAND SLAM SUCCESS

1990

At just 21, there was much that rested on Craig Chalmers' shoulders during Scotland's 1990 Five Nations campaign. As if being playmaker wasn't enough, the Melrose fly-half was then given the added responsibility of being promoted to first-choice goalkicker, ahead of Gavin Hastings.

For someone starting only his seventh international against Ireland (previously with five for Scotland and one with the Lions), Chalmers coped comfortably with the task he inherited. It resulted in Chalmers troubling the scorers in all matches that campaign, his five-point addition against Ireland followed by ten versus France, with nine against Wales.

However, holding his nerve to kick three crucial penalty goals in the Grand Slam game against England was easily his most telling contribution. Not a bad return for someone who, in the most bizarre of circumstances, was nearly a non-runner in Scotland's title race.

Chalmers tells an interesting tale of two coaches:

"I only came into the team the season before and the only game I'd lost with Scotland had been against France in Paris.

Whatever side won that won the Championship, and we did get a bit of a lesson. There was a point in time during the 1990 run that I was thinking, *This international caper is quite good.*

"In December 1989, we played Romania and I missed that game. I hurt my knee playing for Melrose – actually, I hurt it on the bus, coming back from Heriot's. We'd won the game and were in the pub next door afterwards. We all got on the coach and I decided to have a sleep, straddling across the aisle, lying on one seat, feet up on the other. Keith Robertson and Gus Redburn were messing around and Gus tried to vault me but stood on my leg.

"It woke me up, but I thought nothing of it. I was out in Gala that night for a few more beers and I got up the next day feeling a bit dusty, but I couldn't move my knee. It was all swollen and I had to retrace my day and work out how this could have happened.

"I started against Ayr the following week but was struggling and got to the point where I was saying this had gone too long, so I went up to Edinburgh and saw Malcolm Macnicol, the orthopaedic surgeon – he looked after various footballers, Geoff Capes, other athletes – who said see you tomorrow.

"He performed an arthroscopy – keyhole surgery – and repaired the damage. I was running three days later, played against Musselburgh eight days later, missed the Scotland trial, played Boroughmuir and got cramp after 60 minutes but was fit and selected to play Ireland. If I hadn't gone to see Malcolm, I'd have missed the start of the Five Nations, maybe even missed all of it. So much for peaceful, scenic coach travel.

"Ireland led at half-time but Derek White scored two tries; the first one, Sean [Lineen] came in on a fantastic line burst on my shoulder, gave it to JJ [John Jeffrey] and he fed Derek. I inherited the kicking duties from Gavin [Hastings] who had

PART III - 1990s

the 'yips' at the time. We went 10–6 down, I kicked a penalty, missed a couple of drop-goal attempts, but off a scrum about 10 yards out, Derek White picked up and just bashed his way into 'Laidlaw's Corner' for the winning score.

"Having taken over from Gavin, I started as place-kicker against France, on anything under 40m. The French game was a bit of a weird one. Gavin's big boot came into play when he smashed one into the wind, then pushed one wide, so that was me back on as kicker.

"It was tough going, then JJ got his head stood on – which would explain a few things – by Alain Carminati, who was sent off. I kicked the penalty, and after that we never looked back.

"Sean Lineen chased a kick from Iwan Tukalo, dribbled on, but Fin [Calder] was given the touchdown, then I hit 'Tuks' with a pass and he managed to shake off a couple of tackles for the try. I converted both, but the highlight of the game for me was in the first half when the French winger [Peyo] Hontas, on his debut, was away down the right and I managed to put in a good diving tap tackle – I say good, it was bloody awesome – to stop him and keep our lead.

"The Wales game was a bit like the Irish game – nothing much in it. Big Damian Cronin scored a try after we'd nicked a line-out, with Gary [Armstrong] going up the narrow side, and Damian proved he could run when he wanted to. I added a couple of penalties and we were up 10–3 at half-time, despite Wales pinning us right back on our own line with a series of tap penalties and scrums. Tries and kicks win games, ultimately, but there are games when it's your defence that either keep you in the game or keep the opposition out. That was some brave stuff in that game.

"Wales scored a converted try by Arthur Emyr to get within a point, but there was still a quarter of the game to go when I hit another penalty. Emyr was an awkward runner, all arms and knees, but he could shift. At one point it took Scott Hastings, Sean and Gary all to stop him. But that was a battle.

"And that was us into a Grand Slam game against England. Test matches, unless it's a World Cup final, don't come close to that game. We all realised it was something special, but everything was riding on that.

"I don't remember much about the week leading up to it; we agreed not to speak to the press, just to let England talk themselves up, which they did, although I think the English media were the ones who really spun it up.

"The game was never going to be pretty. There was too much to lose. It was also terribly windy, making kicking a lottery.

"It was always destined to become very physical up front – good reason to stay well clear and not get caught up in anything. I just wanted it simple; the forwards win it, Gary gives it, I call the moves. What I didn't want was Gary acting like a wing-forward and clearing up the forwards' mess, leaving Kenny Milne to play scrum-half. He enjoyed doing that more than I did, for sure.

"That season, our pack was just awesome, real proper men, real rugby players – physically hard, mentally harder and never willing to take a backwards step. You had leaders in there – Soley [David Sole] was our captain, but JJ and Fin were leaders as well. We also had guys who were willing to be led. Kenny Milne, Paul Burnell, they would run through a brick wall for you if you told them that's what was needed.

"We really took it to England up front. Finlay took a tap – actually it was Gary who gave him it – and he ran at England but was driven back, only for our pack to arrive and drive England backwards. It was quite formidable. We had forwards who were interested in being forwards, not posing out with the backs –

PART III - 1990s

apart from JJ 'seagulling' around, looking to pick up scraps.

"There would have been some better individual players around, but, as a group, they were pretty awesome and gave us real grunt up front. I hate praising them up, but they were good.

"Gavin [Hastings] was another big talker and occasionally he'd say something sensible. He didn't play during my first season; got injured skiing in Colorado. That was something a bit different – although someone jumping on you when you're asleep on the bus takes a bit of beating.

"With him not there in 1989, I was taking the kick-offs and the likes, but suddenly Gavin was back and wanting to do it. I was like, 'F**k off.' He was so good at it, he was the one who kicked the ball straight out in the Grand Slam decider, which gave England the scrum at the start of the second half. They made a mess of it, knocked on, we got the put-in, and Tony [Stanger] scored, plucking the ball out of the air and on to his knee – I mean the ground.

"I don't know though; I could be doing Gav a disservice. He might have worked all of that out in advance.

"It's funny what you remember. The 17 March was our coach Jim Telfer's birthday and it was his 50th. There was no way I was ever going to lose that game and get the blame for spoiling his birthday, that day, that year, the following year, or 20 years down the road. He doesn't forget those kinds of things.

"That said, I never felt we could lose. You can't say it beforehand, but looking around that dressing room, what a bunch of guys to be playing with. There were no weak links there and we had guys who could really get inside the English heads, one way or another."

39

DAVID SOLE ON THE MARCH

17 March 1990 • Five Nations, Murrayfield
Scotland 13–England 7

It was St Patrick's Day, but two other saints, Andrew and George, took top billing that day in 1990 as Scotland and England did battle to decide who would take the Calcutta Cup, the Triple Crown, the Five Nations Championship, the Grand Slam and, possibly even more important, bragging rights for evermore.

After wins against Ireland, France and Wales, the Scots would need to wait just a fortnight to take on England at Murrayfield, an English side which would enter the biggest game in their history off a month of idle reflection.

Even so, they were still a powerful team, front to back, and Scotland would need to keep their wits about them to get the upper hand. Or just outwit them.

Scotland captain David Sole knew the start his side made would be critical. However, Sole calculated that the match started as soon as his side took to the pitch. His ploy, therefore, was to make an entrance like no other, one that would have the passionate home crowd cheering their side before a ball was kicked or a tackle made.

PART III – 1990s

Sole then devised his famous march on to the pitch, a gladiatorial entrance at walking pace, milking the moment and igniting the spirit coursing through the veins of every Scot. And oh, how it worked.

Scotland eventually triumphed 13–7, but some still say the game was won in those opening few seconds as the Scots emerged from the tunnel.

David Sole on making history: "Did I think nearly 30 years on people would still have been talking about that walk? I think if we'd lost they wouldn't have been.

"It was just a special occasion. Ask anyone where they were when we won the Grand Slam in 1990 and they'll probably be able to remember that and exactly what happened. I think less about the walk, more about the occasion itself, and that was just a part of what was a great day.

"Everyone was pretty excited about the game; the first time in history that it had happened, all that sort of stuff. I think even without the hype around the entrance into Murrayfield, it was always pretty exciting.

"It was very easy for us. We were the underdogs by a country mile. England had played superbly well throughout the season, while we just sort of chuntered from one game to the next. In some respects, we scraped through some of the matches; the game in Cardiff was not a memorable match by any stretch of the imagination, we stuttered against Ireland, and even against France we were playing against 14 men for much of the match, so that clearly helped. We were justifiably underdogs.

"Even so, there is something about a Scotland–England match which makes life quite exciting, and that we were both playing for a Grand Slam added a bit of tastiness to it. As I say, I think the atmosphere built on it, and the fact we just had a couple of weeks between each game meant that we could develop our own sense of momentum, through the matches, and try to learn and improve for each game that we played.

"We were massively respectful of the England players. We'd toured with a lot of them the previous year, and a lot of the guys, both forwards and backs, had made up the 1989 Lions side. A lot of us then knew what they were like, knew what their drivers were, knew how competitive and how capable they were, and we knew we would have to be at our absolute best if we were going to stand a chance. I think you go into these things with your eyes wide open and recognise you have to be at your very best for the whole of the 80 minutes if you're going to be in with a shout come the final whistle. Everyone was up for it.

"Because we only had a fortnight between our matches – England had the big four-week break, while we had our free week at the start of the campaign – we were able to maintain our momentum. It was almost like coming together like a club side.

"As we learned how to win tight matches, that stood us in pretty good stead come the final game.

"But if I had one abiding memory from that match it would be the atmosphere. It reached a peak when we walked on to the pitch, then was sustained for 80 minutes. At no point did you get a sense that people were relaxing into the game. You could feel the tension; you could feel the really strong sense of the noise. Clearly it was a home crowd, so that was enormously uplifting.

"Your memories of the game, actually, become those that you see on TV, because they've been replayed. You don't see it at ground level anymore. I have very few recollections of what it was like during the game, but you still know what the emotional response is, when you talk about walking on to the field and what the impact was, and how that felt. The roof came off as we

PART III - 1990s

marched on and stayed off until half an hour after we'd gone into the dressing room and were having a beer.

"We were just really, really lucky to have such an exceptional group of players, in critical positions, all at once. You need to have that, but these occasions are few and far between.

"I think you have to appreciate that rugby isn't Scotland's national sport. It comes a long way behind other sports, in terms of participation and profile. There are more cricketers than there are rugby players in Scotland, for example.

"We are always going to struggle when you put us on a global stage, and as other teams and countries get better, and have greater and more prolific pools to select from. It's always going to be tough.

"Scotland was just very, very lucky in the 1980s into the early 1990s when we had an exceptional group of players who came through together, bonded together and had a common sense of purpose, with a very strong team identity. And that served us well.

"I'd go beyond 1990 and into 1991 when we got to the semi-final of the World Cup, and no Scottish side has repeated that feat yet. It was an outstanding period and I think you have to appreciate some of the common denominators were around coaching and players, and a degree of continuity that existed between 1984 through 1986, with six new caps for the first match, which was very helpful. Many went to the World Cup in 1987, we had a changing of the guard in 1988 and 1989, and a rebuilding which brought its benefits for the next few years after that.

"When you look back over the whole history of Scottish rugby, whether it's 50 years or 100 years, that era of Scottish rugby was one of the pinnacles.

"One of the things it did was create an expectation amongst

the rugby public that this is what it was always going to be like. You go back and obviously that wasn't the case at all. We always produced world-class players – think 1971 and 1974 Lions; there were some outstanding Scottish players in those squads – who played an absolute integral part of those tours, but they never enjoyed the same sort of success with Scotland as we did.

"From a purely statistical perspective, to have such high expectations is probably unrealistic in Scotland."

40

TONY STANGER'S MATCH WINNER

1990

"Scotland with the put-in – the referee deciding I think there was a slight knock forward as they went for the pickup...

"And that's quite an advantage to the Scots because that looked a useful ball for England...

"The pickup by Jeffrey, Jeffrey to Armstrong, Armstrong nicely out to Gavin Hastings, Gavin Hastings, there's a kick through, on goes Stanger, Stanger could be there first... It's a try, a magnificent try for the 21-year-old, his first try in a Championship match, but his sixth try for Scotland in his sixth international, and well, the euphoria around the ground is something else..."

No one on TV has quite called it like Bill McLaren since, but then, not many commentators have had the opportunity to describe a player from their home town scoring arguably their nation's most famous try.

Hawick's Tony Stanger – until the next time – will remain the last Scot to score a Grand Slam-winning try, a touchdown with luck and improvisation at its core.

But for Gavin Hastings overstriking his kick-off to start the second half into touch, there would have been no scrum; but for Mike Teague knocking on as he tried to pick up from the scrum, there would have been no Scotland put-in; and but for Hastings putting boot to ball, there may not have been a try.

Matches and titles can be decided by such miniscule events. Few, however, would give any of those micro moments a second thought. All that mattered in that passage of play was the end result: Stanger's first try in a Five Nations game, and another on his path to the 24 he would eventually score for his country, becoming Scotland's joint-leading scorer of all time.

Not that any came close to the significance of the one that March afternoon at Murrayfield.

Tony Stanger on how 11 seconds shaped his life: "That was my first season in the international team, winning my first caps in the autumn internationals against Fiji, when I scored twice on my debut, and against Romania, when I scored three tries. That was as good as it could have possibly gone for a 21-year-old, new to the team.

"It was a great start for me, but having grown up watching the Five Nations, that next step was just a dream for me. But I was selected for the first game in Ireland, and once in that environment, that was the real introduction; not friendlies, but serious games in a competition, where you had to keep your wits about you and learn very quickly, because everyone was either more experienced – or just very good.

"The first player I faced at that level was Keith Crossan, the Irish winger, who had around eight years of a start on me in that setting, a very tough opponent for me, just setting out, and it was fascinating to see how he went about his business. As the tournament went on, you extended yourself, you improved, things were not so new, you began doing things as second nature almost. But you couldn't be complacent. You had to stay switched on.

PART III - 1990s

"The day of the Grand Slam game, I found myself up against Rory Underwood, England's record try scorer. He was just one of a very good group of England players, however, he was my player; he was quick, elusive and could score tries. He also would go looking for the ball, to be involved.

"That was the style England had played throughout that Championship. Being expansive and allowing their backs to cut loose.

"I knew I was the one who was, most likely, going to have to stop Underwood. It was a challenge I was looking forward to.

"But, equally, I couldn't only be focused on stopping him from playing. It was just as important I kept my eye on the job I was there for, which was the same as him – to finish off moves and chances.

"We backed ourselves on the one-to-one contests; good as England were, there were some positions that it was a no contest. We had the better player in that position and in key roles. But you knew the match would be decided upon the very tightest of margins; getting in a tackle, getting in a pass or a kick, getting in for a score. It was going to come down to little moments that would change the game.

"There was less rugby played back then, with a lot of kicking, turning the opposition, chasing them down. What that meant was that any slight mistake was magnified because it stood out more. It doesn't happen so much today, unless you really take time to slow things down and analyse it. But in those days, it sort of stood out. You weren't really making a load of tackles, so get one wrong, everyone saw it.

"It happened during the England match. I missed one on halfway and Gary Armstrong made the tackle. Because there wasn't much going on, you think the eyes of the world are on you, which, of course, they're not – just Gary's, and he wasn't shy in letting me know. Let's say I was very thankful to a fellow Borderer.

"That, though, was a real introduction. But I always looked at these things as a challenge, where if things didn't go well, you'd learn from it rather than it being something that you defined yourself by.

"Being defined by one moment, or one event or act, I don't really have a lot of say in that when it comes to people remembering my try. I suppose that's the way it will be forever more, or until someone else does the same.

"The try itself, that was off a move that we'd worked on, although it didn't quite work to plan; the ball was always going to be worked to Gavin [Hastings], he was going to draw people in and then get a pass to me. But what we'd rehearsed didn't quite come off. He came wider and cramped up for space, and with neither me nor him with anywhere to go, he kicked ahead.

"There was a split second – what I was saying about the fine margins – where Rory is caught, having come forward to cover the threat of Gavin, suddenly flat-footed and having to turn, when Gavin gets the kick away. In that fraction of a second, I'm already off the mark. You can see why they test reaction times for guys in 100-metre races.

"Those tiny fractions make such a difference over short distances. For me, it was about picking my line and going for it. The full-back, who again had advanced to close down Gavin, wasn't there – one less to contend with. Then it's a clear race – and I already had the jump on Rory, although there wasn't much in it at the end. All you're hoping for is that you're on the right line and when the ball bounces, it bounces for you.

"It wasn't the kindest of bounces I'd ever had, but it was at least manageable, bouncing up and high, rather than squirting across the turf.

PART III – 1990s

"Everyone knew the next score after half-time was going to be crucial – a cliché, I know, but it was fact. With the way the game was, and how we could defend, something we had proved in the earlier matches, just getting our noses in front was going to be such an advantage.

"And nothing was ever the same after that!

"For me, there was never going to be another game like that. It was only my sixth cap, remember, and I ended up playing more than 50 times over nine years. But there is an emotional attachment to that game, which although I played in it will mean the same to those who paid their money and watched from the stand or terracing. It was a shared emotion, with everyone in the stadium – with everyone in the country.

"It's just nice to have been part of that team, and to be part of such a positive memory that means people still want to shake your hand and talk about it today. That's what I remember more now, the people who want to share their memory with you, more than I do about the game or the try."

41

SCOTT HASTINGS AND *THAT* TACKLE

1990

One tackle never defined a career, certainly not when the person who made that tackle is Scott Hastings. You only need to look through his photo album to appreciate how many significant moments he enjoyed or endured – punching the air in a record win against England in 1986; *that* photo of him returning broken, battered and bruised from the 1993 Lions Tour; or his delight at winning the Melrose Sevens with Watsonians in 1996.

However, those who witnessed Scotland's crowning glory in that winner-take-all clash at Murrayfield in 1990 will never forget the Scotland no. 13's tackle on Rory Underwood, although they may not have appreciated how good it was at the time.

Then again, all Hastings was doing was making up for an earlier error.

With Scotland leading 6–0, England no. 8 Mike Teague picked up and drove as the Scots scrum crumbled. His pop pass to Richard Hill brought the white-shirted back division into play, with skipper Will Carling swerving wide of Scott Hastings before connecting with Jeremy Guscott, who, with a dummy to

PART III – 1990s

take Gavin Hastings out of commission, completing the finish.

That was England's first try in Edinburgh since 1980, the day Bill Beaumont's side completed their Grand Slam. An ominous omen? Not quite.

That was England's only score in the first half, the boot of Craig Chalmers putting the Scots 9–4 ahead. Less than two minutes into the second half, Tony Stanger touched down in the corner, but the Scottish advantage was pegged back to 13–7 when Hodgkinson finally managed to land a penalty goal.

With little more than nine minutes remaining, English pressure had the home support cheering every clearing kick, one coming from Stanger, giving England field position on the Scots 22.

Wade Dooley deflected the ball to Jeff Probyn, who sought sanctuary within the English maul. Scrum-half Richard Hill fired the ball out along the English backline, through Andrew and Carling, now supplemented by Simon Halliday and Rory Underwood, who had come in on this attack.

Carling bypassed Halliday but fed Underwood, who went for a gap, outside Scott Hastings, inside Iwan Tukalo. Behind those Scots, clear ground. For a split second, Underwood, the world-class finisher, was gone, beyond Hastings and past his wingman Tukalo. But somehow Hastings caught Underwood around the shins, his arms sliding down to fell the flyer (Underwood was an RAF pilot during the day). The ball was chucked forward in the tackle, and all Scotland exhaled in unison.

There will have been many try-saving tackles through history, but not many Calcutta Cup, Triple Crown, Five Nations Championship and Grand Slam-winning tackles.

Who else but the great Bill McLaren probably summed it up best: "Underwood brilliantly tackled by Scott Hastings. That was a try-saving tackle if ever there was one... and once again there, Rory Underwood was escaping – and he was on his way to a 23rd try. He must have felt that he was through. But Hastings just got him."

Scott Hastings on why he got it so right on Underwood:

"England had played the best rugby that season by a mile and were a good team. But so were we. Every team England had defeated, we played next and had to stave off their backlash from having lost to England in the previous game. No mean feat.

"I had gone into that game fully pumped up and it was me who gave away the first try; I got pulled away, sucked in on the defensive alignment on Will Carling, he got on the outside of me, gave the pass to Jeremy Guscott and he scored. Because they splintered our defence, they'd carved us up. [David] Sole got us under the posts and said that is the last mistake we make today.

"It was hands up from me, and I screwed the nut, because people will tell you I was quite an intense rugby player. I knew that outwith that moment of madness, I needed to contribute and play a part, and I was completely switched on from that point forward.

"The year before, I played alongside Jeremy and Rory Underwood in two Tests for the Lions against Australia. They were razor-sharp thinkers and had real speed. The reason Rory is still England's all-time greatest try scorer is because of his devastating pace. If he got a yard on you, forget it. I therefore knew the threat these guys possessed.

"I always prided myself in my defence, and I could read a play. On that move – and they had loaded their line with both wingers coming up – I just felt Underwood was going to try to run that outside arc.

"It was a bootlaces tackle; the timing had to be perfect. Go too soon, he can nip inside. Leave it too late and he had pace

PART III – 1990s

to burn. I got it spot on, and I knew it was a good tackle at the time. I don't sit and watch it over and over, but if I happen to see it, it gives me a good feeling. I also see it and think, *There wasn't much in that*, between me stopping him and him being gone.

"Some of the Watson's boys reckon I had a better one during my junior years. I'd seen footage of Gerald Davies, the Welsh winger, bringing down someone with a flying tackle at full pace and lassoing them around the ankles, and decided I was going to emulate that during a game. I've got a couple of mates who saw that and talk about it to this day. However, it maybe didn't have the same importance or audience as the one at Murrayfield.

"The other side of that are the ones you do miss such as the 1995 World Cup on Émile Ntamack, when I was ready to smash him and he just checked my stride and scored, and I still go through that tackle in my head because it put France through to play Ireland, and as runners-up in the group we got New Zealand. If I'd made it, maybe history changes. But that's just international sport.

"The Underwood tackle, it's not something I make a lot of, but it has worked its way into folklore now. For me, nearly three decades on, it will only ever be another piece in a jigsaw that saw us win the biggest game there had been in the Five Nations. That is satisfaction enough."

42

THE MELROSE ERA BEGINS

1990

It takes more than one championship, or one trophy, to have anyone talking of an era around the success of a club. No, you need a couple of titles, like six in eight years, and maybe even throw in a national cup victory to be quoted in such terms. And while you're at it, why not develop tens of players for the international team.

For those reasons, from 1990 until 1997, when they made it a league and cup double after beating Boroughmuir 31–23 in the final, Scottish club rugby belonged to Melrose – this was their era.

Back-row warrior Carl Hogg on what made Melrose great: "The catalyst at Melrose was Jim Telfer; ask people what makes a good coach and they'll say great players. But the players only become great if they are given the direction, and the scope, to believe that they can be winners – or in Jim's case, be told they should be winners, and if they weren't winning to do something about it.

"We were very lucky that we had good players being replaced by other good players, and good players aspiring to be great players. For me, in that period of Melrose winning six championships – and a league and cup double in 1997 – the

PART III – 1990s

guy who set the benchmark for everyone was Chick [Craig Chalmers].

"He played for the Lions in 1989 and won the Grand Slam the following year. I looked at him, as a 20–21-year-old and was thinking if he can do that, anything is achievable.

"I don't know about Weirdo [Doddie Weir] or Brush [Bryan Redpath] or any of the rest of them, but for me Craig was the guy who showed what heights you could reach, and who you should measure yourself against; not in terms of the position you played, or the points he scored, but what it had taken to get him where he was as a player, and at whatever level he was playing at. Remember, he was an amateur when he did that – phenomenal dedication. And that did rub off on others.

"Some had to work really hard at it, others not so hard because it came easy. Like Doddie. All he needed was the TV cameras to show up and that was him, Scotland squad.

"We had a group of eight or nine boys, the core group, who played through a good chunk of that period, who were achievers.

"Once that core group was in place, achievement became self-perpetuating. You drive yourself on. Then we started being able to bring in Starky and Wrighty [Derek Stark and Peter Wright], and guys like Rowen Shepherd off the back of that.

"Jim was a hard taskmaster, but what he instilled in the players meant they became just as hard on themselves, just as hard on each other. It was his psychology, his philosophy, and whether you knew it or not, you became part of it. Everyone became a captain.

"You couldn't slack, you couldn't not pull your own weight. There were guys in that team who didn't have the glory or the distraction of playing for Scotland and the likes, but their commitment was nothing shy of 100 per cent, because Melrose still mattered the same to them.

"You just demanded more of each other. If you missed a session, or if you missed a tackle, or a pass, there was as much chance of the criticism coming from a teammate as there was the coach. You held one another to account. It maybe wasn't the place for the shy, retiring sorts to be. But you were in the environment of winners.

"That is how disciplined we were. And people wondered how we won for so many years.

"When I first came into the team, the likes of Keith Robertson was still playing, a Grand Slam winner. Imagine having someone like that in the dressing room. There were boys like Andrew Kerr, back rower, tough as teak, never played for Scotland but had the same commitment as boys who won 60 caps; Robbie Brown, another who was immense over several years; the McLeish brothers, Kenny and Tom; Alan Tait, who was scrum-half before Bryan Redpath. You can highlight so many names, invaluable in their contribution, who it would be very easy to overlook, because perhaps they didn't get to run out at Murrayfield, or World Cups. But they were not lesser players when it came to Melrose.

"Craig Redpath was as good as anyone. Even sat on the bench in the 1990 Grand Slam game but never got a cap.

"He came back to Melrose and gave the same total commitment as he'd done to get on that bench. No slacking, no feeling sorry for himself. That moment had gone. Melrose was what mattered again now. He epitomised the commitment we had in that team."

43

BIG GAVIN ON THE CHARGE

30 October 1991 • World Cup, Cardiff
New Zealand 13–Scotland 6

"Boom!"

"If that isn't the memory for me from this World Cup, I'll tell you, nothing is. That was magnificent." So said the late Gordon Brown during commentary while watching Scotland play New Zealand in the third/fourth play-off game in Cardiff. And all of Scotland agreed.

What he'd witnessed was Scotland full-back Gavin Hastings on the charge, when, having fielded a high kick, he set off up the right wing at full chat, opting to take the shortest route available – which meant shoulder-charging his way through All Blacks tight-head prop Richard Loe.

There was only one winner – the Scotland full-back bouncing off Loe, who went tumbling to the turf.

One or two may point out that the reason Hastings was there that day was of his own making, having missed a crucial kick the previous Saturday against England at Murrayfield. Had he been successful, we would never have witnessed his crashing charge on Loe.

I mean, that had to be better than appearing in a World Cup final, surely?

44

SCOTLAND ENTER THE FASHION STAKES

1992

Scotland had traditionally gone for white jerseys as their change kit whenever there was a colour clash, most notably against France or the New Zealand All Blacks. Indeed, Scotland clinched the Grand Slam in 1984 wearing that very kit, and similarly had contested the third-place game against the All Blacks in Cardiff the previous year bedecked in the same attire of white shirts, shorts and blue socks.

But 1992 meant a change – subtle but hugely effective. A horizontal blue pinstripe transformed the Scotland change kit and made it a commercial success as well. It also proved highly popular with sports editors who would regularly use the white look to brighten up dull newspaper pages.

A success. Unfortunately, the same could not be said for future fashion failures.

45

CO-OPTIMISTS "SELECT" SELECT TAKES THE MELROSE SEVENS

10 April 1993 • Melrose Sevens, The Greenyards

There is always a rewarding feeling when a wee plan comes off. There must have been a real glow then amongst the Scotland Sevens contingent as they saw their team – under the none-too-convincing disguise of the Co-optimists – win the Melrose Sevens, part of their preparation for the forthcoming Rugby World Seven tournament, which would take place at Murrayfield later that month.

Alongside other guests, namely Bay of Plenty and Western Province (who didn't last beyond Boroughmuir in their opening tie), Co-optimists, coached by Dougie Morgan, first took out Stirling County, 31–7, then Edinburgh Accies 26–5, before meeting Bay of Plenty in the semi-finals, the New Zealand province seeing their hopes of back-to-back wins at the Greenyards ended in a 14–12 loss. It was the proverbial final before the final.

It was in that tie that Ken Milligan replaced the injured Tony Stanger, while in the former himself gave way to Dundee HSFP scrum-half Andy Nicol.

It was an eight then which triumphed in the final, the Co-optimists putting on a ruthless display of Sevens rugby, romping to a 61–0 win over Jed-Forest to take the Ladies Cup, and for the all-star line-up of Milligan, Gregor Townsend, Mark Appleson, Dave Millard, Doddie Weir, Ian Corcoran, Derek Turnbull and Nicol to take their cherished winners medals.

46

ENGLAND LOSS TOO MUCH FOR HASTINGS

5 February 1994 • Five Nations, Murrayfield
Scotland 14–England 15

Never has the emotion of a loss in a Scotland jersey been as raw as that displayed by Gavin Hastings minutes after the 1994 Calcutta Cup defeat to England.

If you wanted to see what it meant to Hastings, his tears during an interview with the BBC's Dougie Donnelly showed just how painful that loss had been.

Perhaps it was the circumstances behind the defeat – how what should have been a hard-fought Scottish win was snatched away in the cruellest of circumstances with Jon Callard's late penalty winner after an incident known now as "The Hand of Rob".

It appeared that Gregor Townsend's drop goal would hand Scotland their first win against England since 1990 – and a first in that season's Five Nations.

Instead, referee Lindsay McLachlan of New Zealand spotted Scotland centre Ian Jardine handling in a ruck and penalised the Stirling County man. However, TV evidence pointed the finger at the dark arts having been perpetrated by England stand-off Rob Andrew.

Had the referee bought a red herring because the England jersey of that period carried a dark blue cuff?

It mattered little. Scotland had lost and Hastings struggled to hold back the tears.

I suppose it's too late to consult the TMO? Asking for a still-upset friend.

47

SCOTLAND WIN IN PARIS FOR THE FIRST TIME IN 26 YEARS

18 February 1995 • Five Nations, Paris
France 21–Scotland 23

Black-and-white television was still the norm, an undecimalised Britain still spent pounds, shillings and pence, and we hadn't yet become full members of the Common Market. Concorde hadn't even flown the last time Scotland had won in Paris. Yet each of those historic references were immediately consigned to the dustbin on a sunny, spring afternoon in the French capital after the Scots won a bruising battle in Parc des Princes.

Boosted by an opening Five Nations win against Ireland (not forgetting a win over Canada in their "free weekend" friendly Test), Scotland were in good spirits heading into the French game. Early on, however, it did seem like a rerun of an old movie when France took an early lead, Thierry Lacroix chipping over the onrushing Scotland defence for Philippe Saint-André to get the score.

Gavin Hastings reduced the lead with a howitzer of a goal from five metres inside his own half. Those good spirits were suddenly running freely; Scotland explored various avenues, including out wide. When play was switched, Bryan Redpath (having already had the shirt ripped from his back), swung the ball out through Craig Chalmers, with centre Ian Jardine (who would suffer a Championship-ending broken cheekbone during hostilities) flinging a pass towards Hastings, which Philippe Sella nearly intercepted.

The loose ball bounced to the feet of Gregor Townsend, who tried to dribble but was slide-tackled by Lacroix. However, the ball bounced invitingly into the hands of Townsend, who dodged full-back Jean-Luc Sadourny to score behind the posts, making Hastings kick no more than a gimme. Scotland stretched to 13–5 by half-time, Doddie Weir replacing Damian Cronin, who had damaged an arm.

France, though, were a different animal in the second half. Lacroix knocked over a short-range penalty, Christophe Deylaud a drop goal as the home pack and backs combined to drive Scotland backwards, relieved when Hastings made another penalty look simple and took the scoreboard to 16–11 in his side's favour.

Eventually the Scottish line was broken, not once but twice. Guy Accoceberry attacked the narrow side, connecting with Sadourny, who bounced off Scots markers to earn a try. Sadourny then acted as pivot to take Saint-André's pass, then returned the favour to enable the French captain to outpace Jardine up the touchline and score in the corner. Neither try was converted, costly in the circumstances.

Scotland, down by 21–16, had nothing to lose entering the closing minutes. In centre field, Redpath hit Chalmers, who found Townsend; he was halted by two white jerseys but had the wherewithal to spot Hastings coming up in support, who capitalised on Townsend's sleight of hand, bursting through the flimsy French rearguard to score beneath the posts.

PART III - 1990s

After a 40-plus-metre gallop, and with the scores now tied, Hastings regained his composure to kick the additional points to seal a historic and memorable Scottish win. Scotland had gone from nervy tourists to confident title challengers in just 80 minutes.

That's how fickle sport can be.

48

TOONY, PARIS AND *THAT* PASS

1995

As a player, Gregor Townsend was always capable of moments of genius and flashes of brilliance, interspersed by instances of madness. Doddie Weir said his nickname was Toony, not because of his surname, but because it rhymed with loony. Well, Doddie would say that.

However, Townsend's career at international level had seen his first cap won as a replacement for Craig Chalmers at Twickenham (an injury that ruled the latter out of the 1993 Lions trip to New Zealand) but earn a first start as outside centre. For 1994, the Gala man played at no. 10, but reverted to 13 for Scotland's friendly against Canada ahead of their Five Nations campaign kicking off against Ireland, a match they won in Edinburgh.

There wasn't any need, therefore, to make changes for the game at Parc des Princes, Townsend playing outside Chalmers and Ian Jardine. While Townsend scored Scotland's first try – his own first at international level – that match in Paris will forever be remembered for Townsend's back-of-the-hand pass to set up Scotland's winning move.

As an accomplished Sevens exponent, Townsend was well

PART III - 1990s

versed in keeping possession and moving the ball out of tackle situations. It was how you gained an advantage, either numerically or territorially. With Scotland trailing entering the closing minutes, the Scots appeared bogged down in a crowded midfield, until Chalmers threw the ball left to his fellow Borderer. Townsend was apprehended by Philippe Sella and Laurent Cabannes but somehow managed to flick a pass out to the hard-running Gavin Hastings, who ran home from the French 10-metre line.

Ironically, minutes earlier, Townsend had made an outside break deep into French territory, keeping the move alive by finding Craig Joiner with a backhand flip inside. If only the French had been paying attention and spotted Toony's practice attempt, the outcome might have been very different.

Gavin Hastings, Scotland captain on that day, recalls "right place, right time":

"For me, it was probably the one game where I honestly believed I could exert the greatest influence, both as a player and as the captain. I don't know if that was because I had started my international career with a win against the French in 1986, when I kicked all the points, or that we'd won convincingly against them in the big match we had during the 1990 Grand Slam run.

"My mindset and mentality, and expressing that to the players and my team, was borne out of the frustration that so often, and particularly in the years we visited Paris, there had been games when we flew home knowing we could have won but didn't – not because we weren't good enough, or sufficiently talented, but perhaps because we hadn't entirely believed we could go there, to Paris, and win.

"The year previously, Scott and I had won our 50th caps for Scotland at Murrayfield against France – a remarkable coincidence to land on that number at exactly the same time given how we'd got there, through injuries and the likes, and against France, who we'd made our debuts against eight years earlier. It was a great achievement, doubly so, and a special day, but the result wasn't so special.

"I recall saying to Philippe Saint-André after that game, 'Next year, we will take you in Paris.' He just laughed loudly, shrugged and said, '*Non*, that will never happen.' Okay.

"After they spoiled that celebration, maybe I had in my mind that I had to get one back on them, and where better than Paris – easier said than done, to be fair – but having won against Ireland, we were in a good mood, generally, within the camp.

"As soon as we had beaten the Irish, I said right, we are going to win in Paris. Then when we met up again the following week, having asked how everyone was, I started telling them again: remember, we are going to win in Paris.

"All that week leading up to the game, I just kept repeating the line: we will win in Paris. On a one-to-one basis, this weekend we are going to win in Paris; at the airport, on Saturday we will win in Paris; around the dinner table, tomorrow we will win in the Parc des Princes; at the breakfast table, we are going to beat the French today and we will win in Paris. I just went at it, instilling this belief that we were going to win in Paris.

"I knew clearly if I played well and I kicked well, and if we didn't let too many chances go abegging, then we would have a very good chance of winning. Maybe I'd convinced myself! But we did have a very good group of players who had come together wonderfully well, given we'd only really played together for the first time against Canada a month before.

"The game got off to the usual start with France scoring inside five minutes. No need to panic, they always seemed to do that, so there was no need to get in a flap.

"I kicked a penalty from inside our half, which dear old Bill

PART III - 1990s

[McLaren], in a clip I've still got, talks of as 'one of the great penalty goals of all time', which I laugh at, but it was typical Bill. Gregor scored a try and we were 13–5 up at the break.

"We always knew France would come back hard at us, but I hadn't planned that they'd actually be leading with not very long to go. Toony had missed touch with a kick; France ran it back and scored. I pulled the team in as we were waiting for the conversion to be missed, and I have this on video somewhere, and Craig Chalmers talks about it, where he says, 'The big man gathered us in under the posts and says, "You know, we can still win this."'

"Craig then admits, 'You know, for once, I think I believed what he said!' Whenever I show that to people, they start laughing. And rightly so – it is very funny. But that is Craig's recollection.

"Mine is a wee bit different. I pointed out that we had played very well in this game, and we had come so far and so close that if we didn't go back downfield and at least give ourselves a chance of winning it, we would have let ourselves down and let our supporters down.

"Maybe I was looking at Gregor at the same time and thinking he had contributed to the situation we now found ourselves in, but within a minute or two, we were running at them, keeping the ball in hand, just looking for any kind of opening, and then the 'Toony Flip' came.

"That flash was just so Gregor. Me, it was right place, right time.

"I was running in to help as he'd got a bit tangled up, and next thing I had the ball and was scampering in for the try from somewhere around the 10-metre line – well it was the 10-metre line; I watched it often enough. Conversion under the posts? I wasn't worried about that. It was job done because we had scored close enough to make it kickable.

"All we had to do then was hold out, hang on for 90 seconds or however long it was – it felt like an hour. For me, it wasn't the strongest Scotland team that day. We had probably gone there with stronger sides, but we played bloody well and the forwards got really stuck in and it was a deserved victory. I felt all along we were destined to win, and we did.

"The win was fantastic, but the best thing about that game were the celebrations afterwards. It was utter euphoria and unbelievable partying from when we walked through the front door of the hotel, where we were greeted by Scotland fans, many of whom had never seen us win in Paris, and they swept us up the stairs. At home, I've still got photographs from that night with some friends who had popped in.

"I'd been given a bottle of champagne by one of the committee men as I arrived back at the hotel – that's when you realised this was something a wee bit special – and we just had the most wonderful night of celebration, probably as good a post-match party as we'd ever had.

"It was just an incredible game to play in. Even now there's something still quite magical about it all, and in a career which spanned ten international seasons, you recall special memories, and that clearly was a very special moment in mine – probably up there with Craig Chalmers listening to me and believing what I said.

"Joking aside, it was and remains so special to me because it was the one I had the greatest influence on as a captain.

"Four years on, a much-changed Scotland went back and recorded an unbelievable result with an incredible performance to beat France again, and now that game is our last Paris win, just like 1969 was the one we referenced. Again, a few years have passed, but much the same as we did, you know the current team and the way they play, there is no reason why – just by cutting out a few errors and prompting a bit more control – they couldn't emulate those 1995 or 1999 wins."

49

PETERS' TRY SETS TONE FOR ON-SONG SCOTS

4 March 1995 • Five Nations, Murrayfield
Scotland 26–Wales 13

For a team that had just won in Paris for the first time in 26 years and that had kicked off the 1995 Five Nations with a stylish win against Ireland, for once, no one was getting too far ahead of themselves in the build-up to the match against Wales in March of that year.

For once, Scotland would begin as favourites; while they were two from two, Wales were 0–2, well beaten in Paris, and, having had the best part of a month to dwell on that loss, were truly thumped 23–9 by England in Cardiff. However, no one explained how bookies odds worked to Wales, who were rampant from the off and took the lead with less than three minutes on the clock through scrum-half Robert Jones.

A brace of penalties from Gavin Hastings pulled the Scots back into the game, before they grabbed the initiative with a fantastic counter-attack try from Eric Peters.

The Scots charge had begun in their own 22, Rob Wainwright fielding a punt and passing to Hastings, who, sensing an opportunity to run at the fragmented Welsh side, brought Doddie

Weir in on the move. The giant lock galloped forward and linked with Kenny Logan, the winger weaving his way through Welsh cover and tiptoeing up the left touchline before releasing the attentive Peters on the enemy 22, the Bath no. 8 carrying the remaining yards for a magnificent score.

Inside four minutes, Scotland were disappearing into the distance. Craig Chalmers, Wainwright and Redpath all had runs but were repelled by the red wall, only for loose head Dave Hilton to be shunted in for the try, the prop receiving a congratulatory handshake from his clubmate Peters as he sat on the turf.

Up 20–7 going into the second half, Hastings countered anything Neil Jenkins achieved with the boot. Scotland were headed for another Grand Slam decider with the Auld Enemy at Twickenham. By comparison to the glittering prizes on offer in West London, Wales were 80 minutes away from something much more wooden.

Eric Peters on how he arrived on the end of the "try of the season":

"That was only my fourth game for Scotland, quite a way to announce yourself to those who maybe weren't quite sure who you were, or those who wondered if I should be playing for Scotland.

"The confusion came from my accent and that, while at Cambridge, I played for English Universities. Who else was I eligible to play for? I was asked what were my credentials? Being born in Glasgow off Scots parents was a good start.

"I got my chance to face the Springboks up in Aberdeen, playing for a Scotland Select in November 1994. Scotland A had beaten them at Melrose, so we were the next tier down, if you like, a team of disgruntled characters and others trying to push their way up the ladder.

"South Africa had a few names in their side, one being Joel

PART III - 1990s

Stransky. We lost 34–10, but I was noticed for a tackle I put in on Stransky. The Springboks were doing a move down the blindside which I had seen them do before. Stransky threw a miss or a bit of a dummy and I collected him, picked him up, ran for a bit and then dumped him in a pile, which I'm told brought a reaction from Jim Telfer in the stand, who wanted to know, 'Whooo's thaaaat?' I think that was how I ended up in the line-up for the Canada game, probably not a match that's made it into this publication, although Damian Cronin's toilet break after five minutes was quite unique.

"I suppose to some I had emerged from nowhere, and the press attributed a quote to me about it being more difficult to get in the Bath team than the Scotland side. I never said that, but I was up against Ben Clarke, Andy Robinson, John Hall, Steve Ojomoh and Dave Egerton for a starting place every week, so to break into that company, you needed to be doing something right.

"The team that beat Canada pretty much stayed intact for Ireland, then France, though by Wales we had a few injuries to contend with, though it didn't weaken the team in any way. Wales weren't having a great time of it either, but we would still have to play well.

"We'd had a bit of a clear-out, post-South Africa, and by now the new team was clicking and showing a bit more openness, which I think was down to the new guys not really playing to the old script, hence why we were probably able to score such a good try.

"It won a few 'try of the year' prizes, but if I'm honest, I thought we would just clear to touch as nothing much seemed on when Gavin – who was the leader and made people believe they could go out and perform – was given the ball. Then he jogged forward and shipped a pass to Doddie. I was thinking, *What are you doing?*

"One key part in that score was that Ieuan [Evans] stepped in off his wing to target Doddie, and Kenny was given the freedom to weave his way through. Another was that Chick [Chalmers] was taken out of play illegally, which meant I was the only player Kenny – who did well to stay up in the tackle – could give the ball to.

"I had been running so hard just to catch up, it makes my break on to the pass look wonderfully timed. A try like that certainly grabs people's attention and they've been showing it ever since.

"Kenny would tell you he made the try, and he's probably correct. Doddie, though, would tell you he made the space for Kenny. Either way, it was a great try at an important time in the game, and one that pushed us on in what was a really good season for the team.

"I played in the 1995 World Cup, won the European Cup with Bath and then played all the games in the 1999 Five Nations, which we won, although I missed the France game through an injury, and then the World Cup, which meant beating Ireland in 1999 was my last game for Scotland, at a time when I was vice-captain and in the form of my life. Disappointing. Still, they always show my try."

50

THE YEAR OF THE "NEARLY MEN"

1995

Actually, that "nearly men" label, which was attached to the Scots after coming so close to a Championship-winning season in 1995, is both cruel and inaccurate. The reality was that from unfancied contestants, Scotland progressed step by step through the Five Nations to suddenly become the main rivals to favourites England and, arguably, the most exciting team to watch that term.

It was difficult to get too disappointed when they lost the Grand Slam game at Twickenham, given no one had given them an earthly of being in that position just a few months earlier.

However, it was a Scotland team which grew in stature and grew on the fans. "Nearly men", perhaps, though "nearly champs" would be kinder.

Peter Wright tells his tale of a team which punched way above its weight:

"A big thing people talk about now in sport is momentum, one performance leading to a better one, one win leading to another. I don't think it was part of sports speak in the way it is maybe nowadays, but we generated momentum from the first game in 1995, which wasn't in the Five Nations but a friendly against Canada.

"Our free week, as you had back then when the other four teams played, came right at the start, so the game against Canada brought us up to speed straight away. There were changes to the team, but we seemed to knit together quite well.

"You do just take each game as it comes, but you always look at how the fixtures are arranged, and we always knew the two toughest games would be away from home.

"We knew we'd have a good chance, being at home, against the Irish, who had decent players but were nothing like the team they are now. It was a good win against Ireland. We scored a couple of tries and Gavin [Hastings] was on form, and we won relatively comfortably in the end. A lot of the boys will say it, but that season the Canada game meant we hit the Championship running.

"Then the France game just propelled us forward even faster. I'll be honest, in beating the French, my thoughts were more about meeting them again in the World Cup in South Africa that summer, and how we'd possibly start favourites now, even though it was such a long way off.

"I don't think there was mention of anything Grand Slam or Triple Crown until after the Wales game. There were reasons for that, one being Jim Telfer, who was still kicking around in some capacity or another, the proverbial ton of bricks if you showed any kind of euphoria or celebration.

"The Wales game was much like the Ireland game, even down to the score and the scoring, although the two tries couldn't have been more different – Eric [Peters] finished a brilliant move, where Hilts [Dave Hilton] just got wrestled and dragged over the line. But they all count the same.

"Could we go down and beat England? We thought so. We'd

PART III - 1990s

been counted out by a great many even before we had started that season, but we had a puncher's chance. We were extremely mobile with the pack we had, we could ruck too, and there was some real intelligence in the back row with Iain Morrison, Eric Peters and Rob Wainwright, and not all because they went to Cambridge. They had a bit of rugby nous about them as well.

"We knew what to expect; Chick [Craig Chalmers] said he thought the English back row were slow and quite ponderous off the scrum and ruck, and backed himself to kick three drop goals. He actually only got two, but we had them measured up.

"Where it fell on its backside a wee bit was at Twickenham. I don't think we ever looked like winning it, but we conceded too many penalties trying to stop the driving maul that was the basis of England's game. We lost 24–12.

"Unfortunately, they were frustratingly good at it, but they were playing to their strengths. If you take their scrum – Leonard, Moore, Ubogu, Johnson, Bayfield, Rodber, Clarke and Dean Richards – other than Victor [Ubogu] that was a Lions pack. Actually, it was a Lions team if you see who they had across the backs as well.

"Going to Twickenham then, which had really started to become a pretty impressive stadium – and England had a support behind them as well by then – was never going to be easy, and that's even before you look at the record Scotland had there.

"We had various ploys, most borderline in terms of legality, but the referee Brian Stirling saw everything as being illegal. Hence why Rob Andrew was able to kick seven penalties.

"And, when I say the referee saw everything we did as being against the law, that included my textbook rucking of Will Carling.

"He was lying there, and to my mind, killing the ball and

needed moving. Mr Stirling saw it differently and gave me a yellow card, without looking at me, and only referring to me as 'Blue 3'.

"My claim to fame – the first Scot sent to the sinbin at international level – although it might not earn me a place in any hall of fame. It should; put it to a vote.

"It was disappointing, but then how disappointed could you be getting to play in a Grand Slam decider when you never expected to be there in the first place? I still think the main focus that year was the World Cup, and we had put ourselves in a good place for going there.

"Again, things didn't go to plan after Emile Ntamack's last minute score in Pretoria; although, out in South Africa, I did score my one and only try for Scotland, against the rugby world superpower that was the Ivory Coast. It's amazing how good that try has become over the years. And better than none, I say.

"What happened the following year almost mirrored 1995. We missed Grand Slams, back to back. Sounds quite boastful now, and I suppose it was still the Five Nations. But we were in a good place around that time against some very good teams. Unfortunately, England did for us twice..."

51

CAPTAIN FANTASTIC HAMMERS IVORY COAST

26 May 1995 • World Cup, Rustenberg
Ivory Coast 0–Scotland 89

Scotland were old hands at this World Cup malarkey by the time South Africa staged the 1995 tournament. They had been in the inaugural competition in New Zealand in 1987, and four years on, had come within a couple of kicks of being finalists at Twickenham. Instead, Scotland had to make do with being fourth.

However, leading up to South Africa, the leading question wasn't so much about how a Scotland team which had only just missed out on an unexpected Grand Slam might perform, but did they even play rugby in Ivory Coast?

Côte d'Ivoire were one of just two African nations in the competition, along with the hosts, after topping their final qualifying group. After losing to Morocco, Les Elephants produced more notable results in beating both Namibia and Zimbabwe. The key result, however, had been in the final round of games when the favoured Namibians missed out on the finals when only drawing with Morocco.

The Scots knew little of Ivory Coast, the team, other than some insight gleaned from VHS videos and that they had a squad full of players based in France, and you didn't play there without having a decent skill set.

The Ivorians' unorthodox approach caused the Scots a few issues early on in Rustenburg, until after ten minutes, Gavin Hastings made a great cut back and chip, the ball bouncing into his welcoming hands for the touchdown. He converted that, and his other two first-half tries, as well as adding a couple of penalties. Only Peter Walton's try (his first) prevented it becoming the Gavin Hastings show, as he clocked up 29 points as Scotland led 34–0.

The second half saw him take his personal tally to 44 points in the match – his four tries, nine conversions and brace of penalties a Scottish record, unsurprisingly – as the Scots cut loose, eventually ending the tie with 13 tries (a Scottish record, unsurprisingly) and a final result of 89–0 (a Scottish record, unsurprisingly).

Things might have been different (although not by much) had the Ivorians not lost captain, stand-off, playmaker and inspiration Athanase Dali, who played for Clamart Rugby 92 in France, after 30 minutes through injury. Dali conceded afterwards that his Scots counterpart in all of the above categories (except stand-off) had left his colleagues mesmerised.

"Gavin Hastings is a great player. We spent the entire first half looking at him," Dali admitted.

As for Dali's manager, Pierre Cassagnet, there were positives to be taken from their first World Cup game, albeit while admitting things could have been less damaging.

"We don't think it's humiliating," said Cassagnet. "Maybe around 50 points would have been a bit better..."

Peter Walton on playing alongside "Super Gav": "I'd gone on tour in the summer of 1994 to Argentina but had missed most of

PART III - 1990s

the next season having injured my knee and then been in rehab. I ended up at Lilleshall – in beside all the footballers – with Gary Armstrong, for intensive rehab, which, as you can imagine, was eventful. I hadn't played at all that season but got selected for the World Cup. That was massive for me, although I knew that I was out there as one of the 'also-rans' or in my case, a 'hadn't ran'. What is commonly known as a dirt tracker, someone who would play in the midweek tour games, except there weren't any midweek games. Every match was a World Cup tie, so I did feel fortunate to get selected, even for one match.

"We were still amateurs, remember, so we did the amateur thing when we arrived and that was went out and got hammered. There wasn't even any time difference to worry about. Great!

"That endeared us to the locals in Pretoria, where we were based. You could say we were recruiting supporters.

"For the opening match day, we were at altitude in Rustenburg, which made it bloody hard to breathe. On the way there, we went by bus and got off to have a sandwich, and couldn't breathe while we were eating it because we were actually higher up then than what we would be for the match.

"If that wasn't enough, the heat was a killer too. My fitness wasn't where it should have been. It was torture, and on top of that, my feet were on fire; wearing boots for 80 minutes on a pitch – it was the infield for an athletics track – that was bone hard. I was in agony.

"We weren't sure what to expect from the Ivory Coast. I think there was one lad, a back rower playing in France, he was the only one I knew. The rest we'd 'learned' from one VHS video tape we had, which looked like it had been watched 27 times.

"There were some big guys amongst them, very unorthodox, let's say, in how they tackled or mauled and rucked. But once we'd familiarised ourselves with them, and when they started to run out of gas, simply because they hadn't faced that kind of intensity before, we had the game won.

"While I'm saying I was struggling, and a few others were as well, Gavin was unstoppable. I remember looking at him and thinking, *How the hell is he doing that?* We were told we should be doing this and that, but from where I was, all we had to do was get the ball to Gavin and he'd score.

"It was a measure of what Gav did that day that nearly quarter of a century on, no one has beaten his total in a game.

"The wives and girlfriends were out there for the tournament, the first time they'd been invited by the SRU, but we only saw them after that game, then they all went back to the Sun City resort. My wife and Gavin's wife shared a room and got on great. But some of the others' girls I don't think had much in common other than their partners played rugby together.

"That couldn't have been easy, especially after the pool and the casino lost its appeal. What was great was that any time a tour was mentioned ever again, none of the partners wanted to go!

"As for us, we had another good win over Tonga, then lost the must-win game against France, which set up a game against the All Blacks. It wouldn't be the World Cup without playing them."

52

DODDIE'S DOUBLE NOT ENOUGH TO HALT ALL BLACKS

11 June 1995 • World Cup, Pretoria
New Zealand 48–Scotland 30

Scoring not one but two tries against the All Blacks at the World Cup is something Doddie Weir takes immense pride in – especially when in conversation with wingers who can perhaps only dream of having such a red-letter day on their CV.

When it comes to World Cups there has always been a little bit of history repeating itself between the Scots and Kiwis, a trend that by the third such tournament was well established. Scotland exited the inaugural tournament in 1987 when they lost to eventual tournament winners and hosts New Zealand in the quarter-finals. Four years hence and Scotland's adventure again came to a halt against the men in black, this time in the play-off for third place in Cardiff.

Even before a ball was kicked in anger for the 1995 tournament therefore, it was established that to avoid pre-event favourites All Blacks in the last eight, Scotland would have to finish top of Pool D. That would mean beating France in the final group game at Loftus Versfeld in Pretoria. Scotland lost 22–19, meaning that for a third successive competition, the thistle would go up against the silver fern. Not the news anyone in Scotland wanted, unless you had shares in a half-and-half scarf knitting business.

New Zealand had already beaten Ireland and Wales, and obliterated Japan by 145–17. They had been impressive both as a team and individually, none more so than giant winger Jonah Lomu, who, with his speed and strength, could be a match winner on his own and was well on his way to building a fearsome reputation, albeit just five caps into his All Blacks career.

It wasn't quite as simple as "stop Lomu, stop New Zealand". But keeping him quiet would be advantageous. Unfortunately, Scotland failed on that count almost immediately. Inside five minutes, Lomu sped outside Craig Joiner, evaded the clutches of Scott Hastings, bounced over Gavin Hastings, was eventually felled by Graham Shiel, but still got a pass off for Walter Little to score.

Gavin Hastings kicked two penalties to trail 7–6, then Lomu scored a try of his own as New Zealand made it 17–9 by the break, stretching that to 31–9 with scores from Little and Andrew Mehrtens, who would eventually also land 18 points with the boot. Then came a Scotland try, Doddie Weir emerging from a driven maul to score. It was still just a glancing blow to All Blacks domination; Frank Bunce weaved his way past some flimsy defending to score, while Sean Fitzpatrick found himself wide man to add another on the left to take New Zealand out of sight at 45–16.

Scotland did nevertheless add some respectability to the outcome before the end. With 14 minutes left, Graeme Bachop fluffed his kick when tackled by Dave Hilton. The ball rebounded to Weir five metres out and the big man was driven over for the try, before Scott Hastings added another, converted by brother Gavin, his last points in a Scotland jersey.

At the end, New Zealand headed for a semi-final against

PART III - 1990s

England, Gavin Hastings for retirement, chaired off the pitch by Rob Wainwright and Doddie Weir. Maybe it should have been the other way around?

Doddie Weir looks back:

"How many times have you scored against the All Blacks in a game? That's shut a few folk up over the years. I have embellished the story, on occasions, depending on the audience. I think I may have said I sprinted in from 40 yards or something like that for the tries, throwing the odd sidestep along the way. But the reality was I fell over from a few feet each time. Actually, the first one, I only got the ball down at the second attempt. But no one can take that achievement away from me.

"Being honest, I don't think we were ever going to get close enough to the All Blacks, or stick with them long enough, to cause an upset. They were too powerful, as England found out in their semi-final. Tactically, there was only so much you could do to keep big Jonah [Lomu] out of the game. Every team that played against him spoke of the tactics they'd developed to either close him down or isolate him, but that always took more than one man, several at times, and if they were watching him, it created space for others. He was an immense presence at his peak.

"But he only scored the once that day. Did I mention that?"

53

DODS' HAUL SEES SCOTLAND TO WIN OVER FRENCH

3 February 1996 • Five Nations, Murrayfield
Scotland 19–France 14

The name Dods accumulating points in a Scotland jersey wasn't new; in the 1980s, Peter Dods had bagged a tidy haul during Scotland's Grand Slam-winning season. It should not have been a surprise then to find such traits carried in the genes of younger brother Michael, who became the mainstay of Scotland point-scoring during the 1996 Five Nations, when Scotland came so close once again to the Grand Slam.

Already with four caps to his name, the Northampton utility back started against Ireland in Dublin, scoring his first try in a tight win.

However, at Murrayfield a fortnight later, he proved to be the match winner. Scotland's aggressive and direct approach caught out the French, who early on did well to repulse the likes of Gregor Townsend, Rob Wainwright and Rowen Shepherd.

A try in each half and three successive penalties gave Dods 17 points on the day (he had struck 15 against Argentina and Samoa in previous Scotland appearances), but more importantly a second successive Five Nations win, forcing defeated French

PART III – 1990s

captain Philippe Saint-André to concede: "Scotland should win the Grand Slam the way they played against us."

Where had they heard that before?

Michael Dods on his unexpected promotion to kicker and match winner: "We'd had a poor autumn series – actually it wasn't a series, it was just one game – against Samoa – which we had drawn. That was seen as a bit of a poor result. Scotland A went to Italy and lost, so they made a few more changes. It was a new squad for the Ireland game, but we went to Dublin and won.

"We hadn't been given much of a chance against Ireland, and even less of a chance for the French match at Murrayfield. England had been fancied strongly for the Grand Slam, as holders, but France beat England in Paris and now we were faced by them.

"That France team was the usual array of big stars, an unbelievable side. But all week in training, we were all just talking about what the French were like and what they might do. It was almost as if, as a collective, we just said enough about them. What if we tried this? Imagine if we just run the ball back at them, from the first kick-off? Let's do it and see what they would do. Everyone would expect the forwards to take it, scrum-half to stand-off or full-back kick to touch.

"No one is expecting the kick-off to be run back at them and anyway, we probably knew we'd nothing to lose. Rob Wainwright was captain and said something like, 'Well, if we're all agreed, that's that.'

"From the kick-off, we called a double miss and the ball came out to me, and while I got tackled, the crowd just erupted; the noise was like anything we'd get in the England game. I think that's what I've remembered most from that game. The stands responded because they hadn't seen it coming – this wasn't typical Scotland – but then neither had the French, who were just as surprised, and you could tell they were wondering what was going on – and the tone was set.

"We won the ruck, made yards and our belief swelled that maybe we could take this to them. The speed of the game was intense. We barely had a chance to catch breath, but there was no use in asking anyone to calm it down – this is what we'd asked for.

"We had been running everything and then got a try out of it. Toony [Gregor Townsend] took off through the midfield, the forwards took it on and Brush [Bryan Redpath] got his hands on the ball, but instead of passing it out along the line, he looked as if he was measuring up a kick across field because the French backs had come up.

"In my head, I'm shouting, 'No, don't,' – actually, it was a bit stronger than that – because I honestly felt exhausted but would have to chase it, and I could see the big boy [Laurent] Cabannes had a start on me. But I buzzed past him, although I think he just chucked it, he was so tired running around, chasing the game, and I got in to ground the kick in the corner.

"My goal-kicking wasn't the best, missing a few, but I managed to get a few over as well, though I did feel there had been an extra burden put on me. In the Ireland game, I had been asked to kick, and again it was a bit hit and miss. Rob asked me to kick one into the gale and I admitted I didn't think I could reach the posts – and that wasn't far outside their 22 – so we went for touch.

"Afterwards Jim Telfer asked, *Why did you not kick at goal?* He just looked mystified, and not terribly supportive when I explained why, so against France, I just stuck with it.

"Off my own try, I thought I landed the conversion, maybe it just didn't turn in enough, like an earlier penalty, but I looked to Clayton Thomas the referee and asked the question, and he said no, it had missed. Not the best start.

PART III – 1990s

"I kicked a couple but missed a few, including the conversion off my second try. We won a ruck, pretty much centre field and Bryan just threw a long pass out to me, which I nearly dropped twice before finishing the move in the corner.

"But again, every time you miss, you heap pressure on yourself. I suppose the main thing was that I did kick a few penalties, including the last one in the closing minutes that took as a try in front. It looked great – 'Dods with all 19 points' – but I knew I should have had a barrowload.

"I was following on from Gavin [Hastings], who had an excellent success percentage, which left probably only Neil Jenkins in that 90 per cent-plus category. I mean, we were still a bit of a way off Jonny Wilkinson and Chris Paterson's level of accuracy.

"What disappointed me was that the previous summer, off the back of the World Cup in South Africa, I purposely went to New Zealand and joined Otago, just for the purpose of learning and to take my game to the next level. There were about a dozen or so All Blacks in the team – they had Jamie Joseph, Josh Kronfeld, Marc Ellis, Graeme Bachop, John Leslie, a proper team – and although I only played a couple of times, I was in their match squad regularly, so got to train and work on my game and really practise my kicking.

"That was the time when I was kicking well, but we still hadn't really gone full professional in the UK, so maintaining those highs was very difficult. A few years later, you had kicking coaches and the likes, but back then it was down to you.

"The England game, losing when we had a chance of a Grand Slam – disappointing. But we had punched above our weight and all in, it was a great season and a good set of players to be involved with."

54

ENGLAND LEAVE SCOTS SO NEAR, YET SO FAR AGAIN

2 March 1996 • Five Nations, Murrayfield
Scotland 9–England 18

It wasn't quite an action replay of the previous season, but Scotland surprised a few people – perhaps themselves above all – when for a second successive season they found themselves playing England to win the Grand Slam. Not that England were in contention for that prize, having lost to France in their opening game.

That same weekend, Scotland had beaten Ireland 16–10 in Dublin, with tries by hooker Kevin McKenzie, stealing around the front of a line-out to score, and Michael Dods. The latter scored all of Scotland's points against France in a 19–14 victory. And on to Cardiff, the match hinging on Arwel Thomas' last-minute conversion, which fell past the left post, handing Scotland a 16–14 win and so setting them up for a Grand Slam.

Alas, history repeated itself for the second year in a row, the Scots yet again punished for conceding too many penalties up front. Yet, despite that disappointment, finishing as runner-up in the 1996 Five Nations is fondly remembered by players and fans alike.

PART III - 1990s

Scotland captain Rob Wainwright on why the upset of a Calcutta Cup defeat was easily forgotten:

"It may have appeared unexpected to some, but you know when these things happen, you just think they're going according to plan. Every season you start, you believe you have a Slam, or a Championship, or a Triple Crown in you. People think it could be their year and you could win, but that season it was threatening to happen. It was an amazing year, very exciting and there was just a great feel to everything that was happening. We had a good team, and a good coaching set-up, and we just enjoyed ourselves. There was an energy and we just clicked.

"We'd lost Gavin [Hastings] and Kenny [Milne] after the World Cup – those were the two major retirements. But we had Gregor [Townsend] in at stand-off which obviously changed the dynamic considerably from what Scotland had been doing the last wee while. Other than that, we were a team of grafters; there wasn't anyone you would have described as utterly amazing players. Very good and very capable.

"In recent years, I've been very impressed with some of the Welsh teams that have done so well in the last decade. I've just been so impressed by them being more than the sum of their constituent parts – in other words, it's a great team. And what we achieved in 1996 was through the collective will within the team, having done much the same in 1995, again slightly unexpectedly. But we just said, let's dream and let's go for it.

"We were very organised and knew what we should be doing wherever we were on the pitch.

"The Irish game doesn't leap out at me. Michael Dods played on the wing and was wrongly bracketed as having to play there because we needed to incorporate a kicker somewhere. That was unfair. He didn't just score with the boot, he was a very good try finisher as well.

"He did so against Ireland, and two against France. Playing France at Murrayfield was always a favourite match as a player. It was always right up there. They tended to throw the ball around, so they were usually quite open contests. Just to have the Murrayfield roar at full blast was always quite special.

"I watched the 1996 match not so long ago with the nephew; a) I thought all the scoring was in the first half, and that wasn't the case, and b) the game has moved on so far in 20-odd years. Our skill sets then to now are just chalk and cheese. They are so prepared now compared to us.

"But there were fantastic players around back then: Castaignède, Saint-André, Ntamack, Benazzi, Pelous. Those chaps would have been players in any company, any generation. We had a bit of a tit-for-tat relationship with them at that time. We beat them in Paris, they beat us in the World Cup in Pretoria, we beat them again at Murrayfield. Then we stopped tit-for-tatting until 1999. Since the Millennium, I've enjoyed most of the matches, though there has been a frustration because we should have won more than we have.

"Not the case in 2004, as it was the first game I took my eldest son to see, and we lost by 30-odd points – not a great selling point to a new, young fan. Two years later, I went with a couple of friends. We had pretty crap seats, but we just walked down and picked another couple because there was so many to choose from – the place was half empty. My friends went to get a drink and missed two tries. That'll teach them.

"Anyway, we beat France in 1996 which is what this story is about, and then did the same to Wales two weeks later. Michael kicked a few points again, but my most vivid recollection was of this amazing scrum move that we had, which Toony scored a try from.

"We needed to be slightly left of centre, within five to 15

PART III – 1990s

yards out. We'd practised it, perfected it, got it like clockwork but never got the chance to use it until we got a scrum not too far off the Welsh line, quite late on. So I called it.

"What it entailed was Ian Smith dropping off the scrum on the open side. Bryan Redpath passed to Smithy, then Bryan ran behind him before scissoring inside for Toony bursting in on the angle at speed. Smithy tied up their back row, Bryan would pull their fly-half out and Gregor would go through the hole, and any gap then for Gregor looked like a hole, even with three people dangling from him. All super quick and slick and we scored from it.

"I wasn't involved; it required players who could play and had quick hands. But I still take credit for it as I called it.

"Wales scored a late try, but the young kicker hooked his kick and we clung on and won. Cardiff is a very satisfying place to win.

"That brought us to our nemesis, my nemesis, England. They could win the Triple Crown, or we could take everything. A brief synopsis: Michael Dods three penalties, Paul Grayson six.

"There was a frustration. It wasn't as if we had been run off the pitch. But their rolling maul, and especially Dean Richards, was very effective and nearly impossible to stop without conceding a penalty. The year before we'd lost to seven penalties and a drop goal from Rob Andrew. They sucked the life out of the game, and then you had the further indignity of Brian Moore accusing us of killing the game.

"But things unravelled for us in 1996 at Murrayfield, and me in particular, when I was removed from proceedings, if not physically then most definitely mentally after about ten minutes when my brain was emptied of all reasoning by Jason Leonard's forearm smash to my temple.

"Nowadays, I wouldn't have lasted another minute. Neither

might he. But we didn't have any back-row cover so I just said point me in the right direction and I'll play on. The problem was a huge part of the decision-making on the pitch was backed up in my computer. As a reflection of quite how empty my head was, I gave the line-out-calling duties to Ian Smith, who didn't even attend line-out practice. He'd run around thinking he was a back.

"Sense prevailed and Stewart Campbell took on those responsibilities. But we'd played with a man short, that man being me. Which explains a few of the reasons why we lost.

"However, it was a great wee adventure while it lasted, maybe unexpected, and maybe that's why it's so fondly remembered."

55

McGEECHAN AND TELFER MASTERMIND LIONS WIN OVER WORLD CHAMPIONS

1997

From the moment Francois Pienaar received the Webb Ellis Cup from South African President Nelson Mandela, the British & Irish Lions tour to the Cape two years down the road took on an added significance. Not only would the Lions be visiting South Africa for the first time in the post-apartheid era, and touring a nation they last visited in 1980, they would be going toe to toe with the Springboks, who had gone from rugby wilderness to champions of the world in just a few years.

The Boks win against the All Blacks in the 1995 World Cup final heralded not only new holders of the trophy but signalled South Africa's total rehabilitation as one of the leading Test nations. And, while they had Tri-Nations and tours of their own to schedule around, the significance of a visit from the best the British Isles had to offer wasn't lost on them either.

If the Lions would need the most talented squad they could assemble, so too the coaches would have to be the best available. Ian McGeechan and Jim Telfer had been key to Lions excursions since 1983. It was no surprise then that in the summer of 1996, Telfer was listed to join McGeechan for the great South African adventure.

When it came time to announce who had been recruited on the playing side, five of their countrymen – Doddie Weir, Scotland captain Rob Wainwright, Tom Smith, Gregor Townsend and Alan Tait – were listed. Weir's tour, however, would be cut short by a thuggish stamp by Marius Bosman during the match against Mpumalanga. Another Scot, Grand Slam try hero Tony Stanger would eventually fly out as a replacement.

Rugby may have still been finding its feet in the new professional era, but to fast-track the Lions in that direction, Tait was one of six ex-Rugby League players to board the flight.

By the time the opening Test in the series arrived, the Lions had won seven of their eight warm-up contests, the only loss coming against Northern Transvaal.

In the first Test at Newlands, Cape Town, the Lions – with Smith, Townsend and Tait as starters – trailed 16–12 an hour into the contest, kept in the game by the kicking of Neil Jenkins. He added a fifth penalty before the Lions scored two tries in the last seven minutes. Firstly, Matt Dawson dummied an overhead that completely threw the Boks' fringe defence to score in the corner, then in stoppage time, the momentum off a Scott Gibbs burst was continued through Dawson, Tim Rodber throwing a wide pass left to Jenkins to send Tait in uncontested – 25–16 the final score. "Game, set and match," as the former Great Britain Rugby League star summed it up.

A week later, with the same three Scots starting the second Test, South Africa outscored the Lions three tries to nil at Durban's Kings Park. The home side, however, had a nightmare in the kicking department with six kicks on the day missed. By contrast, Jenkins nailed five penalty goals. With three minutes left, Jeremy Guscott chipped over the series-winning drop goal. The Lions had beaten the champions of the world in their own backyard.

PART III – 1990s

The Lions, with injuries now taking their toll, missed out on inflicting a series whitewash on the Springboks as they restored some pride, winning the third and final Test 35–16, with Smith playing in a third successive rubber, joined in the final tour game by Wainwright.

A disappointing conclusion. But it could take nothing away from a magnificent campaign by the Lions, steered, managed and inspired by McGeechan and Telfer.

"Unknown" Tom Smith on announcing himself to the world:

"A couple of years before the Lions tour I was playing for Dundee HSPF's second XV – badly. During the Five Nations matches, to keep the Scotland team sharp, they were having live sessions and I was invited down to be cannon fodder. I was just a wide-eyed young boy, so we got to scrum against the Scotland pack, practise line-outs, all the usual stuff. Jeremy Richardson was there as well and pulled us together and basically planned to make it hard for them, although he explained it in more industrial terms. There were a few fights after that.

"I finished university and went to Watsonians, then professionalism came and a call-up from Scotland. I had three caps and went on a Lions tour. Funny how quickly everything changed.

"But when Geech and Jim were putting that squad together, it was all change in rugby and they could have whoever they wanted. All previous rules didn't apply. The England team were strong, so there were a few of them and the core of the contingent went on to be world champions, but going for the League boys was quite revolutionary. And then they picked a few randoms, like me. Oh good, cannon fodder again.

"Fran Cotton [the manager] understood the new values; he was quite old school – work hard, play hard – but brought a lot of professionalism into the set-up from the off, given how new pro rugby was. They worked as a very good management trio. In other ways, we were still amateurs. It could get a bit raucous, particularly after big games. Thankfully there were no smartphones and no social media then!

"Once we were out there, you realise there is a reasonable chunk of luck involved; if you have a good day against one of the fancied South African players, the luck is with you. If you have a bad day – and that can happen for many reasons – then you take a step backwards. I had more good days than bad and that was being noticed.

"I was fortunate enough to play against Mpumalanga – the one Doddie got jumped on – and they hadn't been beaten at home for years, and a few years earlier they [as South Eastern Transvaal] put a score on a good Welsh team. We scored 60-something and completely demolished their scrum. The front row that played in that match – me, Woody [Keith Wood] and Wally [Paul Wallace] – then played in the first Test.

"Telfer and Geech were a management who were open to people coming in. They put a lot on what they saw, not just reputation. They watched you in every scenario; in games, in training, in contact, in the loose, with the ball. They really analysed and assessed you and were constantly watching. I learned that later on...

"South Africa had a massive front row. Os du Randt was 20 stone, and Adrian Garvey, who was up against me, was two stones heavier than I was. But after the first couple of scrums, we had the measure of them, and how to move them. We also ran them ragged, which tired them out. There was less and less coming back in the scrum.

"I hardly knew Ian or Jim before that tour but knew them a lot better because of it. They were totally different but really complementary in their knowledge and insight. If you want to know how they've succeeded in rugby, and especially on that

PART III - 1990s

tour, just look at the level of intensity and drive. Incredible.

"Pairing them for that tour, with all the changes that were happening in world rugby at the time, was a real coup; they set the bar for everything else that would come after that.

"Interestingly, Jim had said he'd spotted me playing at the Melrose Sevens one year and thought I moved well and was good with the ball in my hands. The Melrose Sevens. As I said, constantly watching."

56

HAIL CESAR II

31 January 1998 • European Cup, Bordeaux
Bath 19–Brive 18

The inception of the Heineken Cup, the European Cup of rugby, coincided with the arrival of the professional game across Europe. If professionalism was supposed to make the game bigger and better, there was no better way to showcase what the top teams were capable of than staging a cross-border tournament.

In the first season, Cardiff reached the final, but not even home advantage against Toulouse could see them home. A year on, and the French dominated again, this time with Brive seeing off Leicester Tigers.

The question in 1998 was would it be third time lucky for a British club, with Bath reaching the final against the holders Brive? The West Country side had three Scots in their ranks that day: prop Dave Hilton, back rower Eric Peters, who was a replacement, and captain Andy Nicol.

By the end of a thrilling contest, Nicol had become the first British captain to lift the trophy, and thus, the parallels were immediately drawn with another Scot lifting a similar trophy in football over three decades before.

Andy Nicol on winning European rugby's biggest prize and

PART III - 1990s

joining an icon: "I had joined Bath in 1994; this was 1998. I had joined in the amateur era when Bath was the most dominant side in English club rugby. I think they'd won 16 out of 23 major trophies, and we'd always thought ourselves as the best team in Europe. But there was no vehicle to prove that until the European Cup came along, and then it became the Holy Grail for Bath; it was something we were absolutely desperate to win and so driven to achieving. Having won everything there was to win, of significance, domestically, the natural progression was to take our success into Europe.

"That wasn't being big-headed, thinking we would win in Europe as well, however, it was the mindset. Conquering Europe became a huge focus for everyone. Thankfully, that dream was fulfilled in 1998.

"Bath had a winning mentality; you never settled for what you had. But winning was based on having some fantastic players over several years. We didn't make the transition to professional rugby particularly well. We were described, not incorrectly either, as one of the most professional of amateur sides, but one of the most amateur of professional teams.

"We hadn't won anything for a couple of years, and in fact that year – the 97/98 season – we had a bit of a disaster halfway through the season, and even just a few weeks before the final, we had lost to Saracens 50–23. Now that doesn't mean anything – there's no shame in losing to Saracens, who have been at the top of European rugby for several years. But back then, it was nothing short of a disaster for us and we had almost a crisis meeting, discussing everything, even wondering if we should give our match fees back to the club because our performances had been so poor. So, it wasn't plain sailing by any means.

"The final was at the end of January back then, as that was the only time available to play the competition, and we were in the middle of this crisis of confidence.

"We'd had Brive, Pontypridd and Scottish Borders in our group – everyone will remember the infamous 'Battle of Brive' when there was fighting on and off the field when the Welsh club went there – and Bath had lost just one game in qualifying top out of the group.

"The quarter-final against Cardiff at The Rec – which for those that don't know is in the middle of Bath and is like Edinburgh playing in front of 12,000 in Princes Street Gardens – was probably one of the most enjoyable games for Bath, because if you know your history, Bath were created by going across the Severn Bridge and playing in Wales. That tie meant a lot because of the history, and Cardiff brought a good few thousand over with them, which created a brilliant atmosphere, but we won it and then took on Pau – who had produced a shock win against Leicester Tigers – in the semis.

"None of the neutral venue stuff then. We were back at The Rec and won quite easily, and then watched the next day as Brive won on tries scored in their draw with Toulouse. Having played Brive twice already, we now had them in the final.

"To go to south-west France for the final, against the reigning champions, who had been outstanding when destroying Leicester in Cardiff in the 1997 final, to say they had 'home' advantage with the game taking place at the Stade Lescure in Bordeaux – where incidentally, Scotland would play Norway later in the year at the football World Cup – would be an understatement. However, we still had about 7,000 fans out of the 36,000 capacity.

"It was an amazing venue and atmosphere. It was a great win, but above all else it was about Bath's spirit on such occasions. We had never lost a semi-final or a final, and we are talking

PART III - 1990s

double figures in all of that. Knowing how to grind out wins in the big games, that saw us through – that and the belief of Andy Robinson as coach, and guys like Nigel Redman and Martin Haag – two absolute stalwarts of that team – amid names that we had in the back division like Catt, Adebayo, Guscott, de Glanville, Ieuan Evans and Callard.

"We all talk about Jon Callard scoring all the points, and his penalty to win us the cup. But for me, what turned the game around was when we were 15–6 down and had to defend five or six scrums on our own line. Had we conceded then it was game over.

"When Callard was lining up what proved to be the winning penalty kick, deep in stoppage time, it became something of a bittersweet moment. Our kit man [Jon Allen] handed him the tee and just said, 'Come on, JC, remember Murrayfield,' a reference to four years before when JC's last-minute kick beat Scotland.

"Me and fellow Scot Jim Fleming, who was the referee, just looked at each other. I didn't think it was a particularly good time to fall out with anyone. But it still wasn't finished; they missed a penalty, but I dropped the ball giving them a scrum-five and off that, Lisandro Arbizu tried a drop goal – and missed and we'd won.

"That was the realisation of Bath's ambitions. But so many had tried, and so many great captains never got the opportunity I did. It was a very special time, but then, I didn't know or realise the significance of what I had achieved personally.

"A headline in one of the Scottish papers was 'Rugby's Cesar lifts European Cup'.

"It wasn't something I'd even considered, but that headline, and being compared to Billy McNeill of Celtic, being the first British captain to lift the European Cup in football, was something that made you sit back and think *wow*.

"In 2019, that feat became very poignant again when Big Billy passed away. I'd met him a couple of times over the years and it was an achievement that wasn't lost on him. It was just lovely to talk about it – his recollections of Lisbon in 1967, mine of Bordeaux in 1998.

"I think his might be the slightly more iconic image of lifting the trophy, but it's just nice being part of a very exclusive club, with just two members."

WORLD-CLASS: A typical electrifying break from Andy Irvine against Wales in 1977.

ALL EYES ON ROY: But Roy Laidlaw is focused on the try line against Ireland in 1984, a plot of land that will forever be known as "Laidlaw's Corner".

LEADING ENGLAND A MERRY DANCE:
John Rutherford's virtuoso performance was key to the Scots' record win in 1986.

SUCCESS SAVOURED:
Winning Lions captain Finlay Calder and coach Ian McGeechan celebrate beating Australia in the historic 1989 Test series.

ON THE MONEY:
Craig Chalmers with a crucial kick against England in the Grand Slam game of 1990.

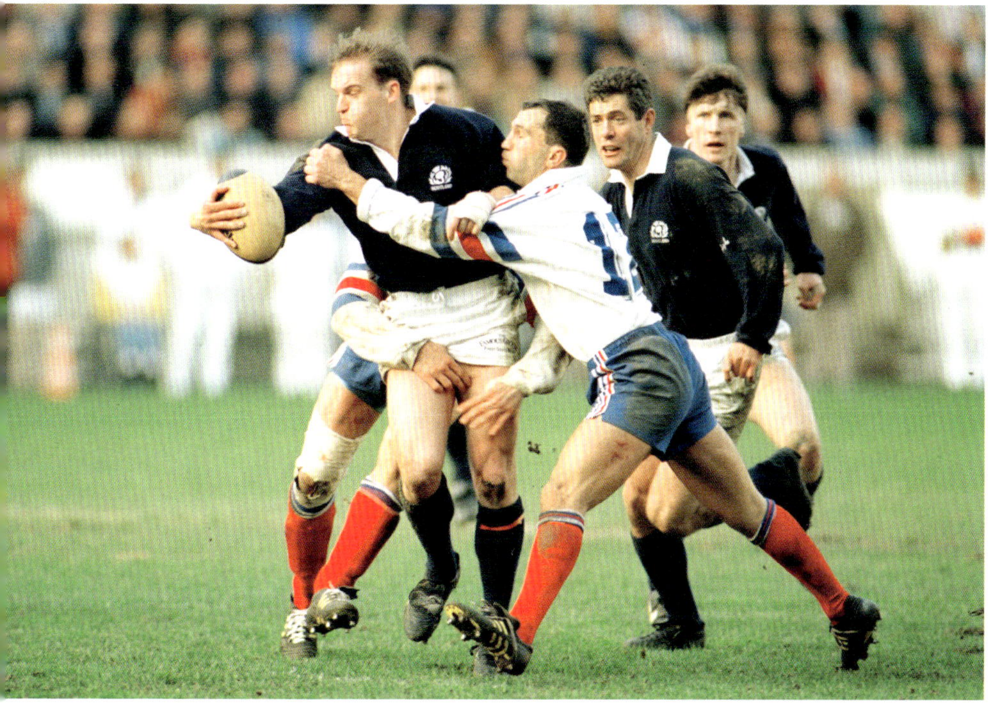

© David Munden / Popperfoto / Getty Images

"THE TOONY FLIP": Current Scotland coach Gregor Townsend setting up Gavin Hastings for Scotland's match-turning try against the French in 1995.

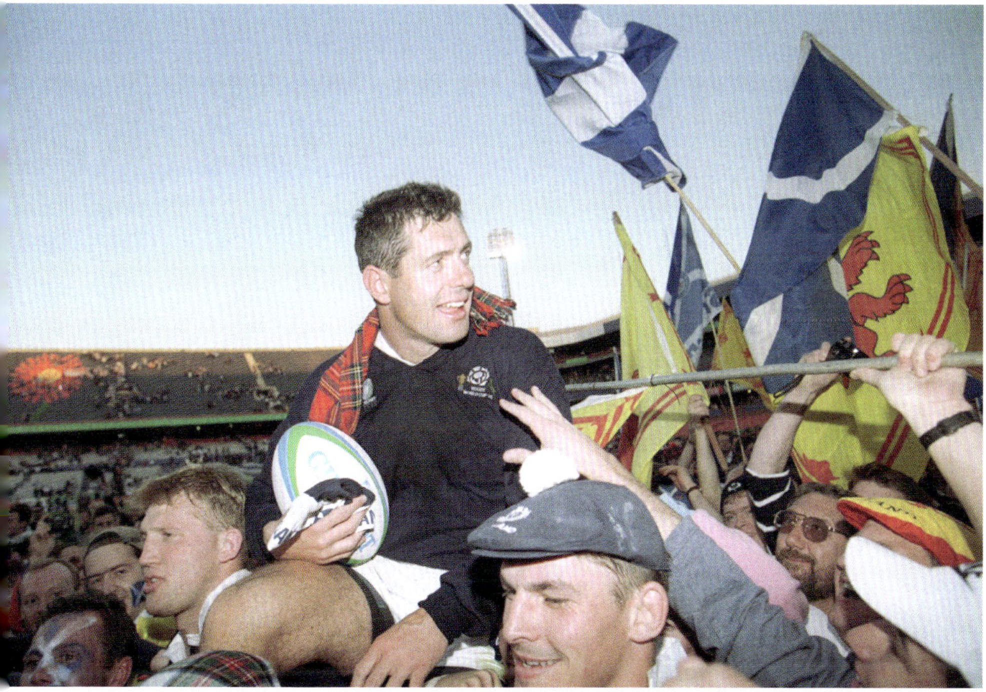

© Simon Bruty / Getty Images

END OF AN ERA: Gavin Hastings retired after the New Zealand game at the 1995 World Cup, chaired off by Doddie Weir and Rob Wainwright.

LEADING BY EXAMPLE: Captain Gary Armstrong sparks yet another Scottish attack during their amazing Paris victory in 1999.

STANDING OVATION: The Millennium Stadium rose as one ahead of Bill McLaren's last match commentary in 2002. Doubly pleasing was Scotland winning the match.

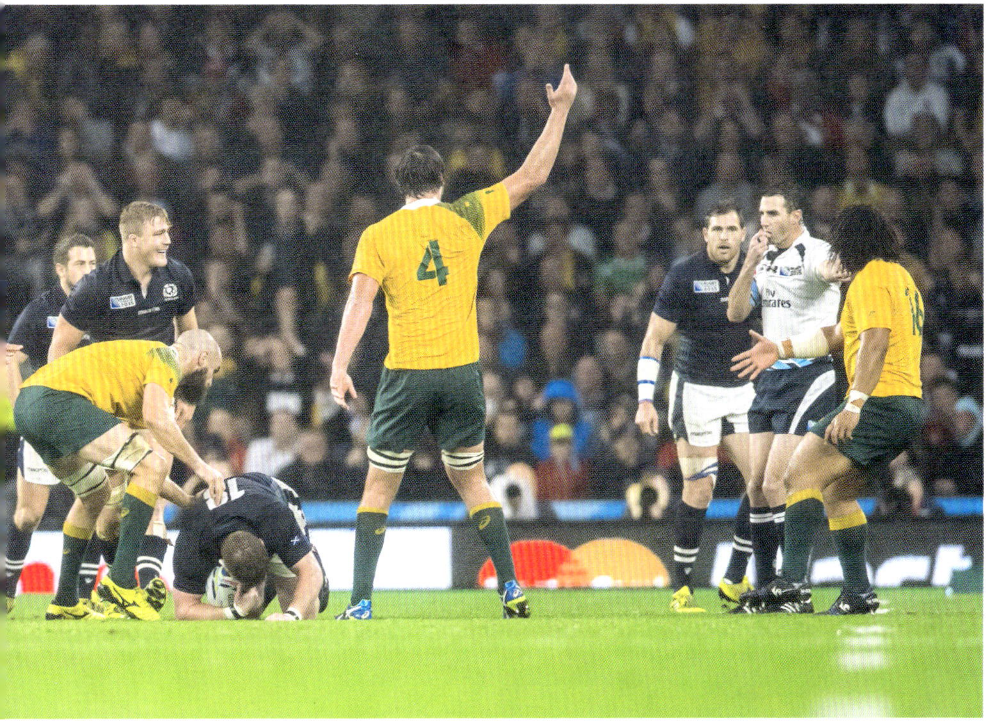

TURNING POINT: The moment referee Craig Joubert made the wrong call at Twickenham in 2015, eliminating Scotland from the World Cup.

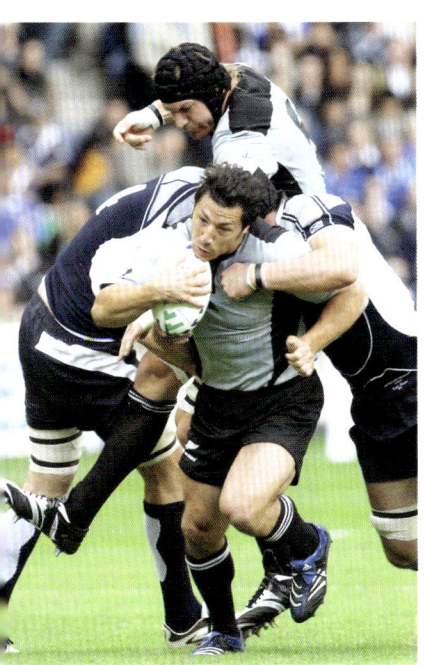

MERGING COLOURS: The 2007 World Cup tie between Scotland and ew Zealand at times left spectators and TV viewers wonder who was who.

© Craig Watson

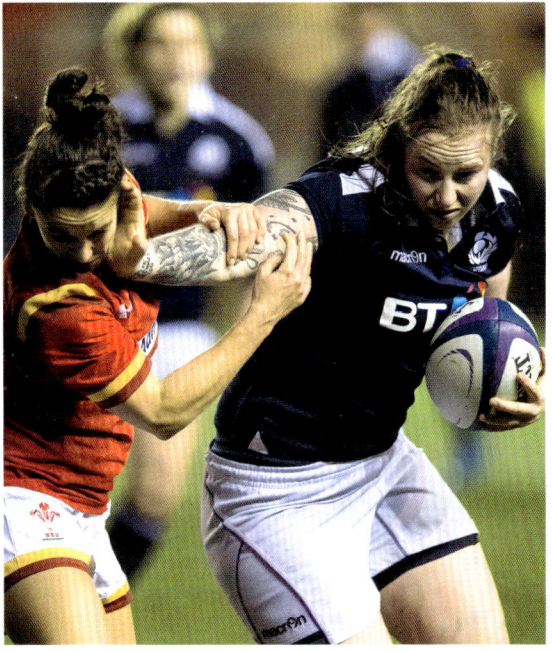

LEADING THE CHARGE: Jade Konkel was the first female to be given a professional contract by the Scottish Rugby Union.

GRAND FINALE: Glasgow Warriors clinched the 2015 Pro12 title with a titanic win over Munster in Belfast.

RUGBY UNITED: New Zealand captain Kieran Read welcomes MND campaigner and Scots rugby great Doddie Weir to the Murrayfield pitch in 2017, as Scotland captain John Barclay looks on.

DOUBLE DELIGHT: Ryan Wilson and Ali Price celebrate Warriors' epic victory over Leicester Tigers in 2017 to secure a European Cup quarter-final place.

NOT SUCH A GRAY DAY: Indeed, seldom has any Scotland side produced such a masterful performance as the day in 2017 when they trounced Australia, Jonny Gray among the scorers.

WHAT A TRY!: Sean Maitland's score against England in the Calcutta Cup win of 2018 was a contender for World Rugby's "Try of the Year".

STILL OURS: Scotland captain Stuart McInally with the Calcutta Cup after the 2019 draw at Twickenham, the first time the Scots had retained the trophy in 35 years.

HAPPY TRIO: Dominic McKay, John Jeffrey and Doddie Weir enjoy Scotland beating France in 2020, before the world went in to lockdown.

57

THE FUTURE'S BRIGHT, THE FUTURE'S ORANGE

1998

So proclaimed a TV advert around that time for a mobile phone provider. Perhaps the message was taken a little too literally by those manufacturing Scotland's rugby kit, because in October that year, the popular pinstriped white number disappeared, to be replaced by the rather garish orange jersey.

But this was no tangerine dream. It was too much for traditionalists, not liked by the players and unloved by fans. Unfortunately, the usual skelping by New Zealand in the World Cup while kitted out in the "council worker hi-viz" (as one Border wag described it) did little to endear it to the masses and potential purchasers.

That said, at its knockdown, sports-clearance-sale price, it became popular with autograph hunters, and, even 20 years on, the odd one can still be spotted, occasionally, on construction sites and building projects across the land.

58

NOW FOR WALES TO DO US A FAVOUR

10 April 1999 • Five Nations, Paris
France 22–Scotland 36

Frank Sinatra used to sing "I Love Paris". Safe to assume then that the famous crooner wasn't a Scotland rugby fan. Indeed, there was little love lost between the Scots and the French capital, thanks entirely to our woeful record when playing anywhere near the Eiffel Tower.

In 1999, the Scots were still revelling in a famous victory from four years hence, but that accounted for our only win in Paris in the previous 30 years, and if truth be told, not many (especially the bookies) believed Scotland could beat even an ordinary French team which had beaten Ireland away by a single point, lost to Wales at home by the same margin, and, more recently, had been kicked into submission by Jonny Wilkinson at Twickenham.

Still, our own performance in West London, losing by three points, in simple terms swung on Wilkinson, on his Championship debut, kicking better than Kenny Logan when it mattered. However, coupled with 30-point tallies against Wales and Ireland, it meant there was some cause for optimism ahead of

PART III – 1990s

the Paris match, and not all of it found at the bottom of a glass of *Châteauneuf du Pape*.

To help the Scots, that graveyard of many a fine thistled XV, Parc des Princes, had become surplus to requirements, the recently new Stade de France now providing the stage, a venue which had already seen some history made by a Scot – but only if you consider Scotland defender Tom Boyd living the dream of many a small boy some ten months previously by scoring the winner for Brazil at the World Cup as an accomplishment.

Therefore, in policing terms, there was no "previous" for the Scots to contend with at Stade de France. After 90 seconds, however, Émile Ntamack had gone over for a touchdown as France came flying out of the blocks.

But on the sun-soaked playing surface that April afternoon, the Scots thrived, turning in a display of running rugby which looked like an amalgam of the very best Sevens and Barbarians rugby had to offer. Martin Leslie rounded off a great counter-attack (Kenny Logan leading the initial break) to score, and within three minutes, Glenn Metcalfe's searing run took him from his own 22 to within a few metres of the French try line, Alan Tait finishing the move.

Orchestrator-in-chief Gregor Townsend scored, only for French no. 8 Christophe Juillet to gather from a short-range scrum, ploughing through Martin Leslie and Gary Armstrong to score.

Almost immediately, Scotland once again scored – their fourth try of the day. Attacking from just inside their own territory, John Leslie's beautifully timed inside feed to Metcalfe allowed the full-back to once more carve his way through French lines, Tait running on his right shoulder, took his pass and crossed for the try. But for a slip, Townsend – once more off John Leslie's direct attack from a set scrum – might have bagged a pair of tries, but Martin Leslie in support picked up to add his own second and Scotland's fifth. Logan banged over his fourth of five conversion attempts and Scotland were 33–12 to the good.

Their lead had been cut to 33–22 at half-time, but in contrast, the second 40 minutes yielded just one Logan penalty. Even now, a 36–22 win still looks great on the CV, and has become even more magical following the ensuing two decades of anguish that perhaps only Paris can produce.

It was a result which, although many wrote it, kept Scotland in with an outside hope of the Five Nations title, dependant on how England faired "away" to Wales at Wembley. Remind me, how did that one turn out?

Captain Gary Armstrong on arguably the most scintillating half of Five Nations rugby the Scots had ever produced:

"It was a beautiful day; sunny, warm, dry, not a breath. The kind of weather you could just thrive in. The only downside was the French had exactly the same conditions, and that usually meant one thing – that they would run like a pack of hounds and tear into you. They didn't disappoint.

"It was almost as if the French believed that psychology, that because the conditions suited them, they had to run everything – and that played straight into our hands. We had the players – Toony, Leslie, Taity – to be more French than the French were that day, and Snowy [Glenn Metcalfe] had a brilliant game, coming into the line with real pace and always a pass at the end of it.

"But Gregor was in his element and just played his natural game; off-the-cuff stuff, the kind of rugby you usually get to run once in a game, but somehow he did it for an entire 40 minutes that day. In fairness, we'd been pretty attack-minded all through the campaign. It was a great game to play in, must have been better to watch, although a wee bit tiring chasing folk all over the pitch. The speed was ferocious.

PART III – 1990s

"It was like an old-fashioned exhibition game, ball in hand and just run. If you did kick, the ball just came flying back at you. France scored three tries in the first half, but we scored five.

"Folk said we never kept it up. But our tongues were hangin' oot at half-time, and to be honest, we just had to calm it down a wee bit.

"France thought there was a chance they could get back into it if they hit us hard up front after the break, but our pack – who maybe never got the credit they deserved that day – proved to be just as gritty as they were mobile.

"I don't think any Scottish side came close to matching how we played that day, or how we were able to amass points, until the England–Scotland game in 2019. But Scotland had nothing to lose at Twickenham when they began throwing it about. We did it from the start in Paris.

"It was an unbelievable way to finish the Five Nations, and it would have been an unbelievable performance had we lifted the Championship that day. Instead we had to rely on others doing us a turn, namely the Welsh – something that, in the right company – has cost me in beer every year since."

59

GREGOR TOWNSEND – INDIVIDUAL GRAND SLAMMER

1999

Enigmatic, mercurial, genius. Gregor Townsend could have had any of those labels attached to him when a player, occasionally even during the same match. The former Scotland and Lions stand-off – and occasional centre – who saw club action with Gala, Northampton Saints, Brive, Castres, Montpellier and Border Reivers – had numerous highlights during his international career. However, 1999 would always take some beating in terms of what he and his country achieved in unison.

Until the 1999 Five Nations, only one Scot, "Johnnie" Wallace (and some may say he did it because he was, in reality, an Australian) had achieved a personal "Slam" (of tries) during Scotland's 1925 Grand Slam campaign, the speedy three-quarter matching the achievements of England's Carston Catcheside the previous season.

Subsequently, only two more players, Frenchmen Patrick Estève and Phillippe Sella, in 1983 and 1986 respectively, had scored against the other four nations during the series.

It was perhaps fitting then that before the Five Nations put on weight by adding the Italians, someone would sign off with

PART III - 1990s

a personal achievement of note. And that would be Scotland stand-off Gregor Townsend. Ironically, "Toony" only got his chance at no. 10 because of an injury to Duncan Hodge, who was carried off early in the second half against Wales, the Scots trailing 13–8. Townsend stepped inside from centre, Alan Tait the replacement in the middle.

Within a minute, Townsend had made his mark with a piece of opportunism. Rob Howley, the Wales no. 9, took a quick tap penalty after the Scots had been adjudged to have gone over on the wrong side at the breakdown. Howley broke, connected with Neil Jenkins, but the Welsh fly-half threw a horrible pass at Scott Quinnell, who fumbled. The ball, however, bounced perfectly for Townsend on his own 10-metre line, and he accelerated away from the advanced Welsh back division to score under the posts to help Scotland win 33–20.

Second up came England, with the Scots putting in arguably their best shift in ages to lose out by just three points (24–21). Kenny Logan kicked three from six, and thereby hangs the tale. Townsend's late score – pouncing on Mike Catt's fumble to make the steal – was the result of a typical "read" by the Scotland no. 10, but was too little, too late.

Ireland at Murrayfield brought another try and a victory. Though, actually, Townsend had managed a try during the "free" weekend in the Championship, when Scotland beat Italy in a friendly Test in Edinburgh.

Against the Irish, Townsend was the instigator of his own try. His pinpoint penalty to touch put the Scots just feet from the Irish line. On their own throw, Martin Leslie took well, but the Irish defence was sound. After Gary Armstrong's snipe had been thwarted, John Leslie ran the ball back towards the narrow side, passing to Townsend, who won his one v one contest against Keith Wood to record his ninth international try.

The Scotland team travelled to Paris, mildly confident that they had the game to beat France, though that feeling perhaps wasn't shared amongst their supporters.

Scotland conceded a try in the first two minutes, but responded with some champagne rugby, with Townsend pulling the strings at stand-off.

Less than 15 minutes had been played – with the men in dark blue already two scores to the good – when Scott Murray took a superb catch off the top of the line-out just outside the French 22. John Leslie made the initial burst, the ball coming back up the narrow side where, faced with a flat French defensive line (in the days before defensive lines were fashionable), Toony threw an outrageous dummy before scuttling over the line to score to make it four out of four against the other Five Nations protagonists – his own personal "Slam".

There may not have been a glittering prize for Gregor. However, his efforts were rewarded the next day as Scotland – thanks to some Welsh intervention – secured a trophy and a title they still hold.

Townsend explains the simplicity of his achievement:

"It was just one of those tournaments when, as a team, we got better and better, and could make and take chances.

"I did get lucky a few times; getting the break of the ball, or a pickup, or an interception. But when you're going looking for the ball, and I always felt I could read certain plays and moves that were coming at us, then the chances would come.

"That year Cammie Murray scored a few, Kenny [Logan] got one against the Italians, John Leslie, Alan Tait – I think he ended up with five that Five Nations. We were playing the type of rugby where the backs were going to get chances to score, right along the line, and through luck, and going for the interception a few times, it paid off for me."

60

WALES DO SCOTS A TURN

11 April 1999 • Five Nations, Wembley
Wales 32–England 31

What the hell, you may ask, is a Welsh win doing as one of Scottish rugby's all-time favourite moments? Some would happily hail any victory against England, by anyone, as being a memory to cherish. However, this one was definitely something to celebrate.

Even after that Paris win the previous day, even the most ardent Scotland fan would have been hard-pressed to make England anything but favourites entering what they believed would be their Grand Slam clincher.

Wins over Scotland, in their opening tie at Twickenham, Ireland and France had set up Lawrence Dallaglio's team to take the title against a Wales side that had somehow managed just one win, in Paris of all places, and even that was by a single digit in a match which saw 67 points scored. And to take the final Five Nations Championship, England wouldn't even have to leave London; due to the building of the Millennium Stadium in Cardiff, Wembley became a satellite state of the principality that term.

Apart from the sea of red-and-white scarves and flags adorned by dragons, the pre-match entertainment came courtesy of Tom Jones and Max Boyce. You would have paid good money to see those headline acts, but what followed is now part of Welsh and Scots rugby folklore.

England led 31–25, but Tim Rodber was penalised for a high tackle on Colin Charvis. With the game well into stoppage time, Neil Jenkins pumped a huge kick to touch on the England 22. From a shortened, three-man line-out, Chris Wyatt tipped the ball to scrum-half Rob Howley who set Scott Quinnell in motion. He juggled the pass; however, his cross-field drift dragged England's cover defence to the right. They had numbers, but they were ineffective as Scott Gibbs, on a counter-angle, burst into the line on the crash ball, running through Rodber and Neil Back's attempted tackles, evading the diving Matt Dawson, swerving past full-back Matt Perry, before his outrageous skip outside Steve Hanley took him home for a try the Lions centre was celebrating long before he grounded the ball.

"He's like the leader in a buffalo stampede, that lad Scott Gibbs," proclaimed Bill McLaren. However, it was now 31–30 . . . to England.

"But the goal has still got to be kicked," McLaren reminded the TV-watching world with a measured calmness, matched only by stand-off Neil Jenkins, who, slightly to the right of the posts, landed the extra points with the last kick to seal a dramatic Wales win. Or not quite.

"It's not over yet," cautioned McLaren. Indeed, injury time appeared never-ending as, from a scrum, England engineered the space for Mike Catt to have a drop at goal, but he skied it. Shane Howarth, the Welsh full-back (although he wouldn't be considered Welsh for much longer), called for the mark, kicked for touch and the game was over.

PART III - 1990s

The vast majority of the 76,000 at Wembley celebrated, as did all of Wales. Four hundred miles to the north, another spontaneous party got under way.

Scott Quinnell reflects:

"Afterwards, there were those saying that Gibbsy and me should drop one of the Ts from our name.

"But to be honest, the last thing on any of our minds was that the win would give Scotland the Championship. No, it was about giving Wales a win and the fans a performance I think they deserved at the end of a hard season.

"That try – Howley to Quinnell to Gibbs. It could have been a move straight out of the Lions playbook, given how many of the 1997 tourists there were in the England side.

"The reality was it was actually more from our Rugby League background; Gibbsy and me had both played 'up north', where you ran different lines and angles all the time, either to make ground or bring others into play.

"We knew how it might work, but we'd only ever talked about it, never even practised it. Maybe that late in the game, when you're desperate, you try desperate things. It worked a treat! Looking back at it, we only had a few yards to work in, but I think that's what made it impossible to defend. I literally threw my pass just a few feet to Scott, but because he hit the line flat out, the English defence were all wrong-footed. They might have got a hand on him, but they weren't going to stop him.

"I think somewhere that try was voted the greatest ever scored by Wales. I couldn't be sure, but it certainly is the most talked about. No matter where I go, someone will always remind me about it, be it an Englishman who'll say his side was denied a Grand Slam, or a Welshman, delighted at our win and a fantastic day at Wembley, or a Scotsman, who sat back and watched others do the hard work for them."

61

WHEN SCOTS WON A CHAMPIONSHIP BUT LET A BIGGER PRIZE SLIP AWAY

1999

Scotland's 1999 Five Nations triumph celebrated its 20th anniversary recently. It might not be held in the same esteem as previous Grand Slam successes, however, it remains the last tangible prize gathered by Scotland's rugby team.

Scotland's only failing that season came at Twickenham, a venue where, at the time, we hadn't won for 16 years. However, for Kenny Logan, an integral part of the Championship win, a bigger prize – which was well within Scotland's grasp – eluded them that season.

The wins against Wales, Ireland and France delivered Scotland a title, however, with hindsight, Logan reckons the Scots lost more than just a match that day against England.

Why Kenny Logan is still kicking himself . . .

"Let's go back a few years before that. In 1995 and again the following year we played England twice in Grand Slam matches and lost them both. No one remembers the losers, but we knew that we had been quite close to winning something and, with a bit of luck, we might win a Triple Crown or a Championship again.

PART III – 1990s

"Sometimes when you're that involved, you forget how hard it is to win a tournament. On that, it's 20 years now since we won the last Five Nations. That shows how difficult it is to win something substantial in the Northern Hemisphere – and how good we were in the 1990s.

"Thinking back, the last Five Nations wasn't any different really from every other one I'd played in, except we had recruited a few players along the way, and that, for once, the Championship wasn't the biggest tournament in the country that year because the World Cup was going to be played.

"By the end of the Five Nations tournament, that team would be up amongst the very best Scotland has ever produced, not just because we won it, but because of the style we played with. To be part of that was wonderful. We scored 16 tries that season; France and Wales were next on nine. We were, at times, unstoppable.

"One or two wee things happened that could have worked against us but worked for us. We started against Wales with Duncan Hodge at stand-off, but he broke his leg during that match. The switch that came moved Gregor [Townsend] in from centre, and Alan Tait filled in for Toony. All of a sudden, the dynamic of the backline had changed and Gregor produced his best-ever period at no. 10 for Scotland and scored a try in every game. I don't think that would have happened if he'd been in the centre all year. That switch had a huge impact on what we did that season.

"Taity as well was just on fire and was just part of an incredible paring with John Leslie in the centre, while the back three was me, Cammie Murray and Glenn Metcalfe at full-back, so options there. And all of that came about because Duncan was injured. But there would be another side to that story.

"I had played from 1992, and there were times where you

celebrated touching the ball, never mind scoring a try with it. For the first two years all I did was chase it. In those days, you chased it, not to get the ball but to take the man; the theory was you would get better field position that way.

"Today, you put the kicks up high to get up on it and catch it and carry play forward that way. In the 1990s, if you jumped, the opposition could take you out in the air. Basic rugby got quite repetitive in that any time you saw the ball, there was an opposition full-back holding it. The only reason I took up place-kicking was to see the ball more. But in the 1999 season, it was like Christmas.

"However, that season wasn't as good as it might have been.

"My biggest regret was that we lost to England by three points and I missed three kicks. I still blame myself for that. We could have won that day, and maybe even have had a Grand Slam. I know things don't always work out that way, but that England game has never left me.

"The kicks I missed were the ones I'd normally get, the big long ones. People forget: before that game I hadn't kicked for two weeks with a cruciate strain. I had been strapped up, so I hadn't played for Wasps, but I needed to play for Scotland because no one else could or would kick, and Hodgy was crocked.

"My big thing was that I'd started goal-kicking that season and was basically learning on the hoof, teaching myself, so it's not a surprise if your technique isn't what it should be. When I made a mistake, I didn't have a clue what I'd done differently. A routine? Did I need one? Did I have one? Goal-kickers didn't get support then; you were on your own, or most of us were. Today they have coaches, analysts, you name it.

"Chris Paterson was the prime example of someone who could block everything out and go through the same routine

PART III – 1990s

with the same result virtually every time. Where I struggled was the concentration, shutting everything out. That wasn't me as a person and I did get distracted. I could do it now, easy. But then I could get sidetracked, and it was costly.

"Everyone was saying Jonny Wilkinson has a kicking coach and he's the best in the world. Hello? That was why he was the best in the world. I did get some private sessions with Jonny's coach, Dave Alred, and he made a massive difference, but you needed him weekly, not monthly. In the end Gareth Rees, the Canadian international, who had been the Wasps stand-off but who lost his place because I had started kicking, was the one who helped me. Credit to him – he could have got his place back by leaving me to it. But I did get better, though only after that England game.

"I tried to get him up to Scotland, but the SRU wouldn't buy it. I'd go back to Wasps and kick brilliantly – why? Because I had Gareth there daily. I was out of my routine, and kicking is all about routine. But that was the way it was then. Nowadays, you'd just say I'm not kicking. Some might still be relieved at that.

"I had three bad days kicking. A game against Italy, a 28-all draw against Wales and the England one. That's not looked upon as being bad because I missed the long kicks. But those were the ones I was favourite to get.

"Jonny said to me, 'You're learning to kick with 70,000 watching; most have a man and a dog.' He was right, and I haven't changed my mind in the years in between.

"But maybe I'm just being too hard on myself, or maybe greedy. Fact is, our achievement is still something that should be celebrated.

"That season, for me, was the best time Jim [Telfer] had as a Scotland coach. He really grasped the professional element;

about rest, about the expansive game you now had to play, and that if you had attacking weapons, use them. It wasn't all about rucking. The new game was about running and Jim got it better than those who were still trying to tell him how to play!

"I've always believed teams play how their coaches are, and for that season, it was a different Jim. I was pleased for him when we won because he'd dissed all those who said his teams could only play the one way. Really? I think we proved every one of those experts, those doubters, wrong."

62

WHEN GALA PARTIED LIKE IT'S 1999

1999!

Every rugby club will have one season that will set it apart from all others, usually based on success on the pitch. It could come in the guise of a tournament win, or a famous victory, or just an injection of a "feel-good factor" that spreads beyond the club rooms and into the local village or town. And it is for those reasons that 1999 will long live in the memory of Gala's players and supporters – if they can remember it, that is.

Promotion to the top flight of the Scottish league system was followed in quick succession by a win at Murrayfield in the Tennent's Velvet Scottish Cup Final when a Chris Paterson try helped sink Kelso 8–3, while the Netherdale club made it a treble of trophies by taking the Melrose Sevens, beating guest sides Cambridge University and Stellenbosch in the quarter- and semi-finals respectively, before seeing off another South African visiting team, Villager, 28–5 in the final.

However, while those successes were memorable, so were the celebrations.

Gala's club captain in 1999 Richie Gray reminisces about the good time had by all in the home of the Braw Lads... or at least what he remembers: "I'll give you the 98/99 season in one: Scotland won the Five Nations, and Gala won everything else Scotland couldn't enter!

"The previous season we had won the Border League, so there was a bit of a team in the making. We were in the Second Division and I had come back after a couple of years away. We needed to beat Musselburgh away to get promoted. We got absolutely hammered on the Saturday night, and well into Sunday – might even have been Monday for a couple – celebrating promotion, sobered up by the Tuesday and got ourselves ready to play Kelso the next weekend, where we had to beat them to win Premier 2, which we did. The previous weekend had only been a rehearsal for the party we had after beating Kelso; it was so typically parochial that beating another Border team somehow made it bigger and better.

"The week after that we had the Scottish Cup semi-final against Melrose at Netherdale, a cracking game of rugby. The telly cameras were there, Bill McLaren commentating, 5,000 packing the place out, and we won that and had a slightly more subdued celebration as we'd only reached the final; we hadn't won anything yet. You cannae get too carried away, although some did.

"The BBC had Jill Douglas presenting *Rugby Special*. 'What was she dain' here?"' one wag demanded to know – not based on Jill's ability but that she was from Hawick and seeing Hoggy [Carl Hogg], who played for Melrose. Typically parochial, or was it paranoid?

"That midweek, we'd arranged to play Langholm, on a Thursday night, ten days before the Cup Final, because we'd decided we had to keep ourselves sharp – and it snowed. It was so heavy, we had to have the lines cleared to play the game. In our minds, this was us preparing properly – we needed to stay

PART III - 1990s

battle-hardened, so there was no chance we were going to call it off.

"We played our first team in the first half, then played the other guys in the second half – like that 40 minutes was going to make a difference to any of us – and then it was up to Murrayfield for the final itself.

"There was 20,000-plus at Murrayfield that day. They weren't all there to see us; that finals day, they were all just about Borders teams – Duns were there to play for the Bowl, Jed-Forest in the Plate final, and ourselves and Kelso contesting the Cup – so it was a busy place, and the occasion all the more memorable for beating Kelso to win the Cup – a league and cup double.

"Promotion won, title clinched, semi-final win, Cup Final victory. Four weekends out of five we were getting melted, and then a double-header.

"Our performances had earned us the team of the year award, which we all trekked up to Murrayfield to collect on the Friday night before the Melrose Sevens. Needless to say, you cannae win and not celebrate, so we did and got hammered, and then headed back doon the road and got back to Gala at about two in the morning.

"I wasn't in the Sevens team – but I was on Radio Borders commentating. The guys who were playing had just about sobered up enough to play their first tie – and we started in the first round – beating Stewart's Melville, then getting past West [of Scotland], less comfortably than the first tie. I think it was fair to say fatigue had set in, or the drink had seeped out our system.

"But we got through to play Villager in the final – our fifth game, while they had only played four – but by now, the thought of winning the Ladies Cup and rubbing salt in the Melrose wound, and adding another trophy, had got everyone jumping, especially one of the experts on Radio Borders.

"The whole team – Michael Dods, Chris Paterson, Nathan Hines, Kevin Amos, Gary Parker, David Gray, Craig Townsend, Gareth Brown and Tam Weir – were brilliant, but Mossy [Chris Paterson] was just phenomenal. He'd been on telly in the Cup semi-final and been man of the match in the final, but I think that the Melrose Sevens was really the first time a TV audience got a look at him properly in terms of what a brilliant runner he was; super fit, super quick, he could just glide past people, which is why he picked up man of the tournament. I'm telling you, there was nothing we didn't win.

"We had a team of characters who had given their all to make it a special couple of years for Gala and maybe that's why so many folk just enjoyed the moment in terms of the celebrations.

"In the club rooms one night, which would hold a couple of hundred, there must have been a thousand folk. That's when I was crowd-surfed to the bar. The local curry house sent down big pots of chicken curry. There were still kids running about on the pitch playing touch at three in the morning. It was mad.

"It was a never-ending party. We played, got pissed, played, got pissed, for about a month. It went into the Sevens season, then through to the Common Riding season. We were just constantly pissed. That team was loved in the town, where all the boys were known.

"We had an open-top bus on the Sunday morning after winning the Cup, and I said to Dodsy, 'There'll be no one here; this will be embarrassing.' We came along Channel Street and around the corner and there was literally a sea of maroon and white – thousands had come out.

"The shirts we wore, with the hooped band around it – the socks were hooped as well to make us look big – carried sponsorship from a local business, Cheque Cashing, and they became iconic – everyone wanted one. Less so the orange away tops.

PART III - 1990s

The shorts were sponsored by the Kingsknowes Hotel, and you had to wash your own. We're talking some boys getting their wives and mothers to do them, others who couldn't work a washing machine doing their own. So the shorts were maroon, or burgundy, or was it claret, or purple or slightly pink?

"One thing that kept its colour were the white T-shirts with 'Maroon Army' across the front. We sold hundreds, spotted daily in Gala and during the summer walking about Ibiza or Majorca or Benidorm. Naebody inside them, just walking themselves..."

PART IV
2000s

63

ENGLAND DENIED THE GRAND SLAM

2 April 2000 • Six Nations, Murrayfield
Scotland 19–England 13

The excuse note, read out loud on more than one occasion during the 2000 Six Nations Championship, was that Scotland weren't really the title holders as this was a new tournament thanks to the introduction of Italy into the series. Putting that extreme pedantry to one side, the truth was that the inaugural Six Nations had been instantly forgettable for the previous year's champions.

From the first match in Rome, when all resistance was kicked out of Ian McGeechan's team by the boot of Azzurri fly-half Diego Domínguez (whose haul at the Stadio Flaminio included a conversion, six penalties and three drop goals), a great many Scots longed to get the old Five Nations back, rather than this newfangled Six Nations upgrade. Defeats against Italy (34–20), Ireland (44–22), France (28–16) and Wales (26–18) had reduced Scotland to wooden spoon favourites.

The reality, therefore, of the final Sunday of the newly extended competition was that it would be nothing more than a face-saving exercise for Scotland. Then again, reality has never been high on the agenda when it comes to facing England, whatever the circumstances.

There was little, some even went as far to say nothing, that suggested England would falter in their pursuit of the Grand Slam. Little, perhaps, other than they'd failed when faced with exactly the same scenario the previous year, losing on the final day to Wales. Could lightning strike twice?

Additional electrical input would not have made conditions any more demanding; it was chilly, windy and wet – extremely wet. It was never going to be a day for running rugby as there was a constant threat of aquaplaning on the treacherous Murrayfield surface. Instead, the game deteriorated into a forward-orientated struggle, which, to be fair, suited the Scots as they restricted England's possession and left their back division as spectators.

England led at the turnaround, 10–9, thanks largely to a Lawrence Dallaglio try. Scotland kept pace thanks to Duncan Hodge's accuracy from the tee, however, England simply should have carried more of a lead into the second period.

The longer the game went in what were by now dire conditions underfoot, the more it felt a try from either side would win the contest. Scotland's masterplan may have been to quell the English pack, but they also coped with, and made best use of, the dampness, emphasised as the clock ran down to single digits.

With eight minutes remaining, and 12–10 to the good, Gregor Townsend's vision saw him send a kick across field, behind England's defence and wide of full-back Matt Perry, who, rather than trying to pick up the slithering ball, chose to side-foot the ball through the puddles and into touch. It was a huge territorial gain the Scots were desperate to capitalise on.

Playing the percentages, Scotland hit their front jumper, the 7'1" Richard Metcalfe, making his debut, who tipped the ball away from the clawing grasp of Simon Shaw. Scotland drove,

PART IV - 2000s

then Nicol sent a deft kick over the rucking forwards, no doubt in a bid to tempt a fumble. The ploy worked.

Austin Healey was beaten by the bounce, or lack of it, and, just metres from his own line, attempted to run laterally, only to be hit by a superb Hodge tackle, meaning the English again only had one out, a touch kick. Scotland had made but a few feet off that initial line-out, but crucially had run 90 seconds off the clock. From the immediate throw, Jason White, near the tail, set up the next attacking platform for a Scottish pack who motored on, albeit running on reserve tanks.

Nicol had a snipe, was thwarted, then Murray had a breenge, only for the ball to slip from his clutches, thankfully sideways, where replacement Gordon McIlwham recovered, laid it back, and Hodge picked up to dive in at the deep end. The degree of difficulty wasn't registered, but by converting his own try – the rain running off the end of his nose as he lined up the kick – Hodge had bagged all of Scotland's points to lead 19–10. Crucially, Scotland were a score and a bit ahead with four minutes to go.

Healey, with the ability to create chances out of nothing, went on a jinking, weaving run in midfield, on to the 22. Mike Tindall, Mike Catt and Wilkinson all probed, but five metres out, Dawson knocked on. However, under immense pressure, the Scotland scrum collapsed and Wilkinson brought it back to 19–13 with a few minutes to go.

England's dream of a 12th Grand Slam all but evaporated though as Murray was launched into the Edinburgh night sky to make a steal of Burke and Hare proportions on an England throw, tipping the ball into the hands of Nicol, who sent a kick skimming over the ground and into the English half, where Dawson and co., try desperately as they might, just couldn't get deep enough into Scottish territory to be a threat.

Scotland celebrated the final whistle, skipper Nicol, bloodied and battered, climbing into the stand to receive the Calcutta Cup. In a far more low-key presentation, England became the first recipients of the Six Nations trophy. That was just rubbing salt in an open wound.

Man of the match Duncan Hodge looks back, through the rain:

"I will say my memory on matches isn't great. Others have total recall, but I'm not one of them. But it would be difficult not to remember big parts of that afternoon, just because of the significance and the end result.

"It wasn't a great tournament for us. As champions from 1999 – a season when I'd missed most of the games after breaking my leg against Wales on the opening weekend – we lost our first game in Rome, the Italians inspired by the occasion, then we had lost the next two, but played quite well against Wales ahead of the last lot of games.

"England, on track for a Grand Slam, had been scoring points for fun, putting up 40s and 50s in matches. They arrived favourites by 20 or 25 points to beat us. But that didn't make a huge difference to us.

"My immediate recollection of the game was how horrendously bad the conditions were. The first half was okay, nothing we weren't used to. We knew it would be wet but that it would deteriorate during the afternoon. The forecast we'd been given all week was totally accurate. The second half was wet and freezing cold.

"England were on top in the first half and potentially could have been more ahead. They'd been 10–3 up, I got it back to 10–6 and with a couple of minutes to go in the first half, they had a five-metre scrum and were parked on our line through several phases, but we held out and got the ball back down the field and eventually, deep in stoppage time, I put over another penalty. We were within a point when they should have been out of sight.

PART IV - 2000s

"We had a real sense of belief after that because we hadn't played particularly well, and they had but had nothing to show for it. Then we came out, and the weather had turned, then we get the crowd behind us, and England begin making mistakes. It just bubbled from there.

"My try came by chance. We had a couple of lunges for the line and had fallen short, and my intention was to clear out a ruck Gordie McIlwham had set up, but the ball floated back and all I had to do was grab it and dive over. But because it was so wet, I basically grounded the ball in a puddle, and it squirmed away from me.

"There was no doubt I got the ball down and scored, but the first thing I did, and you can see me, is look for the referee to make sure he'd given it. I have a great photo of the try and my immediate reaction, where me, Budge [Pountney], Jim McLaren and Richard Metcalfe are giving the referee a good stare just to make sure he'd seen it.

"My son is now of an age where he's started to take a bit of interest in what his dad did once upon a time, and him and his pals were watching it one day. I didn't watch the entire game, but what was noticeable was how the adrenalin must have been pumping when I took the conversion, because I took no time over it. I planked it down and kicked it.

"England had been pretty lippy when Dallaglio scored; they had a lot of leaders, club captains, big cheeses in their team, and they'd been winning all their games. There was a good bit of chat flowing early on. Now you looked up and they had their heads in their hands and there was nothing coming back at you.

"We were really happy at winning, but because it was played on a Sunday, there was no after-match following the game, and nowhere seemed to be open in Edinburgh that night. From memory, celebrations were kinda low-key."

64

A HIGH-WATER MARK FOR THE GAME IN SCOTLAND – LITERALLY

29 April 2000 • Rugby League Challenge Cup Final, Murrayfield, Bradford Bulls 24–Leeds Rhinos 18

Since the inception of the Super League in the mid-1990s, Scotland had been a port of call for various Rugby League matches. Tynecastle had been a venue, but with the ongoing debate of when construction of the new Wembley might begin – or even when the old one might come down – the League authorities looked elsewhere for a suitable venue to stage their showpiece, the Challenge Cup Final.

Murrayfield was chosen as the venue for the 2000 final, and by the time all the various ties and rounds had been played off, two sides remained: holders Leeds and the Bradford Bulls, who were no strangers to the Scottish capital, having previously visited as part of the "On the Road" tour.

However, just days before the final, Edinburgh found itself battered by torrential rain over a 24-hour period, leaving Murrayfield and many parts of the surrounding area underwater. A massive clean-up operation got under way to shift the mud and silt that had been channelled into homes and businesses in the area, as well as the national rugby stadium.

PART IV – 2000s

It was a race against time. Would they manage to get Murrayfield playable, and the stadium itself habitable, for Saturday?

By Friday afternoon, the answer was yes, even if there were still tell-tale signs of the huge deluge – like a high-tide mark in the tunnel and dressing-room areas.

Nevertheless, the match went ahead and it was Bradford and their fans who celebrated, beating Leeds 24–18. Two years later, Wigan beat St Helens as Murrayfield again hosted the final, albeit in slightly drier circumstances.

65

SCOTS WRECK IRISH TITLE AMBITIONS

*22 September 2001 • Six Nations, Murrayfield
Scotland 32–Ireland 10*

Under normal circumstances, a win of this proportion would be recalled for years to come. Except this is the Six Nations win few can remember, perhaps because they are looking for it in the wrong place.

Due to an outbreak of the highly infectious foot-and-mouth disease in mainland Britain, Ireland's travel plans were curtailed, meaning that, having won against Italy and France in their opening ties, they could not complete their match schedule until the September and October of the following season.

The Scots had, during the normal course of events, played out a high-scoring draw with Wales and beaten Italy, securing mid-table safety. They, therefore, had nothing but pride to play for when they faced the Irish at Murrayfield. In contrast, Ireland had everything to lose – and ultimately did.

Both Celtic nations missed relatively easy penalty attempts early in proceedings, meaning it was not until the 23rd minute the deadlock was broken.

Centre John Leslie made the telling insertion, carrying from

PART IV – 2000s

his own 10-metre line deep into the Irish half and passing to Chris Paterson outside him. The Scotland winger cut inside, weaving across the pitch to make space and time, then released skipper Budge Pountney to run the score home. Four minutes from the interval, the Scots added a second try, and then several attacking waves resulted in Tom Smith charging over for the score and a 17–0 half-time lead. Even at that juncture, Irish title and Grand Slam ambitions appeared holed.

Ronan O'Gara put a minor dent in the Scots lead, to which they replied with interest. Off a driven line-out on the Irish 22, Bryan Redpath looked to loop around Gregor Townsend, only for the Scotland fly-half to dummy and go it alone, pulling in the last remnants of the Irish defence before sending Leslie in.

With three minutes of normal time remaining and chasing respectability, Denis Hickie set off but lost possession. Townsend chipped over the Irish backs, with Scotland full-back Glenn Metcalfe showing some deft soccer skills to keep the ball alive, leaving replacement Andy Henderson to gather and stroll in for an international debut try. Scotland were 32–3 up.

Girvan Dempsey bagged a consolation try for Ireland, and although they hammered Wales 36–6 in Cardiff and concluded with a win over England in Dublin, their Grand Slam dreams had already been crushed under the Edinburgh sun.

Scotland captain Budge Pountney on a game the Irish wouldn't forget in a hurry – even if many others did: "We'd never, ever experienced anything like it, and hopefully no one will ever again. Because of foot-and-mouth, it was a different type of season, that's for sure. It was just such a bizarre set of circumstances. But playing your last Six Nations game in September, as a warm-up to the autumn Tests, that was interesting.

"No one hardly ever talks about this game; in fact, sometimes you're hard-pressed to remember the season because you always, invariably, start in February, March and wonder where the Ireland game went.

"To score four tries in a game, be 30 points up on Ireland, wreck all their plans and ambitions, and still have no one talking about it, that shows how peculiar it all was.

"If you watch that game, the first thing you'll notice is how bloody quick it was. It verged on chaotic at times, but it was a really good performance against a top Irish team – O'Gara, O'Driscoll, Horgan, Clohessy, Wood, Davidson, O'Kelly – which, to make the point again, makes it all the more ludicrous that this isn't mentioned as one of Scotland's standout performances around that time.

"There are worse Scotland performances that have been mentioned and written about more!

"It was strange, picking up from the game against the Italians when you couldn't actually remember the Italian match. That break probably helped us more than it did them and proves the point that games in hand are not always an advantage.

"We didn't have to worry about what we'd done or had to do. This was a one-off game, and, basically, the coaches said just go and play with a bit of freedom, at home, and enjoy it. It gave us a blank card to play off; no history before, none afterwards.

"There was much more riding on this one for the Irish, and we caught them cold. We wanted to inject pace into the match because we believed that would win us the game.

"We still had Gregor [Townsend] at stand-off and John Leslie outside him, so there were real attacking options amongst the backs. With Jason White in at lock, we had four back-row players in the pack, which made us really mobile and very quick to the breakdown.

"The year before we had taken a real walloping off the Irish

PART IV – 2000s

in Dublin. If we were going to beat Ireland, we had to play a game that was quick, and that was wide, and we had to get the ball off the floor as quickly as possible. Ireland had a 40 or 50kg advantage on us. That was huge but wasn't such a big factor if you kept it moving.

"I got the first try, because of the good support player I was, although it was made easy to keep up with play because Mossy [Chris Paterson] wasn't exactly running in a straight line. My thinking was if I keep running, he might come back to me, which he did. But there were bits and pieces of all the tries that made them quite good, a bit like that season – extended season – in general.

"You can imagine how the Irish felt after that match. Actually, I'll tell you. All the arrangements had been made well in advance, certainly before the Scotland–Ireland game was rescheduled, but I was supposed to be attending my brother-in-law's wedding in Bangor that day and obviously missed it because I was playing.

"I know I screwed his day up because they were Ireland fans, all watching it on TV. I said I was sorry, but..."

66

BILL MCLAREN RETIRES – AND SCOTLAND "RETIRE" FROM WINNING IN CARDIFF

6 April 2002 • Six Nations, Cardiff
Wales 22–Scotland 27

All good things must come to an end, and on 6 April 2002, Bill McLaren gave his last commentary for the BBC. Unfortunately, it coincided with the Scotland rugby team deciding that, as a mark of respect, it should also be the last time they win in Wales. Of course, they will put it right eventually. But until then, we can only reflect (or test the memory to the max) on what was a good day in Cardiff for the Scots.

The "Voice of Rugby" may have tried to make it low-key, but from when he first offered Gareth Edwards a Hawick Ball in the Angel Hotel, pre-match, and through the rest of the day, the TV cameras were on the broadcasting legend, recording his every response, especially when the stadium joined in a chorus of "For He's a Jolly Good Fellow".

By close of play, Scotland's XV (and replacements) were also being hailed as good fellas, having done a number on the Welsh.

In this match, which began with a minute's silence in memory of the Queen Mother (yes, it's that long since we won in Cardiff), fly-half Gregor Townsend became Scotland's most capped

PART IV – 2000s

player, winning his 66th cap. But it was his opposite number, Stephen Jones, who kicked Wales into a somewhat ominous 9–0 lead.

That was until hooker Gordon Bulloch managed to plant the ball on the Welsh line for a try having been driven over by the Scottish pack. Before the half-hour, Scotland led, Bulloch scoring a virtually identical try off a clean Scott Murray line-out catch and drive, Brendan Laney hitting the conversion, then a penalty, to give Scotland a 15–9 half-time advantage.

A Rhys Williams try, converted by Jones, nudged Wales ahead 16–15. Laney and Jones swapped two penalties apiece, each successful kick seeing a change of lead. Wales were ahead 22–21 with a minute of normal time remaining as Townsend restarted. Scotland regained possession from a knock-on, and went for broke with some direct running at the Welsh defence.

With the game already into injury time, George Graham smashed on into the Welsh 22, then Tom Smith, setting up another ruck. Then a loud blast on the whistle as the ball popped out on the Welsh side. "You cannot play the ball in the ruck," said French referee Joël Jutge, pointing the finger of fate at centre Mark Taylor.

Home hearts and bodies sank at that call, but such had been the ferocity of those final 60 seconds that players of both sides lay strewn across the field. By the time they were tended to, we were over two minutes into stoppage time when Laney struck his fifth successive kick of the day, and Scotland were 24–22 to the good. However, there was even more injury time to be added.

In the fourth minute of added time, centre James McLaren hoofed upfield and somehow pinched possession. It gave Laney a drop-goal opening, but he missed, injuring himself in the process. As he writhed in pain, referee Jutge was telling everyone, "We play, we play." Wales were happy with that call and tried to run out from their own 22. However, when replacement flanker Gavin Thomas held on in the tackle, Scotland won a penalty.

With Laney crocked, the first and only act by substitute Duncan Hodge, as the clock ticked on to 85 minutes, was to make the clinching kick. While the conclusion may have been dramatic, if truth be told, this was a match of poor quality between two bottom-half-of-the-table teams.

"Scotland the winners, 27 points to 22." Those were Bill McLaren's last words from the commentary box for the BBC, heading for retirement with a Scotland victory and a pat on the back from co-commentator Jonathan Davies.

Stuart Grimes reflects:

"I started on the bench and came on just before the hour. Watching on, it wasn't what I'd describe as being a memorable game. Both teams were toiling that season, and there was a lot of pride being played for, which made the closing minutes really intense.

"But I can't really remember many matches where the commitment was like that so late on. I was packing behind George Graham, my Falcons teammate, and remember telling him to keep going, not to go down even if he was under pressure, and him replying that he was effing trying!

"Scott Murray was awarded the man of the match but for me it should have been Brendan Laney. He was a good guy and a good player, and he kicked well that day and had to. But I don't think he maybe got the recognition he deserved.

"To some, maybe to many, he was just another Kiwi parachuted into the Scotland set-up. The attitude to that from elements of the media and support was that he wasn't good enough to be an All Black, so Scotland would just take him.

PART IV – 2000s

"He was a big lad, which again gave some the impression – or the excuse – that he wasn't the physical specimen he should have been. But that wasn't the case; he was quick and strong and decent under pressure. The irony was, of course, that in what should have been his moment of glory, he injured himself trying to seal the win, leaving Duncan Hodge to come on for the clinching penalty.

"We all knew Bill McLaren was retiring, so he was awarded a commemorative Scotland shirt after the game by Ian McGeechan, a nice touch. It was a much easier presentation than it would have been had we lost.

"It was Rob Howley's last game for Wales that day, but at the dinner that evening, John Leslie told me he was going to concentrate on club rugby and wouldn't be playing for Scotland again. That was a shocker, to be honest – although nothing compared to the shock of still talking about that 2002 game as being our last win in Cardiff."

67

SCOTLAND CAST ASIDE
33 YEARS OF HURT AND HISTORY

16 November 2002 • Autumn Test, Murrayfield
Scotland 21–South Africa 6

When not even your oldest player was born the last time you beat an opponent, it's always a good reason to set the record straight. And when on their last visit you came off second best in a high-scoring World Cup tie, that's even more motivation to get it right this time.

Those were the scenarios facing Scotland when they faced the touring South Africans in their autumn Test in 2002. Not since 1969 had the Scots defeated the Springboks, while the memory of a 46–29 loss during the 1999 World Cup was still raw enough to hurt.

Scotland, fresh off a 37–10 win over Romania, appeared more at ease in the greasy environment, although neither side had gained an advantage by half-time, all square at 6–6.

In the second half, however, Scotland's kicking game – expertly directed and deployed by Anglo half-backs Bryan Redpath of Sale and Leeds fly-half Gordon Ross – paid dividends. With Brendan Laney giving Scotland a 9–6 lead with the boot, the green-and-gold line was eventually broken by Budge Pountney after concerted

PART IV - 2000s

drives from the Scotland pack, although the award only came after referee Nigel Williams awarded a try, then consulted the inconclusive video evidence, which he chose to ignore.

Winger Nikki Walker added a second try late on – although whether contact was made with the ball was questionable – following some horrendously careless play from the Boks behind their own goal line.

Time to rewrite the history Boks – we mean books.

Skipper Bryan Redpath on an emphatic 21–6 win and some midweek psychology: "I was captain and the week before we had played Romania, and although we'd won relatively well, 37–10, the mood in the camp was a bit subdued. I said to Geech and Jim [Ian McGeechan and Jim Telfer], let the boys go out for a few beers on the Wednesday, just to relax them, to let them chill a bit, and we'll come back into camp and get stuck into preparing for South Africa – and they agreed to it.

"They knew we weren't going to go mad, although there were a couple who took a bit of watching.

"We had studied South Africa in training, and virtually everything we'd prepared for was how they looked to be setting up; bullying us, being physical and taking us apart up front. Then the weather changed, as can happen in Edinburgh in the autumn ... and spring and summer.

"We knew their hooker Lukas van Biljon was a big ball carrier at the time, as were their second-row players, so we knew if we targeted them, stopped them, then we could upset what they had prepared for. We also wanted to get after Butch James at no. 10, who was a big player for them in how he could dictate play. We needed him on the back foot and scrabbling for space.

"Ultimately, that's how it worked. We had a kicking strategy to force them back – I kicked a lot more than normal – and just kept pressing. While we had amended our game plan because of the weather, they stuck to theirs, which meant they were trying to run in the rain. Never easy.

"We did have some good, accurate kickers right across the backs – Gordon Ross outside me, Brendan Laney outside him, Chris Paterson in the back three – so we could put the ball over them and get them turning from virtually anywhere, and when we went long, we had some quick, big lads in the backs, good chasers – Andy Craig, Nikki Walker and Stuart Moffat at full-back, who didn't win a lot of caps – to make sure we kept what territory we gained.

"The term 'good chaser' conjures up an impression of guys who just run after the ball but do it at speed, and create a real presence, and that does become a very good attack weapon.

"The Springboks had some quick players in their back three, but we also knew a couple of them weren't natural or, being honest, very good kickers, so might choose to run rather than clear their lines. We read that one spot on.

"It took a wee while to get the breakthrough, coming from Budge [Pountney] and then the second try came when they were trying to exit and I caught the kicker, who lost the ball over the line, and Nikki Walker pounced for the touchdown.

"The change in weather was significant. It always surprised me how many teams took playing in the rain and the wind and the cold so badly. They didn't fancy it, but we were celebrating and shouting for more of the same.

"The weather played a part, but that whole week was all about telling ourselves we had nothing to lose. Not many folk could remember the 1969 win (by 6–3), and, of course, so much had changed in South Africa in that time, which was one of the reasons why we hadn't recorded a victory since. We had won A and B games against them, one being in Melrose, but we had never won a Test.

PART IV – 2000s

"Before 2002 they had put some real scores on us since their comeback into international rugby, and after waiting 33 years, we could have had another win the following summer on tour before the World Cup, when we lost in Durban only by a late penalty, and again in Jo'burg by a handful of points, though in both games we led at half-time.

"We got close to them because we played it smart; we knew we couldn't take them on in an arm wrestle for 80 minutes – we had to use a bit of savvy. And that's how we won the game in Edinburgh that day – although I'd like to think my sports psychology on the Wednesday had been the significant part."

68

SCOTLAND JOIN THE CENTURY CLUB – PATERSON HITS 40

13 November 2004 • Autumn Test, Perth
Scotland 100–Japan 8

You would never want to be on the receiving end of such a mauling. However, there has always been something about teams at any level managing to reach three figures. Prior to Japan's visit to Perth in 2004, the biggest score the Scots had clocked up in a home match was 48–0 against Spain during the 1999 World Cup.

That came four years after Gavin Hastings had inspired an 89–0 win over Côte d'Ivoire (Ivory Coast in old money) in the same competition.

No one had set their sights on a record-breaking performance from the Scots on that November evening. Indeed, any kind of result would be embraced by the hosts, who that year had drawn a blank in the Six Nations and lost three successive Tests, home and away, against Australia, the only respite coming in the form of a 38–3 win in Wellington against Samoa.

Within 90 seconds of kick-off, Scotland had scored their first try, Newcastle Falcons flanker Ally Hogg set up by Allan Jacobsen and Chris Cusiter. However, after such a buoyant

PART IV – 2000s

beginning, people sank back down in their McDiarmid Park seats as the Japanese came straight back with a try by winger Hayato Daimon.

It wasn't until the 20th minute that the Scots hit double digits, the ball passing through the hands of Dan Parks, Ben Hinshelwood and Chris Paterson to set up Hugo Southwell. From that point, Scotland turned the screw.

Paterson followed a penalty with a try, dancing his way through on the wrong wing, and was soon joined on the growing list of try scorers by Dan Parks and Jon Petrie for a 36–8 interval lead. Thereafter it was one-way traffic. Paterson chased a Parks kick, booted ahead and fell over the line. Mike Blair then also chased a Parks cross-field chip and somersaulted over the line. Five points and 5.9 for artistic content from the Perth judges.

Centre Andrew Henderson crossed for the score after Scotland again bullied the Japanese into basic errors. Blair stabbed a kick through off the outside of his boot, the ball running for Paterson to bring up his treble with Southwell in attendance. Graeme Morrison scrambled in for his first international try (he wouldn't score again for nearly four years), Sean Lamont added another, open-side Donnie Macfadyen ripped the ball from a maul to dive in for the score, then sub hooker Robbie Russell cut up the blindside from a line-out.

It was left for Hugo Southwell to slice his way through the now-decimated Japanese defence to set a new record score for the national side, and there was yet time for a 15th try as the clock ran into the red, Russell making it a brace with an excellent individual effort. The resulting conversion from Paterson brought up the ton, a figure which the BBC's scoreboard graphic had obviously not been designed for.

Paterson's haul of three tries, 11 conversions and a penalty was the second-biggest individual tally by a Scot in a single game, after the 44 points Gavin Hastings amassed against Côte d'Ivoire. It also took Paterson beyond Andy Irvine as Scotland's second-leading aggregate points scorer, once again with Hastings out in front, and over the 300-point mark in his 48 Test appearances.

Over the next two weeks Scotland would lose to Australia again, this time at Hampden, and South Africa. Out of 12 Tests in 2004, Scotland won two. The Japan result barely papered over the widening cracks under the tenure of coach Matt Williams.

This wasn't Japan's strongest side by any means, but that is a minor detail today. But to paraphrase a famous Norwegian commentator: Ryohei Miki, Koichiro Kubota, Seiichi Shimomura, Yukio Motoki, Hayato Daimon, Keisuke Sawaki, Wataru Ikeda, Takuro Miuchi, Hajime Kiso, Naoya Okubo, Hitoshi Ono, Takanori Kumagai, Ryo Yamamura, Takashi Yamaoka, Yuichi Hisadomi, Mitsugu Yamamoto, Masahito Yamamoto, Feletliki Mau, Takatoyo Yamaguchi, Kiyonori Tanaka, Masatoshi Mukoyama and Hideyuki Yoshida, you boys took a helluva beating...

69

THE KICKING TEE DELIVERY BUSINESS JUST GOT REAL

2006

For years at Murrayfield, Scotland's tried and trusted place-kickers (and oh, how we needed those guys for many years, when, let's be honest, they weren't taking many conversions) wouldn't have to go searching for the kicking tee as it was delivered straight to their boot.

The remote-control model car had, in its various guises, provided a quick and practical method of getting the tee to the players with the least amount of fuss, even if in a moment of devilment, many of us longed to be the buggy driver, teasing the kicker to reach for the tee, then scooting away at the last minute. Childish, I know.

However, in a moment which might have been akin to Alan Partridge lying atop his hotel bed, Dictaphone in hand, and spouting all kinds of weird and wonderful ideas, someone came up with the nugget of having the remote vehicle in the shape of a rugby ball, with the sponsor's name emblazoned up the side of it, and – wait for it – topped off with an infamous game bird.

Well done to whoever arrived at that genius, and an even bigger well done to all place-kickers who kept their face straight, and their kicks straighter.

70

HADDEN INSPIRES DEBUT CALCUTTA CUP WIN

25 February 2006 • Six Nations, Murrayfield
Scotland 18–England 12

Scotland had been in a bad place through 2005. Wooden spoon avoidance disguised real issues as Ireland, Wales and England all rattled up 40 points apiece. Coach Matt Williams wasn't working and, indeed, wouldn't be by the April. The inevitable came on the back of the unexpected, Ian McGeechan resigning as director of rugby at the SRU to head for Wasps.

The SRU looked to Edinburgh coach Frank Hadden, firstly on an interim basis, but after beating the Barbarians and Romania, it became a fixed role.

Kicking off the 2006 Six Nations with a win over France helped buoy the long-suffering Scottish support (who quickly bought up the 10,000 unsold tickets that remained for the Auld Enemy's visit), but successive home victories that season would mean defeating England for only the second time at Murrayfield since the Grand Slam decider in 1990.

What resulted was a hard-fought, dour, pragmatic Scottish win. Chris Paterson and Charlie Hodgson shared penalties, the latter adding another before Paterson with a brace and a Dan

PART IV – 2000s

Parks drop goal from around 25 metres out edged Scotland 12–6 ahead. Again, Hodgson outscored Paterson two to one to leave the match poised 15–12, before the *coup de grâce* three minutes from time to clinch the win.

Paterson's unerring accuracy was only half the story, however. Defensively, Scotland tackled like men possessed. Jason White made 17, Simon Taylor and centre Andrew Henderson 16 apiece, even scrum-half Mike Blair hitting 15. Above them all, though, was Ally Hogg, who made an impressive 20 tackles. That said, had he not been halted a foot short of the English line with ten minutes of standard time remaining – Andrew Sheridan and Mark Cueto in unison on the stop – Hogg could have been a try-scoring hero, or even a try-making hero (had he passed to Alastair Kellock outside) as well, rather than just a hard-hitting one.

It wasn't pretty and neither was Scotland's final-day win in Rome. But three wins and mid-table sanctuary (third place, and ahead of England) categorised 2006 a success.

Ally Hogg explains the numbers game:

"People would ask how can you make 190 tackles in 80 minutes? Simple; you don't have the ball very much. The back row did play well that day. Alan Tait was defence coach and like most who had been over to Rugby League, really had you drilled in how to stop your opponents.

"With what had happened with Matt Williams, which was awful, Frank [Hadden] gave us new purpose and a spark. He was just going to play like he had with Edinburgh; get the ball, get it wide.

"We had beaten France the first game up, which was Frank's first Six Nations match and lost narrowly to Wales in Cardiff when Scott Murray had been sent off and suspended. While we may not have been favourites against England, and therefore overconfident, equally, I don't think we were overawed either.

"There was a bit of a buzz after the French game because while we had to defend hard, we'd also scored two tries in that game through Sean Lamont. The team was playing a more direct, quicker-paced game, just like Edinburgh.

"Frank had assembled a very mobile pack and there were some guys in there who maybe weren't household names but who were in because they suited that style, like Dougie Hall at hooker, who was good in wide channels, and Bruce Douglas next to him, who was an excellent ball handler. The back row was a big unit and very mobile. The game plan was very different to what Matt Williams had adopted.

"Stretching the game was the plan, but that quick-tempo style was difficult to maintain against England, because they were a powerful team, and the conditions didn't help us. The pitch was very heavy; it was wet, and all they did was chuck sand on it, which only made it heavier. Neither side could run very much.

"The upside of that, though, was that it was a good day not to have the ball, daft as that may sound. You could apply more pressure by kicking long, getting it down the pitch, turning England around – their big men didn't like that – and then hitting them hard deep in their half. That was why the tackle count was so very high.

"If you could apply pressure in the set piece, which we did, they would give up penalties, which is what happened, and Mossy [Chris Paterson] kicked everything.

"I fell half a yard short of the try line in the closing minutes. That would have got me on *A Question of Sport*. Unfortunately, it wasn't to be. But lifting the Calcutta Cup at the end, that's not something you forget."

71

KICKING MASTERCLASS FROM PATERSON SEES OFF WALES

10 February 2007 • Six Nations, Murrayfield
Scotland 21–Wales 6

Much of sport is about repetition and practice, doing the same thing over and over and over again, so that come the big-pressure moments during match time, your technique doesn't fail you. Like a golfer being hot with his putter on the green, or a snooker player having such control of the cue ball that it looks as if it could be on a string, or a cricketer middling everything, from a forward defensive push to an exhilarating cover drive. Maintaining that method so you can deliver when it matters is the difference between being good and great.

Chris Paterson certainly belonged in the latter category, thankfully for Scotland. For during a period when Scotland, the team, underachieved, the boot of Paterson overdelivered, with his display against Wales during the 2007 Six Nations emphasising that point.

In what was a disappointing tournament for the Scots – which included a horrendous home performance against Italy – Paterson delivered Scotland's only win with a place-kicking masterclass. What else would you expect from the player who, statistically, was the best in world rugby?

Having reached the 500-point mark during a heavy loss to England at Twickenham, Paterson's first success against Wales after six minutes was relatively simple after Welsh prop Duncan Jones had gone offside at the breakdown in front of the posts. Hooker Rhys Thomas then didn't release when isolated, and Paterson from 15m inside the Wales half made it 6–0, which became 9–3 when loose head Adam Rhys Jones was caught offside. Paterson was having a good day, entirely thanks to the ill discipline of the Welsh front row.

Stephen Jones, the Welsh stand-off, was matching Paterson in terms of accuracy, making it two from two before half-time.

Early in the second half, Paterson, operating as the left wing, fielded a Dwayne Peel box kick and, as he returned the kick, was taken out by Ceri Sweeney. Paterson, from the 22, was deadly, and again from similar distance on the other side, making it 15–6.

Jones narrowed the leeway with another penalty of his own, before Mossy banged over two more goals to clock up his magnificent seven, his 21 points against Wales surpassing his own best of 20 set in 2003.

One month later, and following on from the Italian debacle when Paterson scored a try and was again perfect with the boot, he struck six from six against Ireland, his metronomic consistency only undone by Ronan O'Gara. Scotland 18, Ireland 19 – or to be more exact, Paterson 18, O'Gara 19.

Chris Paterson on the loneliness of a long-distance goal-kicker: "I remember that Wales game and the seven penalties. I don't think it was a particularly memorable game – 30 points, all kicked.

"But for me there was the satisfaction of a job well done again.

PART IV – 2000s

I relished the responsibility and my role and the position I'd been given. You could be a match winner – or loser – but even when you produced perfection, you don't get anything near the same adulation as a try scorer. It never worried me though, not in the slightest. I think most place-kickers get a personal satisfaction that all their hard work has paid off.

"To excel with my skill, I had to shut myself off from what was happening around me. Even if we'd scored a great try, I had to ignore it. And even if you land a really crucial kick, you go through what you've just done, the self-analysis, examining what you did to make the kick a success, because you might be asked to do exactly the same 30 seconds later.

"Remember what I said about not getting the acclaim of the try scorers? The funny thing from that Wales game was that even though I scored seven from seven, a match-winning performance, Simon Taylor got the man of the match award!"

72

THAT JERSEY AND *THAT* GAME

24 February 2007 • Six Nations, Murrayfield
Scotland 17–Italy 37

Not all memories are happy memories, no. 17.

The difference between a good kit and a bad kit can quite easily be dictated by the results achieved wearing them. There is therefore no chance of Scotland's change kit for the 2007 Six Nations being looked on favourably.

It is almost impossible then to think of that shirt (predominantly white but with blue side panels, yellow shoulders and red piping – yes, red piping) without recalling the first six minutes of the game against Italy that season, when the Azzurri ran in three tries in the opening six minutes, the first after just 18 seconds, to lead 21–0.

Scotland rallied but still lost 37–17, a culmination of poor judgement, catastrophic handling errors and failings in attack and defence. Above all else, it was the jersey to blame.

Forget a memory, more of a nightmare.

73

STRICTLY KENNY

2007

Why do people enter reality TV shows? Is it the money? Is it for self-promotion? Is it because they like seeing themselves on TV? Is it because they have a point to prove?

In the case of Kenny Logan, it was for the latter; coaxed, cajoled and coerced into signing up for the 2007 series of *Strictly Come Dancing* by wife Gabby, Kenny partnered Ola Jordan, his best weekly scores coming when dancing the American Smooth and the foxtrot; his worst tally coming in the samba – although he did finish last in the cha-cha-cha.

And the paso doble.

And the Viennese waltz.

And the rumba.

However, despite some savaging by the judges, Kenny – who had seen off the sporting challenge of snooker player Willie Thorne and footballer John Barnes – survived longer than wife Gabby and partner James Jordan – husband of Ola – who bid farewell to the show first, bowing out in the fourth week of competition.

Amazingly, Kenny and Ola were the ninth pair to be eliminated as Alesha Dixon won the overall prize. Kenny, however, had to content himself with bragging rights in the Logan household.

"Footloose" Logan gives his version of events (other versions are available):

"Learning to read at 30 was my biggest achievement. Beating the wife in *Strictly* was my second-biggest achievement. And she can never take that away from me. She may be a better dancer, but like sport, it's a result-driven business. She was knocked out in October, I lasted to December. Sorry...

"The producers at *Strictly* wanted a couple involved. Gabby was signed up and they asked me, and I said, 'No chance.'

"I went to pick her up one day after rehearsals and they sat me down and said, 'Will you do it?'

"Having said no, and been adamant about it, I then said yes but realised I had just signed a contract with ITV at the time, to do the 2007 Rugby World Cup, so it was a no again.

"Gabby, though, was not having it. She looked at the dates and said the only date I couldn't do was if Scotland beat the All Blacks so I said, 'Count me in.'

"Today, because of how Scotland are playing, I'd hang around for the New Zealand game, but back then it was a kind of inevitable conclusion.

"Learning to dance was a great experience and good fun. Hard work but, once you got into it, that will to win kicked in. My departure was funny. In the end, Len Goodman said, 'I think you've done enough,' to which I replied, 'I think you're right,' – although in saying that, Jim Telfer once told me the same – and I got 50 caps after that.

"I haven't kept up with the dancing. It was quite time-consuming, and anyway, I proved a point and I retired at the top, undefeated – in this household, although I seldom mention that..."

74

SCOTS WELL BEATEN BY NEW ZEALAND – OR MAYBE NOT

23 September 2007 • *World Cup, Murrayfield*
Scotland 0–New Zealand 40

In getting back with tradition, Scotland suffered World Cup defeat in 2007 at the hands of New Zealand at Murrayfield. A 20–0 half-time lead for the Kiwis was doubled in the second half, Dan Carter, Doug Howlett, Byron Kelleher, Ali Williams and captain Richie McCaw all scoring tries in what was a one-way rout for the All Blacks.

Except, they weren't the All Blacks that day. New Zealand played in their change kit – silver shirts with black flashing, black shorts and black socks. Very different from their normal daywear.

Unfortunately, Scotland's home kit for that season were navy tops, adorned with large white and silver panels. Close up, both jerseys looked different and distinctive. However, at a distance – as it was for the close-on 65,000 in the stadium – at times it was nearly impossible to distinguish between the two teams, other than the fact one kept scoring.

It was a difficult day for the Scots, made all the more impossible for their supporters with the unintentional kit clash.

Lessons were learned and promises made that it would never happen again. Which is why we had exactly the same scenario in the 2018/19 season when Cardiff and Glasgow Warriors met in the Champions Cup.

Scott Lawson was the Scotland hooker that day: "I played in that game and remember the complaints, post-game.

"At the time, it didn't seem to be an issue for the players.

"All I remember was chasing shadows as the All Blacks ran riot.

"They might not have looked it but, trust me, that was the All Blacks, regardless of what they were wearing."

75

OUT OF THE BLUE

8 March 2008 • Six Nations, Murrayfield
Scotland 15–England 9

When everything seems lost, or at least has been misplaced sufficiently for you to believe it may never be found, Scotland throughout its rugby history has managed to pull out the most unexpected result from nowhere. Amazing that so often that can be against England. Why is that, I wonder?

In amongst those tales of the unexpected, Scotland's 2008 Six Nations victory over the Auld Enemy features highly.

The Scots had been comprehensively trounced by France in their opening tie, and while Chris Paterson had another perfect day with the boot in Cardiff, there was nothing Scotland could do to halt the growing momentum of a Wales XV (30–15 winners) that was putting together a Grand Slam-clinching campaign.

Scotland did manage a try against Ireland in Dublin, through Simon Webster, but that barely grazed the chin of the Irish, who won 34–13.

There was little therefore that would suggest Scotland would lay a glove on an England side, which, although beaten by Wales first time up that season, had contested a World Cup final just months earlier.

Conditions were perfect ahead of kick-off; it was wet, windy and the pitch had already begun to cut up badly, even during the warm-up, as skipper Mike Blair belatedly led his Scotland side on to the field. Nothing like keeping your adversaries waiting.

If the conditions made for a pragmatic approach in both camps, from respective coaches Frank Hadden and Brian Ashton, then Scotland's ability to suffocate their more illustrious opponents meant there was little rugby played. The game then reverted to a kicking contest between Paterson, and his deputy Dan Parks, versus Jonny Wilkinson.

Paterson gave Scotland the lead inside the first ten minutes, England coming in from the side at a maul. Play was delayed while medics dealt with a head injury to wing Rory Lamont, meaning a rejigging of the Scots backline, with Paterson – who had started at no. 10 – being put on the wing, with Parks deputising at stand-off.

It was their counterpart Wilkinson who took the plaudits next, however, making it 3–3, kicking a penalty to take his overall points tally in international rugby to 1,093, having shared the world record at start of play with Neil Jenkins of Wales.

English prop Andrew Sheridan gave away a needless penalty on the half-hour, then Simon Shaw failed to roll away at a ruck in first-half stoppage time, both offences punished by Paterson. In between those scores, Wilkinson had missed a 48m attempt, leaving Scotland 9–3 up at the interval. With less than a minute gone of the second period, the deadly Paterson landed his 30th consecutive kick after England had been penalised for not releasing, although that call from referee Jonathan Kaplan was almost reversed after a sarcastic pat on the back from Nathan Hines on the luckless Sheridan.

When Iain Balshaw held on to the ball for too long, Paterson protected his unblemished record by allowing Parks to kick from

PART IV - 2000s

inside the English ten as the wind swirled around Murrayfield. Thankfully, points were not awarded for artistic impression, just for the ball going over, and Scotland were 15–3 up. The PA system blasted a chorus of "Magic" (Pilot's 1974 hit for all you music lovers out there) through the stadium. Indeed, it was if you weren't clad in wet, white shirts.

England were always going to come back at the Scots and Wilkinson struck twice within five minutes, his second wind assisted from 41m to peg Scotland's lead back to six points at 15–9.

In desperation, England coach Ashton replaced Wilkinson and captain Phil Vickery with Charlie Hodgson and Matt Stevens for the last ten minutes, but the dogged Scots continued to frustrate, every piece of possession pinched welcomed like a try. But who needs tries to win the Calcutta Cup.

Scotland full-back that day was Hugo Southwell:

"When you look through the Scotland team from that game it would surprise some with the names that jump out: Graeme Morrison, Nikki Walker, Scott Macleod, Alasdair Strokosch. All really good players, but how many would have had those guys as the first names you'd mention as players who'd played in winning Scotland teams against England?

"Simon Webster, who was probably best known as a winger with Edinburgh, started at no. 13 because Frank Hadden saw an opportunity to play him there, believing he offered up a potential threat if he got the ball sooner, and stuck him at centre rather than out wide – so directly up against the Falcons midfield of Wilkinson, Toby Flood and Jamie Noon. Not exactly conventional thinking.

"But a lot of the credit for that win should go to Frank Hadden as coach. Our game plan really was to take England on up front, to such an extent it negated any threat they might hold amongst their back division.

"It was a simple but effective plan but had to be followed to the letter. What is often missed is that in putting in the tackles, and winning the breakdowns against a bludgeoning England pack, your discipline has to be immense. Don't give away needless penalties. Don't kill the ball, don't stray offside, don't be lazy after the tackle. I can still hear it now. Do any of that, you knew the consequences against the likes of Jonny Wilkinson.

"Instead it was England who committed all those punishable offences, and Chris [Paterson] punished them. Listen, nothing in that game was going to make a 'best of' DVD, unless it was about kicking goals under pressure. Don't forget the one Dan [Parks] flopped over as well.

"It was a horrible day, weather-wise. You would always get people saying, 'Oh, this suits the Scots,' but it was still horrible – although the sun was shining when we won. That was my second successive win against England at Murrayfield, and it wasn't pretty that day either – either in terms of the weather or the performance.

"Two years later, again in a season when we struggled for results, we pulled out a draw against England, 15–15 when it was Dan who kicked everything. In three games, I never lost as a player against England at Murrayfield. That stacks up pretty well against quite a few in the game."

76

EDINBURGH GO FOR ARTISTRY OF A DIFFERENT KIND

2009

Once seen, never forgotten.

No Scottish rugby fan will ever forget the first time they clapped eyes on Edinburgh's special kit for the 1972 cup clash with Glasgow. Neither will they have erased that particular kit from their personal hard drive!

To be honest, Edinburgh had merely followed someone else's lead – on this occasion, French side Stade Français who, over a couple of years, had produced some strange and interesting designs for both domestic and European Cup matches. Well, you know what they say: if you can't beat them, join them – although with this one, Edinburgh probably beat them – only to then beat themselves the following year with an even more outrageously garish "special".

We haven't seen anything quite as abstract or colourful since, although I fancy, like a great many things, it will only be a matter of time before we do.

PART V

2010s

77

SCOTS CLEAN UP IN DUBLIN THANKS TO PARKS DEPARTMENT

20 March 2010 • Six Nations, Murrayfield
Ireland 20–Scotland 23

On the road in the Six Nations (and even when it was just Five), Scotland's recent record has been pretty abysmal. Incredibly, while gaining a reputation as a watchable, attacking force, Scotland's last away win anywhere in the Northern Hemisphere's main event – other than in Rome – came nine years ago, in March 2010, a season when even the Italians managed to beat the Scots 16–12. The trip to Dublin, however, would be different.

Somehow, while being 0–3 in the campaign, Scotland managed to gain a draw against England, 15–15, a kicking contest with Dan Parks going up against Jonny Wilkinson and Toby Flood.

Entering the final match that season, Scotland needed to beat Ireland at Croke Park to avoid the wooden spoon, not an easy assignment given that Declan Kidney's team still had Triple Crown ambitions following 20–16 and 27–12 wins over England (away) and Wales (home) respectively.

Scotland scored first, Parks handed a penalty straight in front of the uprights, but the visitors' lead was short-lived as Johnny

Sexton looped around Gordon D'Arcy, threw a fake pass and accelerated through the dark blue defensive line before another dummy and a well-timed flick inside to Brian O'Driscoll to cross for the try – amazingly, his first in that season's tournament.

Fifteen minutes in, Scotland regained the lead. From turnover ball on halfway, Kelly Brown popped the ball up for centre Graeme Morrison, his feed inside on the 22 finding Johnnie Beattie in full flow, the no. 8 crashing over and through Paul O'Connell, D'Arcy and Geordan Murphy for a great score.

A slender 8–7 lead for the Scots became 14–7 by the interval; Donncha O'Callaghan's reluctance to roll away handed Parks another penalty, while the Australian-born no. 10 was given time and space working behind a dominant Scotland pack in stoppage time, receiving Hugo Southwell's feed to slot a long-range drop goal.

Scotland continued to play at pace and take the game to the Irish. Sean Lamont's break forced the hosts to once more deliberately slow the ball down, and Parks punished them once more.

In a bizarre exchange, Ronan O'Gara looked to replace Sexton as he lined up a penalty. O'Gara came on, went off, Sexton cut the deficit to 17–10 and was then withdrawn. Scotland's defence and lead was tested as Ireland saw their prize slipping away. They produced a try through Tommy Bowe, converted by O'Gara, to pull level, the Irish kicker again on the mark with a penalty to negate Parks' effort two minutes earlier. With four minutes remaining, it was all square at 20 points apiece.

Ireland kicked away possession, enabling Scotland to punch their way back into Irish territory. When Parks got his hands on the ball with just under three minutes of match time remaining, he hoisted a deep cross-field kick to land in Ireland's 22. Full-back Rob Kearney fielded but was ambushed by Simon Danielli and Nick De Luca. Isolated and by now pinned, Kearney held on, an act that did not escape referee Jonathan Kaplan.

Three metres in from touch, and a metre outside the Irish 22, Parks went through all of his routine painstakingly. The partisan locals made sure they registered their displeasure at what they saw as time-wasting, but Parks remained cool, his nerve unwavering. The ball disappeared into the floodlights, Parks, still on the follow-through, beginning his celebration immediately with a leap and punch of the air. The clock though had only reached 79 minutes.

The Scots held on, however. Italy lifted the wooden spoon, Ireland lifted nothing and Scotland fans lifted the roof. Not an instant classic, but almost a decade on, now looking like a vintage year.

The match through the eyes of Dan Parks:

"We wanted a win to avoid the wooden spoon. Ireland were chasing history and a Triple Crown and were a really good team. I think that's what made it such a tight game. So much was riding on the outcome.

"Johnnie Beattie produced a great finish for his try, and bang on half-time, I was given a free hit at a drop goal. Another penalty and we were in a good place at 17–7, but Ireland were at home and desperate to win, so they were always going to come back at us.

"I never felt at 17–17 or 20–20 we were going to lose it. We might not win, but losing didn't worry me. And then I manufactured a couple of kicks that, from a personal level, were really pleasing; the first was the one that gave Nick De Luca and Simon Danielli the chance to chase down Rob Kearney. He was desperate to keep the ball in play, in Irish hands. That may have swayed the referee slightly, who would have known he could have kicked for touch.

"My penalty, it was one of the sweetest I'd ever taken. And at what a time. I knew it was over as soon as I'd struck it – again, really pleasing under those circumstances. I've never been that demonstrative, but my celebration was more in relief than anything. Running back to halfway, I was hoping I hadn't been too exuberant. You know, I was frightened it could come back to bite me.

"There was a minute to go, perhaps more taking in stoppage time, and I was suddenly very aware they had O'Gara on the pitch – not quite enough to make the hairs stand up, but you knew what he was capable of doing given half a chance. Thankfully, we never gave him that opportunity.

"At the end, we had a lot of family and friends over seeing us. One or two made out we had gone on a lap of honour, but it was anything but. A lap of relief more like, having finally won. There were no celebrations, just a quiet contentment that we had won a very good game.

"Most of the boys wandered around, waving to some of the Scotland fans who had stayed on and recognising some of the people we knew in the stands. We were just relieved to have managed a win to end the season."

78

NO CRIES IN ARGENTINA AS SCOTLAND TAKE HISTORIC SERIES WIN

2010

A year into his tenure as Scotland coach, Andy Robinson took his team to Argentina for a two-match Test series. Things had started brightly for the former England no. 2, with a maiden win over Fiji in the autumn Test followed by an unexpected 9–8 victory over Australia.

However, in their final match of 2009, Scotland lost an equally dour game against Argentina, 9–6. The chance of revenge would be served up the following summer, however, after a Six Nations campaign which offered much but didn't quite deliver on results, two games against the Pumas took on a new degree of difficulty.

The first Test would be played in Tucumán, a location where Argentina, now three places above the Scots in the world rankings, had previously seen off all comers. Amongst the Scots representation was Rory Lawson, starting at scrum-half, and reserve back Jim Thompson on the bench – cousins, but perhaps more famously, grandsons of the late Bill McLaren.

The game, watched by 30,000 in the Estadio José Fierro, began badly for the Scots, going behind to a Gonzalo Tiesi touchdown after three minutes, and conceding another when Juan Manuel Leguizamón crossed over. His later indiscretion, however, cost him a yellow card, enabling Dan Parks to punish the short-handed Pumas with a drop goal on the half-time whistle to go with his three penalty goals, making it 13–12 at the interval.

Scotland, defensively, tightened up for the second 40, meaning Parks could make every opportunity with the boot count. Indeed, Parks repeated his first half dosage – three penalties and a drop goal – to give Scotland a 24–16 win, and a first-ever loss for Argentina in Tucumán.

In contrast, it was the Scots who began the second Test in Mar del Plata with a bang. Two minutes in, Scotland drove a line-out to within a few metres, lock Jim Hamilton wrenching the ball from the pack to dive over. Even that early, the seven-pointer gave Scotland an advantage they wouldn't relinquish, and with Parks again on the mark from the tee, Scotland held out to record a first-ever Test series win in the Southern Hemisphere.

Try hero Jim Hamilton fondly looks back on an "old-style" tour: "I remember we were pretty poor in the lead-up to that trip but ended up having a brilliant tour. To win both of those games, against what was a very good Argentinian side, particularly when they were at home, with most of the big players available and backup to hand, it was a real tonic to the season we'd had in the Six Nations.

"We'd come good against Ireland right at the end in Dublin and somehow managed to get a draw before that against England. But losing in Italy, and to a Shane Williams try in Wales – a game where Thom Evans broke his neck and Chris Paterson ruptured a kidney, as if things weren't bad enough – didn't help, having started with defeat to France at Murrayfield. The results didn't make it the easiest or best of campaigns as we headed out to South America.

PART V – 2010s

"My favourite part of going to Argentina was that it was like being on an old-school tour. Yes, it was great winning two Tests, and great playing as a team in really tough conditions. But by far the most enjoyable part was being able to let our hair down, have a drink during the week, a beer or wine, enjoy the local delicacies if you like – which meant eating as much steak as you liked – and then training hard.

"Because we weren't in Buenos Aires – the games were in Tucumán and Mar del Plata – we could do a bit around the town because there weren't as many people watching us. It was a great trip.

"But then came game day and it just got better. The stadiums were football-like, with fences and moats around the perimeter of the pitch, and you had to walk along these dusty streets to get into the old grounds. I loved it.

"Then of course, all the atmosphere and scenery made it a great experience, but what topped it off were the results and the challenge you faced from the Pumas, especially for the likes of me and the other forwards. It you wanted to test yourself against proper international forward players, then that was the place to go.

"Scotland always considered they had a good pack themselves, some big units and useful with it: Allan Jacobsen, Ross Ford, Moray Low, Al Kellock and the 'Killer Bs' – Brown, Barclay and Beattie. A proper unit, and we fancied it against other teams in the Six Nations or touring teams.

"But that said, Argentina were a mean bunch, hard as, 'borderlining' when it came to legality, and it was a real test of manhood if you were up against their pack, which was never going to take a backwards step. They had an almighty scrum, were good in the set piece and weren't short on physicality. Because of the way rugby has evolved, those elements have been neutered in some ways. But still in 2010, and especially out there, it was the accepted norm.

"Anyone who knows me knows I quite enjoy that side of the game. Add in the cauldron-like atmosphere in the grounds, it was proper Test-match rugby. Let's just say the entire trip equated to my values in the game.

"We won the first Test and Parksy [Dan Parks] kicked like a god. The reason, however, that he had as many goes was because we were giving it to them up front, and they were conceding penalties and yellow cards, and the more they conceded, the more frustration set in.

"My try – our try, our only one in two Tests – came just a couple of minutes into the second Test, which was a much tighter, cagier affair. I'd love to say I danced and bobbed and weaved myself in from 50 metres, but it was just a straight, training-ground, driving maul from a line-out a couple of metres out. And remember, I was filled up on red meat and red wine, so was probably carrying a few more kilos than I would have been normally. But that ballast came in handy. Surprised my score has never featured on a compilation DVD, especially as it was such a rarity – my first and last.

"I saw something recently where someone was saying that of all the Scotland players with over 25 appearances in the Six Nations, I had the worst win percentage. I played 63 times for Scotland. We'll cut out the dubiety and just say no one with 63 caps has a worse win percentage than me. Like I care. It's nice to have a stat of your own.

"All I know is in Argentina, I gave my everything, I scored my only try and we won a Test series which not many can lay claim to. So am I bothered about any other spurious stats and contrived facts? No, not really."

79

SCOTLAND DEFEAT THE WORLD CHAMPIONS

20 November 2010 • Autumn Test, Murrayfield
Scotland 21–South Africa 17

It's not every day you defeat the world champions. It could be supposed that's why Scotland's football fraternity have never forgotten Wembley in 1967. Well, they need to hang on to something.

Unlike their soccer brethren all those years ago against England's class of 1966, Scotland's rugby players weren't the first to inflict a defeat on the 2007 world champions. That honour belonged to the All Blacks.

Nevertheless, to beat the holders of the Webb Ellis Cup was still something of an achievement, particularly given the Scots were coming off the back of a seven-try, 49–3 pummelling by New Zealand the previous week.

Against the Springboks, Scotland made a sluggish start at a sodden Murrayfield, conceding early penalties to enable Morné Steyn to give the tourists a 6–0 advantage. That was soon wiped out, however, by Dan Parks, their lead reduced with a penalty, levelled with a drop goal that flopped its way over.

Parks had his eye in. When South Africa dropped a scrum

on the 22, Parks was good from that distance, and again from midway inside the Boks half – when penalised for offside – to put Scotland into an unexpected 12–6 lead.

When Scotland themselves were punished for offside, Steyn came good with his third successful effort, and he was on the mark again early in the second half to tie the match at 12 points apiece.

After a superb line break by Richie Vernon, Scots aggression was rewarded when desperate South African defending saw them enter a ruck from the side, Parks doing the needful, and he did the same on the hour mark after yet another South African infringement in the scrum to make it 18–12.

As sleety rain swept Murrayfield, so South African ambition was being frozen out by the ever-accurate Parks, who was then presented with his easiest kick of the day when Australian referee Stuart Dickinson, who had frustrated Peter de Villiers' team throughout with some questionable calls, pinged flanker Juan Smith for going off his feet at a ruck. Parks chipped in his sixth penalty for all 21 of Scotland's points.

With ten minutes remaining, a try to warm the crowd, although it sent a chill through the Scotland supporters as Willem Albertz picked one off the tail of a line-out to batter his way over for the try. Almost as if to prove what an unsung, professional job Parks had done all day, Steyn's replacement Patrick Lambie hooked his conversion outside the near upright, leaving it as a two-score game, 21–17, which is how it finished.

Not pretty, but effective.

Rory Lawson, Scotland's winning captain, on drawing inspiration from the late Bill McLaren and being on the "balls":

"I broke my hand five weeks before the All Blacks game. Andy Robinson asked if I'd captain the team. I tried training and I realised by Tuesday there was no chance I was playing against New

PART V – 2010s

Zealand, which was disappointing. My hand just hadn't recovered well enough, although I kept training without doing the team stuff, trying to get my hand strength back and reduce the pain.

"I watched the All Blacks game, a tough one to watch personally and from a team perspective, then went back into camp on the Monday. At that stage I was still doubtful. There hadn't been a significant improvement in my hand – it had been screwed and plated just a couple of weeks before and was still tender, with a lot of scar tissue around it.

"But Mike Blair had been concussed against the All Blacks, and Greig [Laidlaw] had gone on to win his first cap, so Andy came to me and said, 'I need you to be playing. You are going to be right, aren't you?'

"So I spoke to the doctor and the medics and they said, 'We'll get you playing,' and I went through the week training, which was pretty miserable; the weather wasn't great, but I viewed my role as just trying to energise everyone and generate some belief from somewhere, after having had 40 points put on us by the All Blacks, and me only having one hand to do it with.

"But I was fortunate, not having played in that game not being affected by it, and then coming in to lead the team. Personally, though, I was having an awful week in training. I was chucking all sorts of pies to Dan [Parks] off my left hand. The strapping on my hand had to go over the back, with the padding, then around the palm, which for any player in general, let alone a scrum-half, isn't ideal.

"Parksy just took the piss out of me, Monday, Tuesday, Wednesday, about how bad my passing was. But I knew I had to be right and you find belief from somewhere.

"We had a day off on the Thursday, and I'd gone down to Hawick to see Mum and Dad and Nana, gone for lunch, visited Papa's headstone, and then gone and got some Hawick Balls, while generally thinking what I was going to say to the boys.

"On the eve of the game you have the team meeting, and then the coaches leave and you're left with the team. It was pretty daunting.

"Papa was going to feature in my speech to the guys before dinner. I was shaking a bit, because I was captaining a team with guys significantly more senior than me – Chris Paterson, Nathan Hines – in its ranks.

"What I said was that the All Blacks game was flushed. We're taking on the world champions tomorrow and we can show what we're about. And then I told the story of Papa, and the Hawick Balls, and a few of the boys had met him, and how he'd dig into his pocket and pull out a poke of sweets, and say, 'Go on, son, have one of them – it'll give you an extra yard of pace,' and to the front five, 'You should maybe have two.'

"I just said, 'Look, whether you grab a Hawick Ball leaving here or not, it doesn't really bother me.'

"But I wanted them to put that picture in their head, that if we win every race by a yard, and get there a yard quicker than the South Africans, whether that was line speed, or ball in hand, or quicker to the ruck, or in speed of thought, even if those yards are just inches, if we add them all together, we'll do enough to get us over the line. I concluded by saying, 'Just think tonight about where those yards and inches will come from, don't get too fired up just now, and tomorrow we'll light Murrayfield.' I went to bed quite happy.

"I woke up next morning and I could barely feel my hand, it was hammering it down with rain and blowing a hooley, and then in the tunnel I stood next to Victor Matfield, their captain, who is 6'8", about a foot taller than me. This wasn't how I'd envisaged it.

"However, it all came together. The conditions played a huge part, we fronted up, stayed in the fight and although it wasn't pretty, we won. The power of Hawick Balls..."

80

EDINBURGH LIVE THE EUROPEAN DREAM

2012

It was a year of so near and yet so far for Edinburgh, a season when they turned into cup specialists with a string of performances that belied their woeful domestic form in the PRO12 league, culminating in a special contest against former kings of European rugby.

Sandwiched between basement side Aironi and Treviso in the league table, what could have been an instantly forgettable term remains one fondly remembered by rugby followers in the Scottish capital, thanks to Edinburgh's Champions Cup run.

Drawn in the same section as London Irish, Cardiff Blues and Racing Metro 92, few gave Michael Bradley's team much of a hope of making the knockout stages, particularly when their PRO12 form was so woeful. To put it in some context, by the end of their Champions Cup campaign, Edinburgh had won as many games as they had out of 22 league ties.

Things began well on the road, beating London Irish by a point, followed by a match against Racing that Edinburgh shaded, again by a point, with 95 scored in total. A 25–8 reversal in Cardiff was in itself reversed, 19–12 back in Edinburgh, before Edinburgh concluded with an impressive 27–24 win away – secured by replacement Phil Godman's drop goal off the last tangle in Paris – and a 35–11 victory against the Irish exiles to top their group.

That set up a quarter-final tie against an impressive Toulouse team, topping the French Top 14 league and pool winners (four wins, two losses) ahead of Harlequins, Gloucester and Connacht, only the second time in history Edinburgh had made it to the knockout stages. Few foresaw it, but all of Scottish rugby appeared to jump on the Edinburgh bandwagon ahead of the Murrayfield clash. And a packed stadium wasn't disappointed when Mike Blair scored in the opening minutes, Greig Laidlaw converting.

However, Lionel Beauxis kicked three penalties in addition to a Timoci Matanavou try to put the French visitors 14–7 up at the break. Laidlaw, though, replied with three penalties of his own, plus a dropped goal to send the 37,881 crowd – then, a Scottish club record – home delighted.

Edinburgh's sortie came to an end, squeezed out 22–19 by Ulster at Dublin's Aviva Stadium, Ruan Pienaar the match winner for the Irish province. And so the European adventure was over for Edinburgh. Just seven years to wait until the next time.

"New boy" Grant Gilchrist tells his tale of when European quarter-finals were the norm:

"There were a few of us came through that year into the first team: me, Dents [Dave Denton], Matty [Matt Scott] hadn't been in the team long, even Stuart McInally. It was our first real year of playing regularly, and to begin with I was just delighted to be playing.

"We did get the feeling, because of what was being said and the interest around the club, that this was pretty special. But

PART V – 2010s

when you're young, it's difficult not to get caught up in it all.

"I remember during that run, guys like Chunk [Allan Jacobsen] trying to keep us grounded, telling us he'd been at the club more than ten years and that it was only the second time he'd been given a chance to play at that stage in the European Cup, so basically, this wasn't normal. I should have listened.

"Playing for Edinburgh was a goal of mine from a very young age. I was good mates with Stuart Edwards and his dad Henry was the forwards coach at that time. We'd come through and watch Edinburgh when they were at Myreside, and then Meadowbank, genuine supporters, so most Friday nights were spent watching Edinburgh. Playing for them, that was my ambition.

"That season we struggled for any kind of form in the League, but in Europe it was one of those magical cup runs as people call it. We saved all our best rugby for the Heineken Cup. That wasn't intentional, that was just the way it happened.

"I was still actually in the Academy when I played my first Heineken Cup game down at London Irish, which we won 20–19, but the Irish full-back [Tom Homer] had a kick in the last minute to win it and missed.

"We did have a rub of the green; there was that crazy group game against Racing [Metro], which finished with us winning it 48–47, that was a basketball score! We were something like 14 points up at one stage, then 24 points down, then Tim Visser scored our sixth try, which Greig [Laidlaw] converted to put us a point in front, and even then, Juan Martín Hernández had the chance to win it in the last second with a drop goal from the 22, and missed it. Mad.

"The game against Toulouse was really special. We went from playing in front of six or seven thousand, and for the quarter-final, nearly 38,000 turned up. You wondered where they'd been the rest of the time. It just showed how important it was, not just to Edinburgh, but there was a real support from all over Scotland.

"The Toulouse game was by far the biggest game I'd ever been involved in up until that point, and to beat the team which two years earlier had won the tournament was incredible.

"The stadium wasn't full, but it felt like it and the atmosphere was amazing. It was one of those games where you can remember the noise; it wouldn't have been as loud, but the game against the All Blacks a couple of years ago, when Stuart Hogg was tackled in the last few seconds, I remember being at the bottom of the ruck and just listening to the noise. I thought he must have scored. Those kind of moments stay with you for ever.

"The semi-final wasn't so great. But in 2012, and just 21 years old, it was easy to think, *This is all right, this is just the norm*. You soon learn differently, as we found out against Munster in 2018, a game we should have won. Again, it makes you realise those days are special..."

81

ANSBRO AND STROKOSCH SPILL BLOOD FOR THE CAUSE

5 June 2012 • Summer Tour/Hopetoun Cup, Newcastle
Australia 6–Scotland 9

Scotland's single Test in Australia in the summer of 2012 looked like the Scots had packed up their own weather and flown it out to Oz.

The game in Newcastle was played in dreadful conditions – wind, driving rain and a sodden pitch. It was virtually a home from home. Unsurprisingly, Scotland made full use of nature.

It was always unlikely there would be much rugby played in such poor conditions, and both sides were entirely inadequate when it came to ball retention and holding on to passes. That meant any penalty offerings would be well received.

By the half-hour, Greig Laidlaw – operating at stand-off for this one – had scored two penalty goals (having missed his first), although that advantage was reduced by Mike Harris, who then, two minutes into the second half, had tied the game 6–6.

It wasn't that there was inactivity for the next 40 minutes. But the endeavours of both sides just weren't being rewarded, as trying to establish a base in which to play from was almost impossible.

With around ten minutes remaining, Harris tried a pot at goal from a few metres inside the Scotland half, but his kick barely got bar high and dropped short.

But in stoppage time, and despite Scotland having carried for just 98 yards during the game, an opportunity offered itself to Laidlaw. From a Scotland scrum put-in on the 22, Aussie loose head James Slipper folded under the pressure applied by Euan Murray, referee Jaco Peyper blowing for the infringement.

With the clock well into the red, Laidlaw calmly kicked the winning points, and Mr Peyper sounded for full time. Scotland celebrations were immediate, but as the bodies piled in on top of match winner Laidlaw, flanker Alasdair Strokosch and Joe Ansbro ran from different sides of the growing mountain of bodies and, in mid-air, clashed heads in a sickening collision.

Alasdair (6'3" and 17 stone on the hoof) rocked back, while Joe, giving away two stones to his sparring partner, landed on his back but was still smiling as he picked himself up. Ansbro, though, was unaware of the damage done, and only when Nick De Luca pointed out the blood running down his face did Ansbro realise he had a large gash around his left eye.

Strokosch, meanwhile, had a gaping wound on his forehead which required four stitches to patch up the damage, while Joe "had a few more" on his eye.

Well, if you can't be a headbanger when you win...

82

TONGA SHOCKER AT PITTODRIE ENDS ROBINSON'S TENURE

24 November 2012 • Autumn Test, Aberdeen
Scotland 15–Tonga 21

Not all memories are happy memories, no. 10.

As a nation, Scotland's footballers have had a long and successful history of making minnows appear like sharks, failing against some of the lesser nations. During the autumn Test matches in 2012, it appeared as if their rugby-playing counterparts has succumbed to the same affliction.

Having been well beaten by New Zealand and defeated again by South Africa, Scotland went for a change of scenery for their last game of the year against Tonga, Aberdeen's Pittodrie Stadium the temporary home venue.

The location may have changed but Scotland's abysmal form continued as the islanders scored a 21–15 victory, their first-ever against us, with only the boot of Greig Laidlaw maintaining respectability as the Tongans outscored the Scots two tries to nil.

Put in context, Tonga's population was just over 100,000 – half that of host city Aberdeen. It was a painful result for the Scots and coach Andy Robinson.

"I'm very angry – there will be consequences because of this performance. It reflects on me," he said. "I've got to look at myself, as has everybody involved."

Next day, Robinson quit.

83

HOGGY AND *THAT* PIC

2013

Scotland's input into Lions tours have, in recent times at least, been somewhat limited. In 2013 Andy Irvine, one of Scotland's greatest tourists, was manager of the British & Irish Lions during their tour to Australia. However, while Warriors prop Ryan Grant would join them later as a replacement for Gethin Jenkins, only three Scots made Warren Gatland's original squad – namely lock Richie Gray, winger Sean Maitland and Stuart Hogg, the Glasgow full-back who, like Maitland, could also guise as a utility back.

Hogg was only 20, the youngest member of the party, and therefore had a position of responsibility from the off – to look after "Bil", the Lions mascot. Despite complaining that he was allergic to the stuffed toy (Hogg believed it made him sneeze and his eyes water, although his hay fever may have been a contributing factor), he was dutiful and diligent in acting as Bil's companion and bodyguard, staving off would-be kidnap attempts from teammates.

Those duties aside, Hogg – like Gray and Maitland – played in five of the ten tour matches. Maitland and Grant made the bench for the first and second Tests respectively, but only Gray

PART V – 2010s

made it on to the pitch as a substitute during the third and Test-series-clinching victory in Sydney. All minor details when it came to celebrating the Lions success Down Under.

Which went some of the way towards explaining why, on the morning after the night before, Hogg – who hadn't played a competitive match in the ten days prior to the deciding rubber – emerged in downtown Sydney wearing only a pair of red Speedos.

Hogg's "budgie smuggler" moment was captured by television cameras, although he seemed unperplexed by their attentions as he sauntered out of the team hotel, beer in hand. You can take the boy out of Hawick ...

84

IBROX MAKES THE PERFECT STAGE FOR SEVENS

26/27 July 2014 • Commonwealth Games, Glasgow

You could never have the home of rugby Sevens not having the sport they gave to the world when it came time for that nation to play host to the Commonwealth Games.

Scotland was always going to have the rugby Sevens tournament at Glasgow 2014 as one of the main events, and the organisers knew it would be popular with spectators and broadcasters alike. It therefore needed a venue of status to house the tournament, and where better than Ibrox Stadium, home of Rangers?

The Glasgow Subway was packed, and the surrounds to Ibrox transformed to welcome the hordes who would watch the rugby – and there would be many. Over the four sessions of play that first weekend of the Games, a total of 171,000 fans – a record for the sport at any Games – watched an enthralling event unfold.

Hosts Scotland made it out of their qualifying pool, beating Canada and Barbados but losing narrowly, by 17–14, to favourites New Zealand. That took the Scots through to the last eight, where they were unable to live with a formidable South African squad.

PART V – 2010s

England, beaten by Australia in their group game, suffered a 15–14 loss to Samoa, while Wales, who qualified for the quarter-finals behind the Samoans, also went out in the tightest of contests, losing 21–19 to Australia.

The Anzac semi-final clash saw the Kiwis win 19–7, while South Africa showed their intent with an emphatic 35–7 victory against Samoa, and in an absorbing final, the South Africans maintained their impressive form to take gold with a 17–12 win against New Zealand.

Scotland Sevens star Scott Wight recalls being centre stage at Scotland's biggest ever sporting event: "The whole Sevens tournament was pretty central to the whole Games, and so were we.

"The good thing was that they split the two days into four sections, which meant you had a morning and an afternoon session, so the crowd were always fresh. Some would have doubled over and taken in two sessions, but it meant that the folk weren't getting bored so the enthusiasm from the crowd never dipped, with a new energy for each session, and that really spread on to the pitch.

"With Ibrox being built for massive football crowds, the spectators being so close to the pitch was brilliant. Even teams like Sri Lanka, Uganda, the Cook Islands, who were there to make up numbers, if we're honest – the crowd got right behind the underdogs most of the time, which was just brilliant and must have been wonderful for those playing.

"I've played all over the world, at every major venue and tournament, and the atmosphere at Ibrox was one of the best I'd ever experienced.

"The Sevens boys were all part of a much bigger Team Scotland, and rugby was an important part of the entire event. It was brought home to me when Lee Jones, Sean Lamont and myself were all asked to model the official Scotland team outfits – shirts and kilts – that we'd wear at the opening ceremony.

"I've still got the kilt. It's been on to a couple of weddings and got folk talking. The shirt? If we ever have a Sevens tournament in Hawaii, that's what I'm wearing to travel in.

"But it was great, training out at Stirling University, staying in the athletes' village and taking part in the opening ceremony, which for anyone from any sport was just a special night.

"There was always an expectation when you pulled on the jersey to represent your country, but you really felt you were part of a much bigger team, playing for all of the people in Scotland, not just those with an interest in rugby.

"We were a wee bit disappointed. We ran New Zealand close, and there was no shame in losing to the eventual winners in South Africa. There was a feeling within the team that perhaps we could have done a bit better, but I don't think anyone at Ibrox noticed too much – they were just having such a great time."

85

WARRIORS ARE GRAND IN PRO12 FINAL

30 May 2015 • PRO12 Grand Final, Belfast
Glasgow Warriors 31–Munster 13

Having been knocking on the door over the previous couple of seasons, Glasgow Warriors made a spectacular entrance in to the winner's hall of fame when they produced a scintillating and clinical display in Belfast as they beat Munster 31–13 to take the 2015 PRO12 Grand Final. It also gave Scottish rugby (well, maybe not so much in Edinburgh), something to celebrate after what had been a dire year in terms of international results up to that point.

Having only just made it through their semi-final, Warriors were on top form as early as the eighth minute when man of the match, Leone Nakarawa, broke the Leinster defensive line to send Ron Harley in for the score.

DTH van der Merwe, scorer of the crucial try six minutes from time against Ulster in the semis, was then put in on the corner by the unstoppable Nakarawa. Stuart Hogg created the third try, showing real speed to break between David Kilcoyne and full-back Felix Jones to create the space, then slipping a pass inside to Henry Pyrgos to run in unchallenged. An Andrew Smith solo effort for Leinster gave them hope, but that was blown away as, on the hour, Pyrgos pivoted to find Finn Russell, who sliced his way through the Leinster cover for the touchdown, before kicking his fourth successful conversion.

Duncan Weir, with a late penalty, applied the finishing touches and it was job done for the Warriors, a fitting send off for one of the ultimate Warriors, Glasgow captain Al Kellock.

Winning captain Al Kellock on his last act before kicking off the boots and putting on the slippers...

"It was between us and Munster who was going to top the table and get top seeding.

"We had some pretty decent tussles with them that season and over the years. We'd beaten Munster in the semi-finals the previous season to reach the PRO12 final at the RDS against Leinster, and the year before that, we put 50 points on them during the league games. In 2015, we knew that at some stage, if we had any ambition of winning the tournament, we would play them in one of the knockout games.

"When I first started, Munster were the winning team in Europe and we would come out on the wrong end a few times. It was special then that we would get to play them in a final, because of that history. It wasn't a strong rivalry as such, but we had come from a place where we had struggled to beat them to now holding our own with them, and beating them. We also appeared to have some epic games against them at different times, beating them 16–15 in the 2014 semi-final being an example.

"In 2015, there was nothing between us, them and Ospreys. Ospreys had finished on 74, ourselves and Munster tied on 75, but we won the tiebreak on matches won.

"That gave us a semi-final against Ulster, a tight match which we somehow squeezed a win from. The conversion, from right on the touchline, that was the making of Finn that night,

PART V – 2010s

showing everyone that he had plenty of nerve and what it took in the big games.

"We were delighted, Ulster less so. It had been a massive game for both teams, but talking to Rory Best after it, Ulster had been desperate to win it. In denying them a place in the final, we had taken away their chance to play the PRO12 final at the Kingspan Stadium in Belfast, their home ground.

"We were into another final, but already we were thinking about the previous year when we got to the final, and were beaten by Leinster. We thought we had made it and forgot there was a final to win and were well beaten 34–12.

"You learn from winning and losing semis and finals. We got carried away with the occasion and possibly tried to do too much during the week leading up to the 2014 final. For meeting Munster, we just concentrated on the game, what it would take to play well and beat them.

"That had been our attitude all season. We carried our form through the important times. We had learned how to peak around the big games, and we had also learned to spread the workload around, something the Irish provinces had been extremely astute at doing for years, either domestically or in Europe.

"What was important that night in Belfast was, that while there was the 23 who were selected and would beat Munster, handsomely – I mean, four tries to one didn't flatter us – all the guys who had played throughout that season, and we had used 52 players to win the league, were there as well because they'd played a part in getting us there.

"We just clicked in the Final, everything clicked, everything worked. We came out the blocks flying and were 21–3 up at one stage. We did things well. That's what you need to do to win any rugby match, but we were consistently good in all areas. For 80 minutes we were on top form.

"I started on the bench. I had been concussed during the semi-final, and couldn't do any training until the Thursday before the final. Gregor [Townsend] pulled me in and said he was going to start with Leone [Nakarawa] and Jonny [Gray]. I totally got that. I thought the year before was the last chance I'd get to play in a final, so even getting on for the last 15 minutes was brilliant, and especially where the game was at the stage, which was virtually won.

"Not starting took nothing away from the moment. As I say, making the 23 out of 52 was the big thing for me. And no way did I think I wasn't getting on. When my time came, I just had to do my job. It wasn't about me, or Dougie Hall, or any of the other boys that were playing for the last time. It was about us winning. We weren't chasing the game, we were just running the time down.

"I was quite involved for all the time I was on, but I knew we'd done it when Nigel Owens looked at me, and gave me a wee nod just before he blew the whistle. And what a feeling.

"I was very, very fortunate that my last act as a professional player was lifting that trophy up.

"Ironically, of course, Warriors again went for the PRO14 title this year, against Irish opposition, and, again with Nigel Owens as the referee. But, it wasn't to be at Celtic Park. Hopefully they can put that loss behind them and come again, just as we did a few years back . . ."

86

SCOTS DENIED WORLD CUP SEMI-FINAL THROUGH REFEREE ERROR

18 October 2015 • World Cup, Twickenham
Australia 35–Scotland 34

Not all memories are happy memories, no. 1.

Scotland have only ever contested one World Cup semi-final, back in 1991. However, with only seconds remaining against Australia at Twickenham in their 2015 quarter-final tie, the Scots led 34–32 and had played superbly well to earn that lead, including three tries from Pete Horne, Tommy Seymour and Mark Bennett, with Greig Laidlaw kicking the rest.

Then off a Scottish line-out, referee Craig Joubert awarded a penalty to Australia for the Scots being offside, penalising prop Jon Welsh, who had played the ball following a knock-on by a teammate – except the ball actually came off Australia's Nick Phipps, making Welsh onside.

Joubert had got it wrong. Brendan Foley landed the kick and the Scots were out.

However, while most would have accepted Joubert's mistake as being a genuine one – and even that the incident fell outside what the TMO protocol allowed in terms of reference – Joubert's antics on the final whistle, when he ran off the pitch, only heightened the levels of criticism aimed at the South African.

World Rugby later conceded Joubert's decision had been wrong and that they would be looking to change how the TMO could be referenced in the future.

News that made everyone in Scotland feel so much better...

87

JADE BECOMES A TRAILBLAZER

2016

Being the first in anything can mean experiencing fame, perhaps even notoriety, or becoming the benchmark from which others will be gauged. The one thing that cannot be challenged or measured is the fact that you were the first, a title Jade Konkel will own for evermore after becoming Scottish Rugby's first full-time female player in the BT Sport Scottish Rugby Academy in summer 2016.

Having started out with Inverness Craig Dunain rugby club, as did her parents and brothers, she progressed through Hillhead Jordanhill and into the Academy set-up, by which time she was already three years into her international career with Scotland, after making her debut against England as a replacement in the opening 2013 Six Nations match.

Konkel, who previously also played basketball for Highland Bears, joined top female French club Lille Métropole Rugby Club Villeneuvois in 2017 and latterly played for English Premier 15s side Harlequins.

88

SEVENS SUCCESS FOR SCOTS DUO IN RIO

6/11 August 2016 • XXXI Olympics, Rio

Eric Liddell won gold (and bronze) at the 1924 Olympics, his feat in the 400 metres made famous in the film *Chariots of Fire*. But Liddell was better known in some parts as an international try-scoring winger for Scotland. Somewhat ironically, 1924 was the last year 15-a-side rugby was played at the Games, the USA taking gold. However, rugby – this time in Sevens format – would return to the greatest show on earth again in 2016, enabling two Scots rugby stars to emulate Liddell with Team GB.

Eight Englishmen, two from Wales, and Scots Mark Bennett and Mark Robertson – the latter from Melrose, the home of the Sevens game – made up the Team GB squad that progressed through to the last eight after topping a group that included New Zealand, Japan and Kenya.

In a tight quarter-final tie against Argentina, Britain made it through with a single score after extra time, then defeated South Africa 7–5 in an equally intense semi-final.

However, in the final, Team GB were no match for the might of Sevens specialists Fiji, who romped home 43–7.

PART V – 2010s

Nevertheless, the great adventure to Rio for Burnett and Robertson resulted in them winning silver medals.

Mark Robertson on travelling halfway around the globe, just to excel in a game his home town gave to the world: "Where I came from, and given that my dad [Keith] played it, I was almost born into Sevens rugby. Coming from Melrose, all I wanted to do when I was growing up was someday play in the Melrose Sevens. As it happened, I played in the final of the Melrose Sevens 30 years to the day that my dad won the final with Melrose. We were 24–0 up at one stage against Stellenbosch, the holders – I had scored two tries – and they came back to win 38–24. But genuinely, playing in that final was the best rugby memory I ever had.

"Once you go away and go into the pro game, while I enjoyed playing Sevens at the end of the season, it wasn't a big priority. It wasn't seen as the top level of the sport; you're trying to aspire to playing national XVs and stuff. But then I got injured and was out for two and a half years, and the only avenue open to me was the Sevens. I always thought I'd go back to the 15-a-side game, but then aged 30, Glasgow were offering me a contract, but I also knew the Olympics was 14 months down the line. At that stage, I'd invested so much into the Sevens, it was a no-brainer for me.

"I always wanted to do something that was different from everyone else. Maybe that had something to do with being a wee bit delusional, being around so many unbelievable players, guys like Chick [Craig Chalmers] and my old man, with everything he achieved. Rightly or wrongly, I grew up thinking I would do something pretty special and different. You need to have that belief, I suppose. Then I realised I was 30 and had achieved nothing. That made me desperate to do something before I really did get too old.

"The whole experience of going to the Olympics was amazing, as amazing as playing rugby at the Olympics. When I started it wasn't even an option. But there we were, with Team GB, out the rugby bubble and all in a big tower block together.

"We were listening to people saying we'd all be one big team, and you were a bit sceptical – but there it was, one big team.

"I'm not the sort to speak to superstars, but Bennett and me were playing the 'snaps' game, and Andy Murray wanted to know how to play it. Next thing, we were in Andy's room explaining the game to him, then sat up for about three hours playing with him, his brother Jamie, all the other British tennis players, playing the name game and realising that he's actually just a normal bloke who liked a good laugh.

"We would play table tennis with other athletes; it was all really good. Then we went to the rugby, and we were so relaxed because we'd been enjoying ourselves.

"The matches themselves, we only had about 10,000 watching us, compared to 40,000 in Hong Kong or 80,000 at Twickenham.

"Coming away with a medal was pretty cool. We thought we had a chance in the final against Fiji; they'd only just edged the quarter-final against New Zealand, who we'd beaten in the pool. If they clicked, you'd be in bother, and they clicked – 29–0 down before we knew it. Silver it was.

"On the pitch, it was all a bit of an anti-climax. I was only getting five or six minutes and wasn't able to make the impact I wanted to make. I was going to retire after the Olympics, but the disappointment of not really getting the game time I'd wanted, or make the impact I'd wanted to make, spurred me on to continue playing.

"I played that last season setting real targets, in terms of what I wanted to achieve and what I wanted to win, so to bow out by making the dream team in the last two tournaments – Scott

PART V - 2010s

Wight also made the team – and beating England to win the Twickenham Sevens, and winning the Player of the Final, and doing it all in a Scotland shirt meant all the things I dreamt about doing, I'd finally done. I could retire content with what I'd achieved, rather than feel as if I'd underachieved.

"The funny thing was that when me and Wighty were sliding about on his grass at the farm, we were picturing ourselves scoring winning tries against England. That's what we ended up doing. As youngsters, though, the main ambition was to play at the Melrose Sevens. Rio was just a bonus."

89

THE TRANSFORMATION IS COMPLETE

21 January 2017 • European Champions Cup, Leicester
Leicester Tigers 0–Glasgow Warriors 43

This victory in itself was historic; in beating the former European Cup winners, Warriors had reached the knockout stages of the Champions Cup for the first time.

The back story to that fact was, in itself, as incredible as Glasgow's six-try mauling of the Tigers; at Welford Road, Leicester were unbeaten against Scottish opposition in five matches in this tournament, the winning margin averaging out at 30-plus points a go. Indeed, in a decade, Tigers had lost only once at home prior to this result, dealt by a team that had won just one of 17 previous trips beyond Hadrian's Wall.

Glasgow's tries came from Tommy Seymour, Mark Bennett, Jonny Gray, Ryan Wilson and Tim Swinson, and a first-half penalty try, while Finn Russell kicked five conversions and a penalty. They led 31–0 by half-time and never relented over the second 40 minutes. Unsurprisingly, it was the Tigers worst-ever loss in the competition.

Warriors coach Gregor Townsend called it a "seminal weekend" for Scottish rugby, and with good reason. Twenty

PART V – 2010s

years earlier, in a quarter-final play-off tie, Glasgow had been annihilated 90–19 by the Tigers at Welford Road, running in 14 tries, with World Cup-winning South African fly-half Joel Stransky accumulating a personal haul of 35 points from three tries and ten conversions.

Fast-forward two decades, and the nightmare of that afternoon in November 1997 was well and truly eradicated by this stunning Warriors win. Unfortunately, the last eight was as far as Warriors travelled, beaten by Saracens 38–13. Where have we heard that tale before?

90

HOGG DOUBLE HAS IRISH IN A STU

4 February 2017 • Six Nations, Murrayfield
Scotland 27–Ireland 22

Stuart Hogg was the 2016 Six Nations Player of the Tournament. Within 20 minutes of the 2017 season kicking-off, the Glasgow Warriors full-back has shown exactly why he was just so highly rated.

After eight minutes of the opening tie against Ireland, Hogg had his first score on the board, as Scotland made their early pressure count. From a ruck virtually on the green line, Laidlaw whipped a pass out to Russell who didn't hesitate in trying to make Scotland numerical advantage out wide count.

The Scotland stand-off through a long ball for Hogg, wide on the right, and when Garry Ringrose missed his attempted interception, Hogg was left with an easy run in for the opening try in the Championship. It wouldn't take long for hogg to show his finishing prowess for a second time.

Midway through the half, Scotland were on the attack once more, Laidlaw linking to Russell drifting left, missing Alex Dunbar – who would completely outfox the Irish with a cunning lineout move later in the half – to seek out Huw Jones who found Hogg outside him.

With support on either side, Hogg's immediate injection of pace had the Irish turned and Rob Kearney faced with a two-on-one, Hogg running at him, Sean Maitland running the touchline. A sideways glance from Hogg was enough for Kearney to buy the dummy and target the winger, allowing Hogg to dive in for another try.

At that point, Hogg had his name on every try scored in the 2017 Six Nations. He would end the season, one of eight players tied on three tries, but his overall contribution to Scotland, and, in terms of being an entertainer, would see him retain his "Player of the Championship" crown for a second season . . .

91

WATSON WALLOPS WALLABIES

17 June 2017 • Summer Tour/Hopetoun Cup, Sydney
Australia 19–Scotland 24

When Vern Cotter moved on after the 2017 Six Nations, Glasgow Warriors coach Gregor Townsend had already been lined up to take over a year in advance of the Kiwi's departure. And with a three-match summer tour to the Far East already in place, neither fans nor players had to wait too long to see Townsend put his stamp on the national team.

If the first leg was staged in unaccustomed surroundings, there was nothing unfamiliar about the opposition as Singapore provided the backdrop, as the rivalry with Italy – ironically the last side Cotter faced as coach – recommenced for Townsend's first game at the helm.

Tries from Ali Price, Tim Visser, a brace from hooker Ross Ford and a fifth and final score from Damien Hoyland saw the Scots to a comfortable 34–13 success. A week later, Australia awaited the Scots at the Allianz Stadium.

Scotland, who had won their previous Test Down Under, started well when Greig Tonks kicked an early penalty, and advantage built up after quarter of an hour when Tatafu Polota-Nau failed to secure Will Genia's erratic pass, kindly

PART V – 2010s

popping the ball up for the scavenging Duncan Taylor to pick it off and give the Saracens centre the easiest try behind the posts.

Aussie full-back Israel Folau replied with a try, bursting on to Bernard Foley's long pass to score. Foley converted, then exited for ten minutes when he took out opposite number Finn Russell with a late shoulder.

With Foley removed as first-up kicker, Australia had to rejig in defence. From a five-metre scrum, no. 8 Scott Higginbotham fed the wide-standing Genia to clear, but his fraction of a delay enabled Russell to close and make the charge down, the ball dropping into the welcoming hands of the Warriors fly-half, who had the presence of mind to run along the in-goal line to make his second conversion as easy as the first.

However, Folau scored his second try before the interval, soaring above Tonks to gather Foley's pinpoint cross kick. Scotland were still up 17–12 but fell behind for the only time when, after concerted pressure from the home team, Genia put his previous aberrations behind him, diving in from just a few feet shy of the line, Foley making it 19–17. This was the first time Scotland had trailed on tour.

However, they responded superbly with what – during Townsend's tenure – would become almost a trademark try.

After half a dozen phases, scrum-half Ali Price went to Russell, who feigned a behind-the-back pass to Ben Toolis, then used Willem Nel's decoy run to shield a pass to Taylor, who, unable to use the slightly advanced Hamish Watson, brought fellow centre Alex Dunbar into play.

Dunbar pulled one defender, then passed to Tonks, who proved such an attraction that replacement Reece Hodge and winger Dane Haylett-Petty tried to tackle him simultaneously. A supporting Tommy Seymour collected, hurdling the human barrier created by that trio to continue the move through Taylor, who passed before Folau arrived to the slightly withdrawn Watson for the try which Russell converted.

With the clock in red, Australia mounted one final charge at the Scotland line, Watson producing an old-school tackle to halt the thundering Tevita Kuridrani's progress, then as Wallabies skipper Michael Hooper drove on, referee Wayne Barnes sounded the loudest whistle blast of the day to signal a penalty to Scotland as the Aussies piled into the ruck. Scotland had completed a memorable win.

A much-changed Scotland side lost the final game of the tour in Suva, going down 27–22 to Fiji. But as Meatloaf might have once said, "Two out of three ain't bad."

Sydney try hero Hamish Watson says:

"It was a team try more than an individual moment of genius; just the right place at the right time.

"The move had bypassed me in the midfield – maybe they didn't trust me at that stage. I joined in support, and the ball came to me with not far to go, and I just got in on the end of it. I took the plaudits and the credit, but there were so many involved with a lot of link-up play between forwards and backs to bring about the score. It was, I suppose, what would be described now as being a typically Scottish score.

"It was a great team move, with great hands and really worked at pace, and a big score for the team, and for Scottish rugby, and for Gregor. That was his first summer with us and that game, and that try, showed the direction he wanted to take the team in and the way he wanted us to be playing the game.

"Scotland had previously won in Australia back in 2012, in a different way, 9–6 that day when it was freezing cold and wet and the most famous thing about that game probably wasn't Greig Laidlaw's last-minute penalty to win, but Alasdair Strokosch

PART V – 2010s

headbutting Joe Ansbro during the full-time celebrations.

"We still celebrated – safely though – because it was a big deal winning that one in Sydney. It immediately stamped Gregor's style on the team, his very direct approach that we'd seen during his time at Glasgow, and showed the supporters the ambition we had to play in a very positive fashion.

"You can't take a win over the home nation in Australia for granted, and that was a great win, but, more importantly, since then we've had bigger and better victories and even better performances. We've been going in the right direction ever since.

"We had led, only for Australia to come back at us. But we had played well to score a couple of tries and didn't feel like it was a game we would lose. It was just about taking the next chance we got."

92

DRIVEN FORD BECOMES SCOTLAND'S MOST CAPPED PLAYER

24 June 2017 • Summer Tour, Suva
Fiji 27–Scotland 22

From winning his first senior cap for Scotland as a replacement during the opening match of the 2004 autumn Tests against Australia at Murrayfield, until overtaking the record previously held by Chris Paterson since 2011 when making his 110th appearance against Fiji in the third Test of the 2017 summer tour, Ross Ford gave tremendous service to his country.

Along the way, in arriving at that total, the man who was first capped while with Border Reivers enjoyed several notable landmark occasions along the way – when he was called in as a replacement on the Lions tour of South Africa in 2009; becoming Kelso's most capped player surpassing the previous best set by John Jeffrey; and when his 76th cap saw him move ahead of Gordon Bulloch as Scotland's most capped hooker.

In addition, he took part in three Rugby World Cups and, on his last tour with the national side, played against Italy (scoring two tries), Australia and Fiji, scoring on the day he completed his record-breaking cap haul.

A great servant to Edinburgh and Scotland.

93

DODDIE WEIR'S BIG ENTRY

18 November 2017 • Autumn Test, Murrayfield
Scotland 17–New Zealand 22

During the summer of 2017, an awareness campaign for motor neuron disease was given added significance with the news that former Scotland and Lions star Doddie Weir had been diagnosed with the as-yet-incurable condition. It was news which shocked all of rugby, but especially in Scotland.

The passing of rugby legend Joost van der Westhuizen in January that year rocked the rugby community. However, word of Weir's diagnosis was felt even more acutely. Weir is a guy who played the game hard, partied harder and who only knew friendship within the game, whether that was from teammates, rivals, or rugby supporters across the country – and, indeed, the world.

That would soon be evidenced in New Zealand where Weir and his family were travelling to as the announcement was made, off to see the British & Irish Lions in their Test series against the All Blacks.

That holiday, however, was soon over, and Weir returned to a country still shocked by the news but determined to do its part to help Doddie and his family over the coming years. After the launch of his Trust and Foundation in August, momentum grew around events and activities to best assist Doddie in his fundraising and mark his achievements as a player who had won 61 international caps with Scotland, dating back to 1990 – his first against Argentina.

The Scottish Rugby Union were quick to align themselves with everything Doddie now sought to achieve and announced that the autumn Test against the New Zealand All Blacks would be their platform to show their support for Weir and give the supporters of the international side an opportunity to show their appreciation of the great man.

Having visited and talked to the Scotland team in the days leading up to the game, Weir now took centre stage as kick-off approached, resplendent in one of his now-legendary tartan suits, accompanied by his three sons, Hamish, Angus and Ben.

The lights were turned down around the stadium, leaving oor Doddie to wander on to the pitch, surrounded by a wall of mobile-phone lights and camera flashes, making an already heartfelt moment even more poignant. As he walked to the middle with the match ball, Doddie's image was played out on the big screens around the ground, the feelings etched on his face mirrored by tens of thousands in the shadows.

Doddie greeted the captains – Kieran Read of New Zealand and Scotland's John Barclay – and match referee Matt Carley, then handed the ball to All Blacks stand-off Beauden Barrett for the kick-off before making his way back to the touchline with a defiant punch of the chest on the way.

When the emotions had subsided, Scotland took an early lead through Finn Russell, but Barrett tied the scores in a tight first half. Scotland, however, had failed to turn pressure to points. Within four minutes of the second period kicking off, hooker

PART V – 2010s

Codie Taylor and the Kiwis took advantage of Scotland's depleted backline – Alex Dunbar was injured – to score out wide, while Damian McKenzie chased on to a prodded kick from Barrett, who then converted, to leave New Zealand 15–3 to the good.

When Sam Cane was sin-binned, Scotland made it count with Jonny Gray scoring a try, converted by Russell, only for the 14-man All Blacks to hit back, Barrett converting his own try to make it 22–10.

Scotland were not done, and with three minutes remaining, Stuart Hogg's kick sat up for Tommy Seymour, who put the ball back inside for Huw Jones to accelerate in for the try. Russell narrowed the deficit to five points. With seconds remaining, Hogg showed a trademark burst through the Kiwi defence, only for the ball to go agonisingly forward when tackled by Barrett. And that was that.

Scotland's 112-year jinx remained intact, a day when hearts were left broken, and not just because of the rugby.

Doddie Weir looks back on an emotional afternoon:

"It was a great gesture from the Scottish Rugby Union to allow me to make my walk on to the pitch. More famous – and it pains me to say – better players had never been given that accolade, so it was special for those reasons alone.

"I know everything I do might look unrehearsed and off the cuff, but we did go through what would be involved before the kick-off on the Saturday evening. I'd collect the ball then walk to the five-metre line with Hamish, Angus and Ben, where they would stop. I always knew that part could get emotional. There was something symbolic about that because that was how things would pan out one day. But I was determined to stay strong, particularly in front of all those cameras and supporters.

"And I was fine, looking forward to it even – then I got a tap on the shoulder. It was Scotland coach Gregor Townsend, who'd left his team in the dressing room to come out and wish me all the best. He gave me a big hug. I cannae remember what he said, but I couldn't say much. That gesture really got me – that ahead of such a massive game, he could make time for me.

"Then it was our cue to walk on to the pitch. The boys reached their mark. I tried to say, 'I'll see you in a minute, boys,' but the noise was just incredible and, having convinced myself everything would be just fine, it suddenly wasn't. Not even a couple of deep breaths could help.

"Kieran Read, the All Blacks captain and the referee were smashing; John Barclay was just special. He's that kind of man. Then the niceties were over. 'Can I have the ball please, mate, so I can kick off?' Beauden Barrett had work to be doing. Just as it should be."

94

SCOTS WALTZ PAST ILL-DISCIPLINED AUSSIES

25 November 2017 • Autumn Tour/Hopetoun Cup, Murrayfield
Scotland 53–Australia 24

In every era, every generation, there will be maybe one, perhaps two matches that will be referenced as a day where a team came close to, or perhaps even touched, excellence.

Scotland hit those heights in Paris in 1995, once more in 1999, maybe in Cardiff in 1982 and again a couple of years later in Dublin when scooping the Triple Crown. As for the 1970s, and ignoring any obvious bias, Scotland managed such performance levels just a couple of times against England, although nothing compared to 1986.

That said, there have been some games of late where Scotland have produced displays that would rate alongside the very best from any decade and none more so than their 2017 destruction of Australia.

With only a Finn Russell penalty to show for early pressure, Scotland's eight-try rout began with a try from Byron McGuigan, the Sale Sharks wing earning just his second cap after Stuart Hogg had called off after the warm-up, who hacked on when Australia's handling let them down. He tried to control the ball but ended up dribbling around the last man in gold, Reece Hodge, to score.

A Brendan Foley chip put Tevita Kuridrani in for a try, the fly-half repeating the ploy after Tommy Seymour dropped the ball, chasing it down and flipping it up for Kuridrani to score and give the visitors a 12–10 advantage just three minutes from half-time.

However, there was long enough left for the major incident in the game to unfold. Hamish Watson was set to perform another piece of "jackling" when prop Sekope Kepu launched his shoulder at Watson's head and was immediately sent off by referee Pascal Gaüzère. And there was still long enough remaining for Scotland to convert their penalty line-out into a try and a half-time lead, Ali Price scrambling in off the driven maul.

Three minutes into the second half, Kurtley Beale scored off a short-range burst for the Aussie XIV to level at 17-all. However, from that point, Scotland upped their game against the depleted Wallabies.

After a series of errors, Sean Maitland, confronted only by locks Rob Simmons and Blake Enever, won a footrace from his own ten to score in the corner, Jonny Gray went over untouched, then Finn Russell took a quick tap instead of kicking for the corner some ten metres off the Australian try line, sending Huw Jones in to score, then McGuigan collected his second and it was 39–17.

Even then, Australia dug in and forced another try, their fourth, replacement lock Lopeti Timani crawling home, but six minutes from the end John Barclay bumped his way in for a score, before the dominant Scottish pack rolled a maul in for a Stuart McInally try.

Australia may have handicapped themselves with the red card, but that self-inflicted wound shouldn't detract from what was a magnificent record-breaking display in all departments by the Scots.

95

MAKE SPACE FOR THE CALCUTTA CUP

24 February 2018 • Six Nations, Murrayfield
Scotland 25–England 13

It wasn't just the win, it was the emphatic manner in which Scotland claimed the Calcutta Cup for the first time since 2008 that delighted many and left some aghast.

England's emphatic pasting of Italy in Rome was followed by a much narrower win against Wales. By contrast, Scotland had a disastrous start to their campaign, beaten 34–7 after a disjointed and lacklustre effort in Cardiff. They had, however, made amends by beating France in Edinburgh in the second round of matches, although as the 32–26 outcome would indicate, Scotland could score points and conceded them with equal ease.

It was a confident England that arrived at Murrayfield, although some of their positivity may have drained away after a coming together, pre-game, between England's star man Owen Farrell and Ryan Wilson, who, once proceedings began, was described as being as "abrasive as an angle grinder – without the safety guard".

Certainly, going behind after two minutes to a Greig Laidlaw penalty after Mako Vunipola clung to the ball on the deck may not have been what they envisaged, or going 10–3 behind after the Scots first try.

Stuart McInally popped the ball to Laidlaw, who worked an intricate scissors-dummy-miss-loop with referee Nigel Owens and Pete Horne before passing to Finn Russell. Faced with a flat England defensive line, the Scotland no. 10 pinged a bouncing grubber kick through behind the English centres, which, having applied a stab at the ball himself, sat up perfectly for Huw Jones to score beside the posts.

Farrell made it two from two with the boot, but that was as close as England would come over the remaining hour of hostilities.

On the half-hour, Scotland produced a try from nothing, Sean Maitland scoring, then three minutes before the interval, Jones made it a double. In centre field, just inside England territory, Laidlaw passed beyond runners Jonny Gray and Grant Gilchrist to Jones, who exploded between Nathan Hughes and Farrell and sprinted 50 yards for the line. And while Anthony Watson and Mike Brown got to the Warriors man, such was the centre's momentum that he carried them over the line as well to score. Laidlaw converted for a 22–6 half-time lead.

Minutes into the second half, Farrell converted his own try before Eddie Jones' side were left rueing their luck, not once but twice. Firstly, referee Owens brought play back for a Scots penalty only after Laidlaw had thrown an interception read by Danny Care, and that was followed by Farrell touching down after he and Watson had hacked on when Scotland skipper John Barclay appeared to spill the ball when smashed by Courtney Lawes. After a TMO review, however, Lawes was deemed to have punched the ball forwards in the tackle and a knock-on was called.

PART V – 2010s

Pivotal moments? You bet. It was left for Finn Russell to land what became the clinching kick for the Scots, Sam Underhill yellow carded for a no-arms shoulder charge on Jamie Bhatti. With no further scoring, the expectant crowd counted down the clock into the red, and Watson's knock-on sparked joyous celebrations from all the home contingent.

The Calcutta Cup was back in Scots hands. Now to defend it.

Nah, that never happens.

96

MAITLAND HITS ENGLAND WITH "TRY OF THE YEAR" CONTENDER

2018

It was one of those tries that looked good at the time and was gratefully received by the Scotland players and fans alike. But who threw that pass, and who made that run? And who sent that other pass out wide, and how close was Sean Maitland to going into touch?

It all happened so quickly that everyone needed a second or third or even a fourth look at Maitland's try just to appreciate fully what a great team score it was.

The play began on the left, between the Scots ten and 22 lines, Greig Laidlaw feeding to Jonny Gray, who quickly brought Finn Russell into play. The Scotland fly-half, with the English defence blitzing on their opposite numbers, threw an elevated pass over the onrushing white shirts, missing Pete Horne but connecting – only just – with Huw Jones, who accelerated between the furthest forward Jonathan Joseph and Jonny May.

Jones raced into the English 22, and although he was felled from behind by the recovering May, Tommy Seymour cleared out the ruck to allow Ryan Wilson to act as scrum-half. He

PART V – 2010s

found John Barclay, who held play up for Laidlaw to join in once again, spinning the ball left to Stuart McInally, who again made good ground, driving England further back.

Farrell made the tackle, but he was unceremoniously tossed aside by Hamish Watson to clear the ball once more for Laidlaw. Squeezed for space down the left, with four would-be England defenders to avoid, Laidlaw picked out Russell, who lobbed the ball over the advanced Watson for Maitland to dive home in the corner.

It was one of Scotland best-ever tries against England. Little wonder it was nominated for "Try of the Year" by World Rugby. It didn't win, but did that matter?

Try scorer Sean Maitland says:

"It was a great team try. I just caught the ball and ran over so maybe they should have nominated Finn [Russell] for that pass or Jonesy [Huw Jones] for the run.

"The try is up there. I scored on my debut against England, when we lost, so this one felt a lot sweeter. The build-up was unbelievable. Finn's miss pass for Huw Jones breaking through was fantastic and then for us to keep the ball alive was awesome.

"You practise these things at training, just hoping you get the chance to do that in a game situation. You could see by the reactions of everyone that it was a special try, though maybe not fully appreciated until you see it rerun.

"You can imagine the stick that was flying around when the try was short-listed and my name was on it!"

97

GEORGE IS HEAD-TURNER WITH CANADA HAT-TRICK

9 June 2018 • Summer Tour, Edmonton
Canada 10–Scotland 48

You wait ages for one hat-trick for the Scottish national team to come along, and then umpteen arrive all at once. What was more remarkable about George Turner's treble against Canada on the 2018 summer tour was that he'd only come on as a first-half replacement for Fraser Brown. We won't even mention the fact that he's a hooker.

Turner's first score in a 48–10 win came minutes into the second half, the tail-gunner on a driven line-out maul. His second score came from short range, crashing on to an Ali Price feed, while his third was a carbon copy of his opener.

Thus, Turner became the first to score a hat-trick of tries since Ally Hogg scored three against Romania in 2007.

A week on and Turner had scored another try – off yet another driven maul – this time after starting against the USA. At the time, his fourth try in only his fourth game put him level with Gordon Bulloch and Ross Ford as Scotland's leading try-scoring hooker – and they had 185 Scotland caps between them.

98

TOMMY SEYMOUR HAT-TRICK VERSUS FIJI

10 November 2018 • Autumn Tour, Murrayfield
Scotland 54–Fiji 17

There was a time when scoring three times for Scotland as a winger was an achievement over the course of a career, let alone in one match. But the expansive style brought to national team performances under Gregor Townsend has meant tries are, in general, more plentiful. Still, a hat-trick in one match is no mean feat. And the autumn Test against Fiji in 2018 is a match Warriors and Lions wing Tommy Seymour won't forget in a hurry.

While the match concluded as a 54–17, eight-try rout to the Scots, they trailed 17–14 in first-half stoppage time, until, with Fiji bending after a double sin-binning, Finn Russell slung a long pass out to Seymour to walk in unopposed.

With Scotland 28–17 up, and Fiji still a man down, Seymour scored for a second time, bursting in on a crash ball from short range near the posts. If those scores were almost training-ground moves, Seymour rounded off his treble with virtually his next touch to finish off a wonderful counter-attacking play.

Fiji stand-off Ben Volavola failed to make touch with his clearance kick, enabling Stuart Hogg to run the ball back. Scotland then launched right through replacements George Horne and Stuart McInally, worked a couple of miss moves, Russell advancing the move through Pete Horne and Chris Harris, who showed great pace and direction, drawing three Fijian defenders before his try-making pass to Seymour, who had held station on the wing to score his 19th try for his country.

Three tries for Seymour in a little over 20 minutes of playing time. It doesn't come much better. Well, probably not a good time to remind Tommy – or indeed his Scotstoun teammate Pete Horne – that it could have been four, and would have been had the Warriors centre exploited the overlap during the first half, instead of trying to dummy full-back Setariki Tuicuvu.

Tommy Seymour says: "I hadn't scored for a while for Scotland. You try not to focus on it, but it's something I was looking forward to doing again."

99

CALCUTTA CUP – A MATCH LIKE NO OTHER

16 March 2019 • Six Nations, Twickenham
England 38–Scotland 38

Sport, at its most basic, is about just two things: winning or losing. Actually, there is a third, of course: the draw, a result which at times can be as good as any victory, or can generate pain the equal of any defeat. As a rule, you need to settle on one of those conclusions, unless, that is, you are involved in a contest which leaves you feeling as if you have sampled all three of those outcomes in the same day – and that's exactly where anyone involved with Scotland found themselves at Twickenham in the spring of 2019.

It would be an understatement to say things started badly for the Scots. They conceded a try after 66 seconds; by the 29th minute, England – who seemed not to have noticed that their Championship ambitions had gone with Wales clinching the Grand Slam in Cardiff – had scored a bonus-point try; they led 31–0. And many bedecked in tartan had already decided the pubs around Richmond were a more attractive proposition. Then ...

It would also be an understatement to say that things clicked for the Scots. Simply, they produced a spell of exhilarating and exceptional rugby, seldom – if ever – seen previously on the international stage.

A modicum of respectability came when they put their first points on the board. Captain Stuart McInally charged down a kick from counterpart Owen Farrell, then raced from his own 10-metre line to score, fending tackles by Jonny May and the backtracking Farrell along the way. Scotland went in trailing 31–7 at half-time; they returned transformed, amid tales of raised voices and a difference of opinions.

Finn Russell's pop pass was carried by Sam Johnson, Ali Price and Sean Maitland making progress before Sam Skinner acted as link man off Price's pass to allow Darcy Graham to dance in from the left for his second try in as many weeks. Within minutes, the Scots had manufactured a third try, the origins being a ruck midway inside their own half, enabling Price to launch the attack with a chip and chase, stalling momentarily before Magnus Bradbury arrived in support at pace to go over. It was 31–19.

After a five-minute breather, Scotland went again; Russell looped a long, cross-field pass to Maitland, who provided the try-scoring ball for Graham. Amazingly, Scotland then drew level as the hour approached. Farrell's midfield pass was picked by game-changer Russell, making the interception, and he sped away and under the posts.

All Scotland needed now was to take the lead – and in the 75th minute, they duly obliged. Russell was again the instigator, the Racing 92 star outfoxing England's defence when he did them with the "eyes", – making it appear he was going to pass deep but instead timed his short pass to Sam Johnson perfectly on the England 10-metre line – the Warriors centre making light of English tackles as he bounced his way over to score Scotland's sixth try of an unforgettable evening.

PART V – 2010s

However, just when it looked like Scotland would celebrate a first win at HQ in 36 years, backup ten George Ford found just enough of an opening to score, saving English blushes and breaking Scottish hearts.

A day of drama and mixed emotions, and for the Scots, a record points haul against England, restored pride, but, above all else, the chance to keep the Calcutta Cup for another year.

It was a draw at Twickenham; but was it a great draw or a bigger disappointment? Scotland coach Gregor Townsend delivers his critique... and a bit of enlightenment about what was said in the dressing room at half-time:

"I've played in a lot of those games, and I've coached in a few of them, and the amount of tries scored, that's what made that game so unusual. Scotland–England games are not, in general, good games. They are more often than not tight, kicking contests and when they have opened up, it's usually been because England are winning them comfortably. I think back to one try in 1994, none in 1995, none in 1996. There was the iconic 1990 game, but that was still only one try-all.

"The last few years have been free-scoring but nothing like 2019. It was great for the spectators, maybe not so good when you have a vested interest in it.

"From our perspective, at half-time we would have taken a draw. With three minutes to go, we certainly wouldn't have taken the draw. That simple.

"The initial feeling was one of disappointment for the players because it looked like another defeat – and a bad one – at Twickenham. This is our biggest game of the year, either England at home or away, every year.

"There's an excitement, there's a lot of time gets put into a game like that, in terms of preparation. And to see the start go so badly, for us, and so well for England, you were thinking,

Well, here we go again. And when you're down by 24 points at half-time, all you're thinking about initially is, *How do we get some respect back? How do we win the second half?* That was the message at half-time.

"To then see the team play unbelievable rugby, the best they'd played for such a long time, things got back to thinking, *Right, we could win this – how do we win this?*

"We got ourselves into a situation that we went ahead, which was incredible, through their great fitness, their great skill. And then, we lose it again. We'll always look at that game as if we lost it again. We'd done enough, we believe. Finn [Russell] put a really good kick in, down to the England 22, having ripped the ball off them. We had 90 seconds, and they were 80 yards away from our line, against a team that hadn't scored since the 30th minute. Really, if we'd got our defensive systems, and made the right decisions, we believe we would have won that game – but we gave them a chance, through the way we defended, through giving them a penalty, through giving them a chance to kick to the corner. Suddenly we were defending in our 22.

"It was an incredible result for it to end up a draw; there had been draws down through the history of the fixture, but never quite one with as many points.

"All teams try to get in that moment – I think they call it 'flow' in sports psychology – when things are happening and you're in control of it. It happens a bit slower for you as an individual. You see things; like a cricketer seeing a ball a bit sharper, or the tennis player has got time to decide his shot then make it.

"But to be able to do that as a team, as a 15, you need to have that understanding of what your teammates are doing, react to that and do the same, in conjunction, as one.

"Sometimes that starts in the beginning of games, just because you've trained all week and everyone knows what each other is doing; you have total concentration and focus on what needs to be done.

"But to do it at a point in the game when there hadn't been any flow during most of that first half – that was incredible. The flow was with England; it looked like everything they were doing was clinical and done at pace, the players were reading each other really well and they were putting points up. Then that flow went to us.

"I think there were two or three turning points; the first one was the response by Stuart McInally to make a big play. Just getting a charge down, or making a big tackle, would have lifted his teammates. But to get the charge down, getting the ball back, and to then run in the score from about 60 yards was tremendous. That maybe stopped the flow. It was the last time that England scored for a long while.

"The captain can set an example. It isn't always sprinting from the halfway line to get a try; a big tackle or a big carry into the teeth of the opposition defence can act as a spur. But it gave us a lift and direction. But to do it as a charge down, and a steal on their captain as well – that was a great example of leadership in action.

"That allowed us to go into the changing rooms with something positive.

"There was no 'stooshie' at half-time. I had a discussion with Finn, on his own, in the medical room, so no other player saw it. I know probably why, when asked what happened at half-time, that is what he remembered. We don't tend to fall out, or disagree; we have a very similar view of the game and a similar way of executing that. I can understand why he would have been frustrated with the score in the first half, and that the game was against us. His natural instinct, as it was mine as a player, is to try and rectify it by saying, *Right, let's make things happen.* That wasn't working in the first half.

"The way England had been playing, if we had forced it, it would have been an even bigger scoreline.

"The game plan we had set out to play, we weren't executing it as well as we could, and sometimes England scored tries which they're always going to score because they're a good team. But just getting back to kicking, and kick chases, that worked and Finn kicked really well after half-time. It gave us a foothold, it made it more difficult for England to score and enabled us to be playing further up the field.

"It's a good thing to have debates. We have 15 minutes between halves, and fortunately he was in the medical room and that gave us a good chance to have a one-on-one discussion. *This is what we're going to do*. Actually, the dressing room was a really calm place. Greig [Laidlaw], who had been on the bench, was speaking a lot with Ali [Price]; our forwards coach was talking about the line-out. The players thought they were under pressure, but he was showing them images to say, *No, the pressure isn't as great as you think it is*. That gave the forwards a lot more belief.

"And Matt [Taylor], our defence coach, he was probably the most positive of everyone, regardless of the score, because we had some excellent defensive sets at the end of the half. We hadn't had those at the beginning, but he was emphasising that if we kept doing it, they weren't going to score against us.

"The two tries at the beginning of the second half – the first one was really good play, going through a few phases, backs interlinking with forwards, with a great finish from Darcy Graham. That would have given the players a bit of belief that when we do get into the English half, or 22, we have the skill to make and score good tries.

"However, the next one, which had the makings of a breakaway try, was a really good chip ahead from Ali that Darcy had actually called, then Ali got on the end of it, Magnus Bradbury at top pace ran away, and that was the moment when the confidence shifted from the English team to ourselves.

"We were running back for the kick-off thinking, *Right, let's keep this going*, and England were going behind the posts to ask questions of themselves about what was happening, like we'd done in the first half. When you have that confident mind set to say, *Right, go for it*, things did flow much better.

"There were parts of our game plan we did in the second half that helped us; as I say, we kicked more, as planned. That gave us field position to play our rugby from. We defended better. But that mindset for playing rugby when we had the ball, of reading the opposition, of seeing the wider picture of what we were aiming for came out in the second half.

"It would have been there before the start. But when the opposition score a few against you, and history is against you, and the crowd is against you, naturally you feel this isn't going to be your day again. However, we stuck with it and it came good for us. Or until three minutes from the end it did.

"The one game that you're okay with a draw is where you have a trophy to retain. It maybe didn't feel like it, but we took the cup back home with us. That was important. If we'd lost the year before, and drawn at Twickenham in those circumstances, and come away with nothing, that would have been really disappointing.

"Retaining the trophy, after everything that happened in the game, was good. It isn't a trophy we win too often and have retained even less. Even if the emotions were somewhat mixed, to see our captain lifting the Calcutta Cup at the end was great."

100

GLASGOW HOSTS BIGGEST PRO14 FINAL EVER

25 May 2019 • PRO14 Grand Final, Glasgow
Glasgow Warriors 15–Leinster 18

Then again, you might expect a record crowd when you stage your showpiece finale in a host city where the home team contests the decider. Even so, that 47,128 would turn out to see Glasgow Warriors take on Leinster on a cold, wet Saturday evening at Celtic Park was still pretty remarkable.

Unfortunately, neither the outcome nor the match lived up to expectations amongst the locals who made up the vast majority of the crowd.

They had plenty to cheer about early on as a Matt Fagerson try gave Warriors the lead, but that was cancelled out almost immediately when Luke McGrath blocked Stuart Hogg's clearing kick and Garry Ringrose responded quickest to score.

Leinster led 15–10 by the break, Cian Healy having scrambled over for a try after the title holders had pressed the Glasgow line, and a second successful Johnny Sexton penalty ten minutes after the turnaround extended Leinster's lead.

Glasgow were struggling to show anything like the level of performance that had seen them secure a final berth after dishing

PART V - 2010s

out a 50–20 thumping to Ulster at Scotstoun in the semi-final.

Then controversy. With 15 minutes remaining, Rob Kearney took out opposite number Hogg – making his last Warriors appearance before his switch to Exeter Chiefs – in the air, an act punishable by only a yellow card from referee Nigel Owens, much to the annoyance of Glasgow fans and players alike. Against 14 men, Glasgow cut the deficit with an unconverted try from replacement hooker Grant Stewart in the corner.

However, in the last five minutes Glasgow were unable to create another opening and the Irishmen celebrated their 18–15 victory, leaving the Warriors contingent to wonder what might have been.

PART VI

2020s

101

MEMORABLE SCOTS WIN – THEN SOMETHING WE'LL NEVER FORGET

8 March 2020 • Six Nations
Scotland 28–France 17

Every picture tells a story, the capture of a moment in time. Sometimes, however, what happens next is the bigger story. This photograph is a particular favourite of Dominic McKay, the former SRU Chief Operating Officer, seen alongside Grand Slam legend John Jeffrey and the inimitable Doddie Weir.

There were plenty of smiles that Sunday afternoon. Scotland followed their Italian win by defeating France 28–17 at Murrayfield, a fourth successive home victory over the French. This was a painful one for Fabien Galthié's team, given they had started with three from three and were looking like Grand Slam champions in the making. Until they met the Scots.

While France were in traditional colours, Scotland wore pale blue, although it was the visitors who were a pale shadow of their previous best that term. Adam Hastings kicked a brace of penalty goals to put his side 6–0 up before France hit their straps. Having repelled several concentrated attacks, Scotland's defence had narrowed enabling Damian Penaud

110 GREAT SCOTTISH RUGBY MOMENTS

to catch Anthony Dupont's crosskick to score. Replacement flyhalf Matthieu Jalibert sank the conversion from wide out.

In the thirty-seventh minute, however, there was a shift in power. Prop Matthieu Jalibert punched Jamie Ritchie, an action not missed by the officials, TV or the partisan crowd and a red card resulted. Hastings was plumb with another penalty before the lead was extended to 14–7 right on halftime.

Hastings' midfield burst eliminated five French defenders. Scotland recycled, Stuart Hogg in space found Sam Johnson hitting the gain line at pace, and his pass out right left Sean Maitland to finish.

France began the second period cutting deep into the Scots 22 points but gave up a needless penalty under the Scots posts. That was the high-water mark of the French travellers.

Maitland began and completed the move for Scotland second touchdown. He first fielded a clearing kick between his 10 and 22, passing inside to Hogg who opted to run, linking to Chris Harris who sliced through the French defence. Price took it on, was held up, and at the second attempt, the ball was churned back. Johnson acted scrumhalf, Ritchie went to Hastings who spun his pass out right where Maitland finished.

Jalibert was on the button to reduce the deficit to 21–10, but Scotland countered with a converted try. Full–back Anthony Bouthier was bundled in to touch midway inside the French sector by Hogg and Blair Kinghorn. Sub-hooker Stuart McInally only found French hands at the resulting lineout, but the loose ball found the hands of McInally again and he galloped over.

The Scots, 28–10 up, were home and hosed; not even a late try from French skipper Charles Ollivon could avert defeat against the invigorated Scots, albeit the critical damage on Les Bleus had been self–inflicted. Murrayfield echoed to a rousing celebration

PART VI – 2020s

on the final whistle, but the cheers would soon become a distant memory as the world faced a deadly crisis, as McKay reflected.

"Within Scottish rugby circles we had become acutely aware of the threat of coronavirus when the Women's Six Nations game versus their Italian counterparts in late February – while the men had played in Rome – was postponed due to the spread of the virus across Lombardy and Veneto in the north of Italy.

"The threat of coronavirus was very real by the France game and in the lead up to the match I had spent time in conversation with UK and Scottish Governments – along with the likes of the SRU's doctor, James Robson – discussing the various precautions we could and should be taking, like regular hand washing, and also about travel plans in the short term.

"It all sounded quite ominous, and there was a heightened awareness of the potential threat, but none of us expected the solution or outcome.

"By the end of that week, sport was being cancelled. Doddie had been 'warned off' going to Cheltenham because of the threat of infection – a blessing as it transpired – as he was going to visit the racing en–route to Cardiff for the Wales–Scotland game, which ultimately was also postponed. It was becoming very real and surreal simultaneously."

The country soon went into lockdown, leaving McKay, like the rest of the nation, feeling somewhat helpless when being mindful of the vulnerable, such as his good friend Doddie.

"Lockdown was such a seismic moment. Everyone had to think of themselves first and foremost, but your thoughts also went out to those exposed and at risk, Doddie being one of them.

"He had the capacity to leave you uplifted whenever you met him, regardless of your mood, quite a unique talent. He just lit the place up. But how could we do the same for him, down a phone or video call, when all he could do was shelter and stay safe.

"I still look at that photo from the France game. It was just a great day, we all enjoyed the game and the occasion. But you do wish there had been more days like that, what with Doddie's condition and how precious his time was.

"That picture remains one of my favourites. I still look at it to this day. As I said, Doddie had the ability to pick you up, give you a positive view of life. He still does, even now."

102

A WIN AT HQ – NEARLY FORTY YEARS IN THE MAKING

6 February 2021 • Six Nations
England 6–Scotland 11

On the evening of Scotland beating England, it was perhaps somewhat ironic that BBC Scotland aired a special on the White Heather Club back in March 1983, along with the proviso "do not adjust your sets".

Television technology had moved on significantly in the four decades since then, but when it came to facing the Auld Enemy at Twickenham, the bi-annual contests were almost always repeats or reruns of what had gone before, except for the odd draw along the way.

The Scots had, however, on their previous trip to London in 2019, shown what was possible in managing to grab an unexpected draw from the jaws of an even more unlikely win.

First game up in the 2021 championship, the Six Nations series was confined to an entirely television audience, due to Covid restrictions. Twickenham is a big place, even more gaunt and stark when empty, when the only real noise was the wind rather than cheering supporters.

Understandably, perhaps, given the surreal atmosphere, this

wasn't a classic. It was a dour tussle for long periods interrupted by flashes of brilliant game management from the Scots with ball in hand, particularly from the dynamic duo, Finn Russell and Stuart Hogg.

It was Russell who set the Scots on their way with a penalty goal landed from close range after just six minutes when England infringed at a ruck. By the half-hour, the Scots were in a slightly more comfortable position.

Russell, who would keep England's back three guessing throughout, planted a steepling kick into the rarified air over Twickers. Owen Farrell awaited its arrival, but the fingertips of Sean Maitland diverted the bladder back into friendly arms, namely those belonging to no. 8 Matt Fagerson. He made yardage while committing English defenders, before recycling.

Ali Price slung a long pass left, Russell introducing Cameron Redpath and Hogg into the attack line, the advance continued by hooker George Turner, faced with the prospect of holding or passing. He opted for the latter, leaving Duhan van der Merwe ten metres out, faced by only Elliot Daly but with the white fringe defence arriving at pace. The Edinburgh wing lost Daly with a shimmy inside, only to catch up with Farrell, Maro Itoje and Billy Vunipola, who he threw off to ram his way over for a score. By the end of the half, the lead was down to two points, and Scotland momentarily down to fourteen. Russell tripped Ben Youngs, Farrell converted for a second time in the half, the plumbed-in crowd noise was turned up to eleven, and it was 8–6 to the visitors.

Russell's enforced time-out completed, he was called back in for kicking duties, Ellis Genge the culprit of a no-arms tackle (a slightly dubious call under closer scrutiny) on the mobile Turner. A stretch of the Russell hamstrings and it was 11–6.

England, having promised a more open, attack-minded

PART VI - 2020s

approach beforehand, eventually cut loose when desperation kicked in. With the clock firmly in the red, they tried desperately to seek an opening from inside their own half. Replacement Courtney Lawes drove in to a dark blue reception committee, only to find "jackler" supreme Hamish Watson standing in wait. The Edinburgh flanker duly robbed his counterpart of his possessions, then wheeled away to boot the ball into the empty seats and begin the celebrations.

"It's up there with anything I'd ever achieved during my playing or coaching career and one of Scotland best-ever results, I would say," admitted national coach Gregor Townsend.

"Those were horrible conditions; wet, windy, no crowd sound. We might be used to the weather, not through choice, but it was a difficult day, and we stuck at them. It was a fantastic achievement from that group of players and well deserved."

England coach Eddie Jones conceded afterwards that he hadn't got the preparations right, and that this was a painful loss. "This stays with you for a long time," said Jones. How right he was, for once ...

103

ITALIAN JOB COMPLETED IN RECORD-BREAKING STYLE

20 March 2021 • Six Nations
Scotland 52–Italy 10

Since 2000, matches against Italy could generally be categorised as never to be forgotten, having created both memories and nightmares over that period.

The year 2021 saw a dream show by Gregor Townsend's new look starting XV. The record–breaking performance – limited once again to a TV audience only – saw Scotland run in eight tries and bag half a century of points in the process. But wasn't that what was supposed to happen?

The easy answer is yes. Arriving in Scotland, Italy's four previous games had seen them concede 50 points in Rome against France, just the 41 at Twickenham, and another 48 against both Ireland and Wales back at the Stadio Olimpico. Not that the Scots were entirely happy themselves, having found out the hard way about top-line sport being about fine margins.

After winning against England at Twickenham, the Scots lost by a point and three to Wales and Ireland respectively. A third successive home game (after the postponement of the France fixture) gave Townsend & Co every opportunity to right those

PART VI - 2020s

wrongs. Not that the Italians paid any attention to pre-match predictions.

On a sun-kissed spring afternoon, Italy began as if they were playing under Roman skies. Six minutes in, the Azzurri were a score up, hooker and captain Luca Bigi peeling off a rolling maul and over in the corner.

One was forgiven for thinking the nervousness talked about in advance by captain Stuart Hogg, covering for Finn Russell at stand–off, was for real. However, the weight of expectation was cast aside as Scotland went up through the gears.

In almost identical fashion, Scotland put their first points on the board when hooker Dave Cherry crossed off a driven line-out. Three minutes on, and Hamish Watson released Duhan van der Merwe to skip over, while fellow winger Darcy Graham only had to run the ball in from three metres in support of Sean Maitland and Huw Jones. Before the half-hour, the Glasgow centre had his own try. Jones, profiting from some quick, precise handling from Sam Johnson, Duhan van der Merwe and Hogg, who added a brace of conversions to put his side 24–10 up at the interlude, by which time, it was all too obvious why Italy had been shelling so many points per game.

Defensively they were a shambles, as Cherry produced a carbon-copy to his first try, on this his first start. No. 9 Scott Steele was then on hand to benefit from an initial drive from centre Johnson, who smashed through prop Danilo Fischetti, then shrugged off Bigi at the second attempt to collect the seventh try.

All that remained was for the rampant Scots to hit the half ton, which they achieved nine minutes from full-time. Italy, manfully trying to achieve a measure of respectability, pushed in to the Scotland 22, only for lock Niccolò Cannone to spill the egg when upended. Fortuitously, the ball bounced into the clutches of replacement scrum-half Ali Price, who threw a dummy to van der Merwe, then sped off with the winger in support. Price, realising the man outside had the advantage of speed and space, flipped possession to van der Merwe, who, despite having half the field to cover, was never going to be captured.

Hogg made it six out of eight conversion attempts to complete the scoring. An excellent showing by the hosts, none more so than by an ebullient Cherry.

"I was delighted to get a couple of tries – you could say they were from my optimum range," recalled Cherry, happy to give others credit for all their help.

"Scoring off the back of a maul, the biggest thing when you have the ball is when to time your own drive. All the guys in front of you are doing the real work. I got time to have a rest and clear my head and just make sure I got there, twice.

"It was a great feeling knowing all the work had paid off. Being honest, I know the score-line said otherwise but I didn't think we were clinical enough at times. Not that I can complain too much.

"Italy were struggling, but you can only play and beat the team in front of you."

104

SCOTS TOWER OVER FRENCH IN PARIS

26 March 2021 • Six Nations
France 23–Scotland 27

Playing on a Friday night, in an abandoned stadium, Match Day 3 coming at the end of a five-game schedule, and Scotland eventually taking their first win on French soil this century. What strange times we lived in back in 2021.

France entered this game – rescheduled following a Covid outbreak in their camp back in February – with a chance of pipping Wales to the overall crown. The arithmetic was basic: defeat the Scots by 21 points and collect a try–scoring bonus point.

The French had the scoreboard working inside the first ten minutes, Romain Ntamack with a regulation penalty. However, their numbers were being reworked within a few minutes as Scotland squeezed the French defence and their resolve. Hooker George Turner broke from a line-out maul and was repelled a few feet out. Hamish Watson similarly held up short. If his dancing feet had waltzed around many a last line, then it was sheer leg power that got Duhan van der Merwe, missile-like, under the French tacklers and over for his and Scotland's first try. Russell converted. Not what was originally scripted.

After exchanging penalties, France found themselves with a five-metre scrum. Grégory Alldritt picked and went, then fed Antoine Dupont, who ran laterally before looping a long pass wide to winger Damian Penaud. He drew and slipped van der Merwe's tackle, then found Brice Dulin inside and the full-back scored. The scores stood at 13–10 at the interval, but Stuart Hogg was only a couple of minutes through a stint in the sinbin.

Against a man down, France showed some eagerness to run. Dulin marked then ran from his 22, brought Ntamack into play with Arthur Vincent downed on halfway. France recycled, Virimi Vakatawa attacked, committing two Scots before slipping a pass, backhanded to Penaud on the Scots ten-metre line. He applied boot to ball, chipping Russell, then kicked on to touch down.

Russell's penalty cut the deficit to 18–13, but Scotland were chasing down the French. A five-metre lineout ended with an untidy conclusion, but with the ball loose, sub hooker Dave Cherry – or should that be the prolific Dave Cherry – gathered and grounded. Russell maintained his flawless display with the additional points. France were in danger of losing the match along with the championship, however, were given a glimmer of hope when second-rower Swan Rebbadj plunged in as French numbers overwhelmed the Scottish defence.

With fifteen minutes remaining on the clock, France had a 23–20 edge. But they needed to score at more than a point per minute if they were to be hailed champions. Just to raise home spirits even more, Russell received a red card from referee Wayne Barnes for an unintentional forearm to the throat of Dulin as Scotland attacked, harsh yes, but a justified sending off, nevertheless.

I mean, this match needed a twist like that at the end! One can only imagine the difference tens of thousands of French

PART VI – 2020s

voices might have made in those closing minutes to the home cause.

But rather than make numbers count, France found Scotland inspired, trying to keep the locals hemmed in their own half. The egg timer was running down, and the egg was in Scottish hands. With Scotland being repelled, Hamish Watson fumbled and turned over possession to Dulin who could have finished the game by putting the ball dead.

Instead, inexplicably, he kept it alive. It remains puzzling even now. But at the breakdown, Mr Barnes considered a Frenchman off their feet at the ruck. That gave Scotland one last possession.

Going for broke and the win, Scotland fired wave on wave of dark blue challengers, all repulsed. Ali Price appeared at the heart of everything as Stuart Hogg, Watson, Cherry and Grant Gilchrist were driven back. But with French resistance exhausted, Scotland executed their coup de grace.

A cohort of Ryan Wilson and Alex Craig were held up short, but off their 20th Phase, Price connected with Adam Hastings who chucked a Hail Mary pass out to van der Merwe, who wrong-footed Penaud with his step inside, and bludgeoned his way through Vincent to score. The Scots inside the Stade de France – otherwise known as "the team" – went wild with delight. One could imagine, however, the decibel levels in Wales being even louder.

All that was left was for Hastings to kick the conversion, twenty-six years after his father Gavin had done the same. As they said in all the best French films, "fin" . . .

105

THIRD SUCCESSIVE SCOTLAND WIN OVER WALLABIES – DO WE GET TO KEEP THEM?

7 November 2021 • Autumn Nations Series
Scotland 15–Australia 13

Sport has a way of throwing up unexpected sequences and runs: unexpected because the team manufacturing such a cycle have, in general, toiled while appearing to save their best for one particular opponent.

So, it was when Scotland hosted Australia in the autumn of 2021. The world was still trying to establish some sort of normality after a global pandemic, but the norm in this fixture, of late, was that those sporting the thistle ran out as winners.

For nearly four decades, Scotland had not found themselves in a similar position. But a 24–19 win in Sydney during the summer of 2017, followed by a 53–24 rout later that same year at home teed the Scots up nicely for the tourists arriving in late 2021.

Scotland had warmed up for the Wallabies with a rousing 60–14 win over Tonga. More of the same was the expectation of both Gregor Townsend and the home supporters. However, the reality was that the Aussies, under the stewardship of former

PART VI - 2020s

Glasgow Warriors coach Dave Rennie, were tougher nuts to crack.

Quarter of an hour in, and while there had been cuts and thrusts from Darcy Graham, Stuart Hogg and Duhan van der Merwe, taking Scotland well into enemy territory, nothing had come of them. But persistence brought reward.

A lineout five metres from the gold line gave Scotland their attack base. Ewan Ashman, called from the bench to replace crocked hooker George Turner, threw to Jamie Ritchie near the tail. He took and gave to Grant Gilchrist all in one move, allowing the Edinburgh lock to locate club mate Hamish Watson to be driven by an attentive Scots pack towards and over the try line. Finn Russell popped over the conversion.

Australia had a try and a player cancelled in double quick time. Michael Hooper barrelled over directly under the posts, but referee Romain Poite adjudged Allan Alaalatoa had connected with the chin of Matt Fagerson as he arrived at a ruck, and the points and the prop disappeared. By half-time Australia had troubled the scorers, James O'Connor sinking a penalty to make it 7–3.

After the restart, the men from Down Under finally clicked. On their set piece from the Scots 22, reserve winger Izaia Perese burst up the side of the scrum, making light of the barrier posed by Ali Price and Russell and gaining good distance. From the breakdown White only had eyes for one man, flanker Rob Leota, and he clattered in from short range. O'Connor added the conversion.

In arrears, Scotland began to spin the ball, and some determined running was matched by some steely Australian defence. Nearing the hour, Scotland edged in front.

The Oz wall had held firm as Scotland sought a way to breach the Australia defence. But when Price came left looking for options, he first fed Gilchrist, who made the ball available for his no. 9, who again probed the narrow side. The ball went through the hands of prop Pierre Schoeman to overlapping hooker Ashman, who gratefully accepted the opportunity of a debut try, incredibly getting the ball down for the score as Perese huckled him in to touch. A swing of five points, now 12–10 in favour of blue.

The scoreline suggested there was nothing between these two teams, and the balance was tipped again in the Aussies favour, fifteen minutes remaining, O'Connor taking care with a mid-range penalty after Ritchie hadn't managed to roll away from a ruck.

Surely the Scots would get one more chance, and a chance they got when Australia were penalised at a scrum, Mr Poite's explanation dividing opinions; Scotland thought he was correct, the Australians thought otherwise.

As it stood, nearing the last ten minutes, Finn Russell picked the right moment in blustery conditions to angle his kick through the uprights and Scotland were two to the good.

As full time approached, Ashman was left with one more task; like a darts player closing out a match, he had to hit no. 6, Jamie Ritchie. Bullseye! The Edinburgh man gathered, his pack engulfed him, and the clock hit red. Job done.

The emotion of the occasion – especially with a full house being back inside Murrayfield – was not lost on man of the match Hamish Watson.

"Having 67,000 back at Murrayfield that afternoon was just amazing and made it a really special day.

"Because it was so tight we had to lift ourselves quite a few times during the game. Australia had won five on the bounce before that. So, they were never going to be any sort of push over. Those last ten minutes felt like an age."

106

MAKE MINE A DOUBLE IS ORDER OF THE DAY

5 February 2022 • Six Nations
Scotland 20–England 17

George Orwell, in his book *1984*, predicted a world where multiple surveillance cameras would watch and judge your every move, and strict Government control would be the order of the day. Entering 2022, in recent times, these facets of life had become the norm in international rugby union, where they were more commonly referred to as the TMO and Covid restrictions.

What Orwell hadn't foreseen was just how long it would take Scotland to produce successive wins over their nearest and dearest rival. Not since beating England in 1983 at Twickenham, then following it up during the Grand Slam winning term twelve months on, had the Scots retained the Calcutta Cup.

Now, with home advantage in 2022, and off the back of their away day success a year prior, did the Scots have the opportunity to replicate that trophy defence.

With the dreaded coronavirus more of an afterthought now, Murrayfield welcomed a full house for this Six Nations opener, although the majority were left subdued somewhat when England fly-half Marcus Smith scuffed over a penalty.

The Scots lost scrum-half Ali Price to an HIA after he found out, the hard way, that going head-to-head with a charging Sam Simmonds has its consequences. Ben White made his debut as replacement and if ever the moniker "super sub" was to be pinned on anyone, then White wore it with distinction.

Seventeen minutes in, a quick lineout found England disorganised. Scotland burst at speed. White's pass found Stuart Hogg, his half-break creating a channel for wing Darcy Graham to accelerate between Ben Youngs and Nick Isiekwe, the Hawick man jigging right then left to evade Joe Marchant, then to release White who cheered himself home, unchallenged, for the try. Finn Russell obliged with the extras, 7–3.

A penalty apiece from Smith and Russell respectively still had Scotland ahead, 10–6, albeit against the general flow of the game.

If Scotland were hanging on, England hung on to their coat tails through another Smith goal, before Eddie Jones' men ground the Scots deeper in to their own patch. Handed a penalty advantage by official Ben O'Keeffe, England exploited their free play, Youngs going left from a crabbing maul to cut loose Smith. From the tee, however, Smith pulled his conversion attempt. Still, England were 14–10 to the good.

It almost got better for the red rose when Scotland captain Stuart Hogg was a wee bit too adventurous in trying to keep the ball in play, only just retrieving his scooped flick before Max Malins pounced a yard from the Scotland try line. It was, nonetheless, England who scored next, Smith this time back on target with a penalty, square in front of the posts.

Against the odds, Scotland were still within touching distance and within a matter of minutes, had tagged the English. Scotland squeezed England, Russell's boot dictating the play. A chip from the no. 10 almost released Duhan van der Merwe out left, and

PART VI - 2020s

when Scotland recycled, Russell again teased with a crosskick aimed in the direction of Graham.

Had he got his hands on the ball, he'd have been favourited to score. Instead, England hooker Luke Cowan-Dickie intercepted with a blatant parry, more akin to the beach volleyball court. To make matters worse, he produced a BAFTA-nominated piece of acting in feigning injury, not that referee O'Keeffe bought it. Yellow card, penalty try, all-square.

Down a man, England had two options; go man-for-man up front and leave a hole for Scotland to exploit amongst the English backs or operate a seven-man scrum. They chose the latter, a costly pick as it soon proved.

On a Scots put-in seven metres out, the whistle blast as England's set piece crumpled meant Russell could put his side ahead with less than ten minutes left to run. He parted the posts, although he was anything but equidistant with his kick, the varying reactions around the stadium testament to just how close it appeared for some.

And, it was still a mightily close contest as England surged forward well past full time, until Elliot Daly was nailed by Chris Harris, Hamish Watson fielded the loose ball and Hogg kicked the ball dead.

"It was a three-point game that could have gone either way," a downhearted Eddie Jones admitted later. "It was a good effort by our team, but Scotland were a bit better and took their chance.

"We don't apportion any blame to Luke [Cowan–Dickie]. He was just contesting the ball in a different area and the referee adjudicated it was a yellow card." That's because it was a yellow card, Eddie . . .

107

YOU WAIT 38 YEARS FOR ONE, THEN . . .

4 February 2023 • Six Nations
England 23–Scotland 29

. . . a bit like London buses, two come along at the same time.

While the conclusion was the same, as was the time in the scheduling, being the first game up in a new Six Nations series, there was little to compare the events of this match to those of two years prior, save for the final score. This was a battle that had everything, including the try of the season, one for the ages.

As ever, regardless of two years ago, England began as favourites, but it was the hoards from the north who, or maybe that should be Huw, drew first blood a quarter of an hour in. Jones found himself in an acre of space (belittling Kevin Sinfield's defensive structure) and carried play to within a few metres of the English line. When Scotland recycled and given an advantage call, Jones was back in station, taking off on to a Sione Tuipulotu grubber for the opening try. Finn Russell kicked the additional point and unlike 2021, the cheers (and jeers) came from 81,000 in the stands.

Max Malins clutched a Marcus Smith crosskick to net the home team their first points, but that gap was extended minutes later with what would be a memorable Scottish score. In the

PART VI - 2020s

twenty-ninth minute, a Jack Van Poortvliet box kick was fielded by right-wing Kyle Steyn, who threw a pass back inside to his fellow wing Duhan van der Merwe just ahead of his own 10-metre line.

Off he set, running through Joe Marchant's diving tackle on halfway, and after speeding beyond Ollie Chessum's flailing grab, like Jones earlier, van der Merwe found himself in open water but with sharks converging. One-on-one with Freddie Steward, VDM's right-cut took him beyond the grip of the England 15, but delayed him sufficiently for van Poortvliet to become the next obstacle, who he avoided with a little hitch-step to the right. The backtracking Alex Dombrandt then arrived, but he was late to the party, the Edinburgh flyer merely using him to push off for additional momentum to drop over the line. An epic touchdown.

By the turnaround however, the home support were more cheerful, Saracens' wing Malins crossed for his second and Owen Farrell split the sticks with a penalty, 13–12 England, stretched to 20–12 following Farrell's conversion of an Ellis Genge try. Scotland were not shaken but stirred.

Scrum-half Ben White fumbled, then blindsided the English cover when he picked up from a ruck to score. Russell converted, then he and Farrell exchanged penalties to leave Scotland a point behind. That was still the deficit entering the last five minutes, but in a sweeping right to left move, Scotland cemented their improbable win.

Steyn made crucial yardage down one flank, the ball exchanged via makeshift scrum-half Tuipulotu, through Russell, the unlikely midfield pairing of Fraser Brown and Richie Gray to Matt Fagerson. He fed van der Merwe outside him, outnumbered and with limited space to work in. But somehow, he managed to evade, shake off or bulldoze five white shirts, Malins the most heroic, to thump the ball down for the try. Russell, out wide, slotted the conversion. Man of the Match and World Rugby's Try of the Year. A decent day's work for VDM, who didn't forget the efforts of others.

"We put a lot in to the first half and to be down, then go further behind after the restart, I think the collective determination we showed to stay in the game was excellent.

"For me the two tries were different, but all part of being a winger and a finisher. Me doing my job.

"The first score came from not very much. In that situation, where I received the ball, you are looking to make ten or fifteen metres or make the gain line. But it just opened up and you just keep running, trying to avoid tackles and hit the gaps you see. If your luck is in, and mine was, you score. On another day you'd get nailed. As I say, all luck.

"The second one, there was a bit more to do, but that distance out, regardless of the defensive numbers, you'd still back yourself to score."

Three Calcutta Cup wins in a row for Scotland was their first such treble since 1972. Back-to-back away victories against England, you'd need a time machine set at 1909 to witness that. Heady days. What were the chances of making it four on the spin?

108

HALFWAY TO PARADISE, SO NEAR AND YET SO FAR

11 February 2023 • *Six Nations*
Scotland 35–Wales 7

Winning individual matches has never been a problem for Scotland. Outside of the All Blacks, those bedecked in tartan, Saltires, face paints and replica tops can all point to outstanding victories and performances against the biggest and best. When it comes to the really big prizes, the memories become slightly less vivid.

Not since 1999 had Scotland topped the tree when it came to winning the biggest international competition in the Northern Hemisphere, although even that was so long ago it was still the Five Nations, rather than Six. However, at least we are still reigning champions in that particular tournament. Be grateful for the smallest mercy, and all that.

When you then win the opening game against England, and a hazardous one at that away from home, you at least put yourself one step towards what might result in a Triple Crown or even a Grand Slam. The last of those came in 1990, long before professional rugby was even a thing, long before shirt sponsors, and long before Murrayfield became an enclosed bowl. The second game up in 2023 saw Wales visiting the Scots capital. Confidence was high in home ranks. Afterall, England had been dropped as Triple Crown contenders, as had Wales, their hopes comprehensively put asunder in Cardiff by a rampant Irish team, the margin 34–10.

Scotland led after the early exchanges, a brace of penalties by Finn Russell separating the sides. That said, there was a steady tightening of the screw by the Scots, urged on by a positive home support and overcoming the loss of international centurion Stuart Hogg (98 caps for his country, two for the Lions) through a head injury.

Nevertheless, the patriotic audience themselves were trying not to make their frustrations audible. Even they had identified this particular Welsh team as something of a distance from being considered even mediocre, and knew Scotland should be winning by more.

On the half-hour, Scotland eventually cut loose. From a lineout, hooker George Turner joined the back of a rolling maul from which he eventually peeled off to ground the ball at the second (or even third) attempt. He only needed one go at grounding George North with a high tackle moments later, a yellow card accruing, and Scotland were thirteen up but a man down.

The numerical surplus for the men in red was speedily put to good use, captain Ken Owens with a try, Dan Biggar with the conversion. But that was as good as it got for Wales, though it should have been better. By the midway mark, winger Rio Dyer had let a try-scoring pass slip through his hands. An escape the Scots would take every advantage of.

Five minutes in to the second period, Russell produced some of his mercurial magic, committing the Welsh drift defence to then slip a back-of-the-hand pass to a grateful Kyle Steyn.

PART VI - 2020s

Minutes later, with Welsh full-back Liam Williams sin binned, the same partnership of supplier and customer earned Scotland a third try. Russell aware of the void created by Williams, cross-kicked for Steyn, gratefully accepted by the waiting wing.

By now, Russell's right boot was operating with the accuracy of a surgeon's knife, and a deft chip found Duhan van der Merwe breaking on to the ball at pace. He took the now-restored Williams and Alex Cuthbert out of commission before casually lobbing a pass inward to the blazing Blair Kinghorn, Hogg's deputy, for try number four.

A bonus point secured, Scotland continued on the front foot and a fifth try would come before the end, Matt Fagerson on the end of Russell's pass popped over the onrushing beleaguered Welsh defence to round off a record-breaking win, surpassing the previous 25-point winning margin dating back to 1924.

It meant Scotland retained the Doddie Weir Cup, and, gave them a two from two start for the first time ever in the Six Nations. No one was getting carried away, least of all captain Jamie Ritchie.

"It wasn't perfect, there were a few clunky bits, but it's good to be winning and having bits to improve," Ritchie said, adding; "We've not won anything yet, we've won two games and looking forward to performing well against France." Heady days.

Unfortunately, the hangover soon followed. The loss to France in Paris meant there would be no Slam, and no Triple Crown either, after Ireland had visited Murrayfield.

Ach, well, it was good while it lasted.

109

ONE IS ALWAYS ENOUGH

3 February 2023 • Six Nations
Wales 26–Scotland 27

It has never been easy supporting Scotland as they have, over the years, often found new and contrived ways to lose matches. This match, however, was a rarity; a new and contrived way to win a match in the Six Nations Championship.

Nothing is guaranteed in sport, though there was a confidence going in to the 2024 series that Scotland could – and there is a lot of heavy lifting around that word – kick on from the previous year where they started with a couple of wins for the first time ever, and, finished the season with three wins and third place overall after beating Italy.

Scotland had comprehensively beaten Wales in Edinburgh twelve months prior, but visits to Cardiff had proven to be losing ones in recent times. Make that one win in twenty-two years of recent times. Whilst 2023 was still fresh in the memory, one might say, for both nations, this was always going to be a tougher ask for Gregor Townsend and his team. Simply, they couldn't face another Welsh side so bereft of confidence and belief, could they?

After 40 minutes, that last question appeared to have been answered with interest. Scotland had run the Welsh ragged,

PART VI – 2020s

leading by 20–0, virtually a pick-up from where they'd left off the previous season at Murrayfield.

Finn Russell opened with a penalty as Scotland forced their hosts backwards from the off. the Scotland pack was dominant and laid siege to the Welsh line. Their defence was resolute, but the battering they were taking was simply relentless. From one lengthy sequence, the Scots turned their 13th phase of play in to a score, Edinburgh loose-head prop Pierre Schoeman drilled his way low through the thin red line to score.

Half an hour in, Scotland increased the margin. They had been able to assemble multiple phases of play, with no respite for Wales who were simply trying to stay in the game. On one such eight-move series, Russell, with a simple show-and-go, outflanked the cover before nonchalantly flipping a no-look pass in to the accepting hands of Duhan van der Merwe who ran it in behind the posts. This was all too easy. Surely a Welsh backlash was imminent. Yes, but not before Scotland added another seven points early in the second half.

Remember that mesmeric touchdown van der Merwe bagged against England? The starting point for his second against Wales wasn't too far removed from that score.

Replacement scrum-half Tomos Williams clearance kicked from the 22 line, straight into the clutches of Kyle Steyn who passed inside to Russell, who from a standing start, zipped through the chasing Welsh forwards, committing flanker Tommy Reffell to the tackle only to offload, one-handed, to van der Merwe on his left shoulder.

The pass gave the speeding winger a straight one-on-one against the aforementioned Williams. While he was working out what it would take to stop the flying wingman, VDM cut him out of the equation, immediately deciding avoiding action was the best policy, using his afterburners to cut a wide flightpath around Williams and pick a safe landing spot in the goal.

Russell made it five from five off the tee, and at 27–0, only a miracle was going to deny Gregor Townsend a victory speech. However, when the time came for Townsend to deliver his words of wisdom, he looked decidedly drained. For Wales, against all odds, so nearly sprung one of the greatest comebacks in international history.

No sooner had the celebratory handshakes concluded, James Botham led the red-clad phalanx over the Scottish line, a double whammy as hooker George Turner was yellow carded for some illegality in the build-up. Ioan Lloyd missed the conversion, the importance of which wasn't even a consideration at that point.

Rio Dyer kept hold of a looping Williams pass to hit the corner, and when Scotland suffered a second sinbinning, this time Sione Tuipulotu for being offside twice according to referee Ben O'Keefe, Warren Gatland's team utilised the numerical advantage, no. 8 Aaron Wainwright launching himself over from short yardage.

Lloyd kicked a second conversion, and Scotland's lead had been reduced now to just 27–19. Wales were rampant by now, and with Tuipulotu still serving his sentence, the home side struck once again.

From a lineout five metres from the line, substitute and debutant Alex Mann was unstoppable as he peeled off to grab a bonus point try. 27–26. Who would bet against the home XV now?

Amazingly, when it would have been almost expected for Scotland to panic and crumble, they showed some real steel and resolve. Indeed, van der Merwe almost made it a personal hat-trick with the clock down to red, but he failed to convince Mr O'Keefe that the ball was on the try line and not atop a

PART VI - 2020s

Welsh boot. It mattered little. After deliberation, the referee called no-side and Scotland had held out.

"I'd compare that game to 2010, when I was an assistant coach," said Scotland coach Gregor Townsend, a match Scotland led 18–9 at halftime, and 24–14 at one stage before losing out 31–24.

"Wales got the momentum and we couldn't stop them. And thoughts of that match were starting to come in to my thoughts the closer they got. But we put a lot of effort into the last five minutes to stave them off. We could have had a couple of penalties, could have had a try, but we saw it through and that was pleasing.

"Nobody wants to lose a game of rugby, but you especially don't when you have been so dominant and so much in control."

110

DUHAN'S TREBLE YELL PUSHES SCOTLAND TO THE FOUR

24 February 2024 • Six Nations
Scotland 30–England 21

One is always welcome, while two is a rarity, but even better. Three is just amazing, but four – four is living in a dreamland, nearly fantasy land. But Scotland could make a fourth successive Calcutta Cup win against England a reality entering round 3 of the 2024 Six Nations.

Some of us (I was a very young boy at the time, honest) can remember such a run before. No, not the one dating back to 1896, but 1972, a sequence detailed at length earlier in this journal.

Scotland were still in the running for the Triple Crown after seeing off Wales first time out, but defeat in Paris had rendered overall honours unlikely. By contrast, England had loftier ambitions, even if they had only stumbled past Italy and Wales themselves.

The pontificating parked, the game started with a bang that would have outdone the One O'clock Gun, England making the noise.

From a scrum on the Scots 22, the ball was spun through the white-shirted hands, Elliot Daly making the telling incision

PART VI – 2020s

to put George Furbank in for the touchdown. George Ford converted, as he did with a penalty shot as England hit double figures less than quarter of an hour in.

Scotland reacted immediately. From scrum ball, Ben White met with Sione Tuipulotu who in turn released centre partner Huw Jones. He made decent yardage before being hauled down by Tommy Freeman and Furbank. But Jones, on his back, had the presence of mind to pop the ball up to Duhan van der Merwe who carried Ben Earl and Danny Care over the line with him.

England's progress was slow, even predictable at times, with the gutsy Scotland defensive line able to push up to restrict space even more. In trying to make something happen, Ford rushed a pass straight on to the forehead of Furbank, his nodded flick accepted by Jones who again fed VDM. The big wing, gathering inside his own half, left Earl rooted on the outside, then skipped out of Henry Slade's grasp to hit the corner.

Russell was metronomic off the tee, a penalty added to a brace of conversions to send the hosts 17–10 ahead, though that was cut by three, Ford given time and space for a needed drop goal, 17–14 at the turnaround.

Some days, even wrong goes right for you. Russell's kick from hand rebounded off the back of Ollie Lawrence but gathered by Cameron Redpath. As England closed on him, Redpath casually turned and headed towards English territory, first wrongfooting and turning England attackers into defenders, then accelerating away to be half-halted by Freeman. Support was instant, Jamie Ritchie bringing Russell in to play, his chip kick bouncing up for van der Merwe, who sprinted over the line untouched to complete his hat trick, thus becoming the first Scot ever to achieve that feat against the Auld Enemy, and the first player in the Six Nations era to score three tries against England.

Ford just about kept his side relevant with a penalty, which was cancelled by Russell, with interest, as he kicked a brace. Six out of six for the superstar fly–half, 30–16 on the big scoreboard.

If Scotland appeared comfortable, replacement wing Immanuel Feyi–Waboso caused some discomfort when he ran Ben Spencer's short-arm pass up the blindside to score.

There was little doubt who the man of the match would be, but as if to confirm the day was all about VDM, he received a yellow card as his individual honour was being announced over the PA system.

"You can only dream about having a day like that – what do they say about dreams coming true," van der Merwe reflected.

"Getting two tries again, I was pretty happy. Then when Finn got the ball in his hands, I just knew he'd try something. When he kicked it, I was just hoping for a good bounce and it just fell perfect for me."

If the free scoring van der Merwe had help sink England, it also proved a high-water mark for the Scots during the 2024 Championship. In Rome, the Scots stumbled to a 31–29 reversal, Italy's first home win in the competition for eleven years, while Ireland beat Scotland 17–13 in the final game to retain the Six Nations title.